OXFORD READINGS IN PHILOSOPHY

APPLIED ETHICS

APPLIED ETHICS

EDITED BY

PETER SINGER

OXFORD
UNIVERSITY PRESS

OXFORD
UNIVERSITY PRESS

Great Clarendon Street, Oxford OX2 6DP

Oxford University Press is a department of the University of Oxford.
It furthers the University's objective of excellence in research, scholarship,
and education by publishing worldwide in

Oxford New York

Auckland   Cape Town Dar es Salaam   Hong Kong   Karachi
Kuala Lumpur Madrid Melbourne Mexico City   Nairobi
New Delhi Shanghai   Taipei Toronto
With offices in
Argentina Austria Brazil Chile Czech Republic France Greece
Guatemala Hungary Italy Japan South Korea Poland Portugal
Singapore Switzerland Thailand Turkey Ukraine Vietnam

Published in the United States
by Oxford University Press Inc., New York

ISBN 978-0-19-875067-3

CONTENTS

INTRODUCTION

To an observer of moral philosophy in the twentieth century, the most striking development of the past twenty years would not be any advance in our theoretical understanding of the subject, nor would it be the acceptance of any particular ideas about right and wrong. It would, rather, be the revival of an entire department of the subject: applied ethics.

I use the term 'revival' because applied ethics is not new to philosophy. The essays in this volume by David Hume and John Stuart Mill fit well alongside modern writings; in the eighteenth and nineteenth centuries these philosophers were doing applied ethics in much the way that it is done today. Indeed, it would have been possible to go further back, and include samples of applied ethics from the medieval scholastics, or from any of a dozen classical writers. From Plato onwards moral philosophers have confronted practical questions, including suicide, the exposure of infants, the treatment of women, and the proper behaviour of public officials. (The continuity is evident in Hume's discussion of suicide, which draws on Seneca's letter on the same topic; while Thomas Nagel's discussion of death takes up a problem raised by Lucretius.) Christian philosophers like Augustine and Aquinas examined with great care such matters as when a war was just, whether it could ever be right to tell a lie, and if a Christian woman did wrong to commit suicide in order to save herself from rape. Hobbes, with the English Civil War freshly in mind, had an urgent practical purpose in writing about the moral basis of obedience to the sovereign. Practical concerns continued with Hume and then with the British utilitarians. Bentham's reforming zeal ranged over an incredible variety of topics, and Mill, in addition to the little-known speech on capital punishment included in this volume, wrote celebrated essays on liberty and on the subjection of women.

Despite this long tradition, for most of the present century moral philosophers kept aloof from practical ethics—a fact that becomes all the more remarkable if we consider the traumatic events through

which most of them lived. There were one or two notable exceptions. C. E. M. Joad wrote on political and social issues, and spoke
at the famous 1933 Oxford Union debate, when the students voted
against fighting for King and Country. Bertrand Russell seemed the
epitome of a philosopher engaged with the concerns of his times,
but his stature among his philosophical colleagues was based on his
work in logic and metaphysics, not on his writings on disarmament
or sexual morality. In any case, these few exceptions could not
produce a body of writings which could be regarded as a branch of
an academic discipline.

Instead of taking up practical issues, moral philosophers limited
themselves to the study of the nature of morality, or (in the heyday
of linguistic philosophy) to the study of the meaning of moral
judgements. This came to be known as 'meta-ethics'—a term which
signified that they were not actually *taking part* in ethics, but were
engaged in a higher-level study *about* ethics. Normative ethics, the
study of general theories about what is good and bad, right and wrong,
was considered an important part of ethics until the 1930s. Then it too
was relegated to a secondary concern, except for occasional discussions of utilitarianism and the different forms it might take.

Ordinary people—and no doubt students beginning their study of
the subject—sometimes still harboured the illusion that moral
philosophy could be of some use in deciding what we ought to do.
Leading philosophers like A. J. Ayer soon put them right: 'It is silly,
as well as presumptuous, for any one type of philosopher to pose as
the champion of virtue. And it is also one reason why many people
find moral philosophy an unsatisfactory subject. For they mistakenly look to the moral philosopher for guidance.'[1] C. D. Broad
went to the trouble of offering reasons for the received wisdom: 'It
is no part of the professional business of moral philosophers to tell
people what they ought or ought not to do . . . Moral philosophers,
as such, have no special information not available to the general
public about what is right and what is wrong; nor have they any call
to undertake those hortatory functions which are so adequately
performed by clergymen, politicians, leader-writers . . .'[2]

[1] A. J. Ayer, 'The Analysis of Moral Judgments' in *Philosophical Essays*
(London, 1959), p. 246.
[2] C. D. Broad, *Ethics and the History of Philosophy* (London, 1952), p. 244.

It may in part have been doubts about the adequacy of those to whom Broad refers which induced moral philosophers to take up practical questions; someone had to be able to do better than the clergy, politicians, and leader-writers! More importantly, those who nodded assent to views like Ayer's and Broad's had not stopped to ask whether moral philosophers could, without merely preaching, make an effective contribution to ethical dilemmas. Does expertise in moral philosophy equip one to clarify the muddy waters of popular moral debates? Does a knowledge of normative ethical theories make it possible to apply such theories to real ethical problems? Can such an application lead to more defensible positions on these questions? The possibility of an affirmative answer to such questions began to be widely recognized only during the 1960s, when first the American civil rights movement, and then the Vietnam war and the rise of student activism began to draw philosophers into discussions of moral issues: equality, justice, war, and civil disobedience. Philosophers who entered these debates as concerned citizens gradually realized that they were discussing ethical questions which were part of the philosophical tradition in which they had been educated. The skills they had acquired in studying and teaching philosophy were suddenly highly relevant.

Gradually the academic world began to respond. Articles on civil disobedience, on racial discrimination, and on war and pacificism, began to appear in publications like *The Journal of Philosophy*. By 1971 sufficient articles in applied ethics had been published for James Rachels to produce an anthology, *Moral Problems*.[3] At that time Rachels could still write, in his introduction, that most students beginning moral philosophy found it disappointingly remote from practical problems, and that 'If practical problems are mentioned at all, it is only by way of illustrating some more theoretical point.' But within five years this was no longer true; and *Moral Problems* was itself one of the most widely used texts in introductory ethics courses. The founding of *Philosophy and Public Affairs*, a new journal devoted to the application of philosophy to public issues, provided both a forum and a new standard of rigour for those bringing philosophy to bear on practical problems. (The prominence of this journal is indicated by the fact that three of the articles

[3] New York, 1971.

in this anthology are drawn from its pages, whereas no other publication is represented more than once.)

The broader community has willingly accepted the relevance and value of contributions by philosophers to practical issues—perhaps they too have not been entirely satisfied with the performance of the clergy, politicians, and leader-writers. This acceptance is particularly noticeable in bioethics, where new developments in medicine and the biological sciences throw up ethical questions which have few precedents. Thus it was no surprise when the British Government appointed a philosopher, Mary Warnock, to chair its Committee of Inquiry into Human Fertilisation and Embryology.[4] In several countries philosophers sit on ethics committees in universities, passing judgement on research involving human or animal experimentation, and in some hospitals they are members of committees which advise on such matters as the withdrawal of treatment from comatose patients. In the Australian state of Victoria, there is now even a legislative requirement that medical experiments involving human embryos must be approved by a committee which includes, among other members, 'a person holding a qualification in the study of philosophy'.

Applied ethics has become part of the teaching of most philosophy departments in English-speaking universities, taking its place alongside meta-ethics and normative ethics. The climate of political radicalism and student activism from which applied ethics gained so much initial impetus has gone; but applied ethics continues to thrive. This should cause no surprise; it is testimony to the perennial importance of the issues discussed, and to the need for them to be discussed with the greatest possible clarity and rigour. Against the long history of philosophical involvement in practical ethical issues, it is the neglect of applied ethics in the earlier years of this century which should be regarded as surprising.

The success of applied ethics in establishing itself as part of the philosophical curriculum has spawned dozens of anthologies, usually arranged so as to cover the major topics which seemed relevant and important when the anthology was put together. Often the

---

[4] See the *Report of the Committee of Inquiry into Human Fertilisation and Embryology* (London, 1984).

articles chosen are selected to provide opposing points of view. For educational purposes, a loosely argued but provocative article may be more effective than one about which students can find nothing to disagree. This collection is intended to serve a different purpose. I have not sought to give expression to alternative viewpoints on each issue. Nor did I set out with the intention of covering every major topic, although I did want to show the range of important topics on which work in applied ethics has been done. My primary aim in selecting from the immense body of literature which now exists in this field was simply to take the best.

Any choice made on this basis will necessarily be highly personal. Moreover the task of choosing the best is made more complicated by the fact that there is no single quality on the basis of which works of philosophy can be ranked. Nevertheless I judge each of the articles which follow to excel in at least one—and often all—of the following qualities: rigour of argument; originality of ideas; illumination of a significant philosophical question; clarity of presentation; and relevance to an important practical problem. The last of these may be considered to be a prerequisite for entry in a collection such as this, rather than a characteristic excellence; but in combination with one or more of the other qualities it can make a marked difference to the overall value of an article. The greater the importance of a topic in all our lives, the more thoroughly it will have been discussed outside philosophy; there is then special merit in adding something new which shifts the discussion to a higher level.

I shall not go through each of the articles which follow, and explain in just which of these qualities I considered them to excel. But for those seeking examples of the kind of rigorous argument that is so important to the subject, I would recommend David Hume's classic essay on suicide, James Rachels's dissection of the alleged significance of the distinction between active and passive euthanasia, Jonathan Glover's consideration of the tempting thought that 'It makes no difference whether or not I do it', Derek Parfit's 'Overpopulation and the Quality of Life', and Janet Radcliffe Richards's 'Separate Spheres'.

Varied forms of originality are displayed by different articles. The essays on abortion, by Judith Jarvis Thomson and by Michael

Tooley, succeed in dealing in new ways with a topic which might have been thought to be exhausted. The same might be said of Louis Pascal's striking essay, on a different but equally well-rehearsed subject. On the other hand the essays by Thomas Nagel, John Harris, Jonathan Glover, and Derek Parfit are original in that they find philosophical issues in questions which had previously scarcely been noticed.

Several of the papers shed light on deeper ethical issues—Nagel, Harris, Glover, and Parfit could again serve as examples. The proper mode of argument in ethics is particularly central to R. M. Hare's 'What is Wrong with Slavery?' Clarity is a special virtue of many of the essays, including those by John Stuart Mill, Harris, Tooley, Glover, Parfit, Hare, Richards, and (I hope) my own.

As for relevance to important practical problems, that is, as I have said, satisfied by all those articles which have been included. But we should not take it for granted. Anyone reading Thomson or Tooley on abortion must gain a clearer insight into where the public debate over abortion—which has for so long been fixated on the question of whether the foetus is 'a human being'—has missed the central issues. To provide such an insight is no small achievement. Similarly, while feminist writers have produced many volumes of essays on the position of women, how many of them have dissected the arguments of their opponents with the care and precision shown in Richards's work? Nicholas Measor's application of games theory to the nuclear arms race is another illustration of the diverse ways in which philosophers can use their skills to challenge conventional wisdom and contribute to public debates on issues of ultimate practical importance.

Although applied ethics has now established itself in academia, it still has its critics. Behind much of the criticism lies the belief that ethics is the realm of feeling and emotion: if there can be no objective truth in ethics, it may seem, there can be no scope for reason and argument. The premiss is, of course, controversial; but even if we accept it, the conclusion does not follow. In general, the articles in this anthology take no stance on the question of the status of ethical judgements. The authors argue from widely accepted premisses; or they seek to persuade by exposing inconsistencies and arbitrary distinctions in opposing positions. Abandoning the idea of objective truth in ethics should not mean abandoning the standards of consistency and relevance we uphold in other aspects of our lives. But I shall not go into such theoretical questions now; the articles which follow are the best defence of the claim that reason and argument have a role to play in the solution of practical ethical issues.

*

For encouraging me to take on this project, I thank Lloyd Humberstone; for advice on the contents, Derek Parfit, Helga Kuhse and Aubrey Townsend; and for secretarial assistance, Lois Osborn. The final responsibility for the contents (and the omissions) is, of course, mine.

P. S.

April 1986

I

DEATH

THOMAS NAGEL

IF death is the unequivocal and permanent end of our existence, the question arises whether it is a bad thing to die.

There is conspicuous disagreement about the matter: some people think death is dreadful; others have no objection to death *per se*, though they hope their own will be neither premature nor painful. Those in the former category tend to think those in the latter are blind to the obvious, while the latter suppose the former to be prey to some sort of confusion. On the one hand it can be said that life is all we have and the loss of it is the greatest loss we can sustain. On the other hand it may be objected that death deprives this supposed loss of its subject, and that if we realize that death is not an unimaginable condition of the persisting person, but a mere blank, we will see that it can have no value whatever, positive or negative.

Since I want to leave aside the question whether we are, or might be, immortal in some form, I shall simply use the word 'death' and its cognates in this discussion to mean *permanent* death, unsupplemented by any form of conscious survival. I want to ask whether death is in itself an evil; and how great an evil, and of what kind, it might be. The question should be of interest even to those who believe in some form of immortality, for one's attitude toward immortality must depend in part on one's attitude toward death.

If death is an evil at all, it cannot be because of its positive features, but only because of what it deprives us of. I shall try to deal with the difficulties surrounding the natural view that death is an evil because it brings to an end all the goods that life contains. We need not give an account of these goods here, except to observe that some of them, like perception, desire, activity, and thought, are so

Thomas Nagel, 'Death' from *Mortal Questions* (1979), pp. 1–10. Reprinted by permission of Cambridge University Press and the author.

general as to be constitutive of human life. They are widely
regarded as formidable benefits in themselves, despite the fact that
they are conditions of misery as well as of happiness, and that a
sufficient quantity of more particular evils can perhaps outweigh
them. That is what is meant, I think, by the allegation that it is good
simply to be alive, even if one is undergoing terrible experiences.
The situation is roughly this: There are elements which, if added to
one's experience, make life better; there are other elements which,
if added to one's experience, make life worse. But what remains
when these are set aside is not merely *neutral*: it is emphatically
positive. Therefore life is worth living even when the bad elements
of experience are plentiful, and the good ones too meagre to
outweigh the bad ones on their own. The additional positive weight
is supplied by experience itself, rather than by any of its contents.

I shall not discuss the value that one person's life or death may
have for others, or its objective value, but only the value it has for
the person who is its subject. That seems to me the primary case,
and the case which presents the greatest difficulties. Let me add
only two observations. First, the value of life and its contents does
not attach to mere organic survival: almost everyone would be
indifferent (other things equal) between immediate death and
immediate coma followed by death twenty years later without
reawakening. And second, like most goods, this can be multiplied
by time: more is better than less. The added quantities need not be
temporally continuous (though continuity has its social advantages). People are attracted to the possibility of long-term suspended
animation or freezing, followed by the resumption of conscious life,
because they can regard it from within simply as a *continuation* of
their present life. If these techniques are ever perfected, what from
outside appeared as a dormant interval of three hundred years
could be experienced by the subject as nothing more than a sharp
discontinuity in the character of his experiences. I do not deny, of
course, that this has its own disadvantages. Family and friends may
have died in the meantime; the language may have changed; the
comforts of social, geographical, and cultural familiarity would be
lacking. Nevertheless these inconveniences would not obliterate
the basic advantage of continued, though discontinuous, existence.

If we turn from what is good about life to what is bad about death, the case is completely different. Essentially, though there may be problems about their specification, what we find desirable in life are certain states, conditions, or types of activity. It is *being* alive, *doing* certain things, having certain experiences, that we consider good. But if death is an evil, it is the *loss of life*, rather than the state of being dead, or non-existent, or unconscious, that is objectionable.[1] This asymmetry is important. If it is good to be alive, that advantage can be attributed to a person at each point of his life. It is a good of which Bach had more than Schubert, simply because he lived longer. Death, however, is not an evil of which Shakespeare has so far received a larger portion than Proust. If death is a disadvantage, it is not easy to say when a man suffers it.

There are two other indications that we do not object to death merely because it involves long periods of non-existence. First, as has been mentioned, most of us would not regard the *temporary* suspension of life, even for substantial intervals, as in itself a misfortune. If it ever happens that people can be frozen without reduction of the conscious life-span, it will be inappropriate to pity those who are temporarily out of circulation. Second, none of us existed before we were born (or conceived), but few regard that as a misfortune. I shall have more to say about this later.

The point that death is not regarded as an unfortunate *state* enables us to refute a curious but very common suggestion about the origin of the fear of death. It is often said that those who object to death have made the mistake of trying to imagine what it is like to *be* dead. It is alleged that the failure to realize that this task is logically impossible (for the banal reason that there is nothing to imagine) leads to the conviction that death is a mysterious and therefore terrifying prospective *state*. But this diagnosis is evidently false, for it is just as impossible to imagine being totally unconscious as to imagine being dead (though it is easy enough to imagine oneself, from the outside, in either of those conditions). Yet people who are averse to death are not usually averse to unconsciousness (so long as it does not entail a substantial cut in the total duration of waking life).

If we are to make sense of the view that to die is bad, it must be on

---

[1] It is sometimes suggested that what we really mind is the process of *dying*. But I should not really object to dying if it were not followed by death.

the ground that life is a good and death is the corresponding deprivation or loss, bad not because of any positive features but because of the desirability of what it removes. We must now turn to the serious difficulties which this hypothesis raises, difficulties about loss and privation in general, and about death in particular.

Essentially, there are three types of problem. First, doubt may be raised whether *anything* can be bad for a man without being positively unpleasant to him: specifically, it may be doubted that there are any evils which consist merely in the deprivation or absence of possible goods, and which do not depend on someone's *minding* that deprivation. Second, there are special difficulties, in the case of death, about how the supposed misfortune is to be assigned to a subject at all. There is doubt both as to *who* its subject is, and as to *when* he undergoes it. So long as a person exists, he has not yet died, and once he has died, he no longer exists; so there seems to be no time when death, if it is a misfortune, can be ascribed to its unfortunate subject. The third type of difficulty concerns the asymmetry, mentioned above, between our attitudes to posthumous and pre-natal non-existence. How can the former be bad if the latter is not?

It should be recognized that if these are valid objections to counting death as an evil, they will apply to many other supposed evils as well. The first type of objection is expressed in general form by the common remark that what you don't know can't hurt you. It means that even if a man is betrayed by his friends, ridiculed behind his back, and despised by people who treat him politely to his face, none of it can be counted as a misfortune for him so long as he does not suffer as a result. It means that a man is not injured if his wishes are ignored by the executor of his will, or if, after his death, the belief becomes current that all the literary works on which his fame rests were really written by his brother, who died in Mexico at the age of 28. It seems to me worth asking what assumptions about good and evil lead to these drastic restrictions.

All the questions have something to do with time. There certainly are goods and evils of a simple kind (including some pleasures and pains) which a person possesses at a given time simply in virtue of his condition at that time. But this is not true of all the things we regard as good or bad for a man. Often we need to know his history to tell whether something is a misfortune or not; this applies to ills like deterioration, deprivation, and damage. Sometimes his experiential *state* is relatively unimportant—as in the case of a man who wastes his life in the cheerful pursuit of a method of communicating with asparagus plants. Someone who holds that all goods and evils must be temporally assignable states of the person may, of course, try to bring difficult cases into line by pointing to the pleasure or pain that more complicated goods and evils cause. Loss, betrayal, deception, and ridicule are on this view bad because people suffer when they learn of them. But it should be asked how our ideas of human value would have to be constituted to accommodate these cases directly instead. One advantage of such an account might be that it would enable us to explain *why* the discovery of these misfortunes causes suffering—in a way that makes it reasonable. For the natural view is that the discovery of betrayal makes us unhappy because it is bad to be betrayed—not that betrayal is bad because its discovery makes us unhappy.

It therefore seems to me worth exploring the position that most good and ill fortune has as its subject a person identified by his history and his possibilities, rather than merely by his categorical state of the moment—and that while this subject can be exactly located in a sequence of places and times, the same is not necessarily true of the goods and ills that befall him.[2]

These ideas can be illustrated by an example of deprivation whose severity approaches that of death. Suppose an intelligent person receives a brain injury that reduces him to the mental condition of a contented infant, and that such desires as remain to him can be satisfied by a custodian, so that he is free from care. Such a development would be widely regarded as a severe misfortune, not only for his friends and relations, or for society, but also, and primarily, for the person himself. This does not mean that a contented infant is unfortunate. The intelligent adult who has been *reduced* to this condition is the subject of the misfortune. He is the one we pity, though of course he does not mind his condition—there is some doubt, in fact, whether he can be said to exist any longer.

The view that such a man has suffered a misfortune is open to the

---

[2] It is certainly not true in general of the things that can be said of him. For example, Abraham Lincoln was taller than Louis XIV. But when?

same objections which have been raised in regard to death. He does not mind his condition. It is in fact the same condition he was in at the age of three months, except that he is bigger. If we did not pity him then, why pity him now; in any case, who is there to pity? The intelligent adult has disappeared, and for a creature like the one before us, happiness consists in a full stomach and a dry diaper.

If these objections are invalid, it must be because they rest on a mistaken assumption about the temporal relation between the subject of a misfortune and the circumstances which constitute it. If, instead of concentrating exclusively on the over-sized baby before us, we consider the person he was, and the person he *could* be now, then his reduction to this state and the cancellation of his natural adult development constitute a perfectly intelligible catastrophe.

This case should convince us that it is arbitrary to restrict the goods and evils that can befall a man to non-relational properties ascribable to him at particular times. As it stands, that restriction excludes not only such cases of gross degeneration, but also a good deal of what is important about success and failure, and other features of a life that have the character of processes. I believe we can go further, however. There are goods and evils which are irreducibly relational; they are features of the relations between a person, with spatial and temporal boundaries of the usual sort, and circumstances which may not coincide with him either in space or in time. A man's life includes much that does not take place within the boundaries of his body and his mind, and what happens to him can include much that does not take place within the boundaries of his life. These boundaries are commonly crossed by the misfortunes of being deceived, or despised, or betrayed. (If this is correct, there is a simple account of what is wrong with breaking a deathbed promise. It is an injury to the dead man. For certain purposes it is possible to regard time as just another type of distance.) The case of mental degeneration shows us an evil that depends on a contrast between the reality and the possible alternatives. A man is the subject of good and evil as much because he has hopes which may or may not be fulfilled, or possibilities which may or may not be realized, as because of his capacity to suffer and enjoy. If death is an evil, it must be accounted for in these terms, and the impossibility of locating it within life should not trouble us.

When a man dies we are left with his corpse, and while a corpse can suffer the kind of mishap that may occur to an article of furniture, it is not a suitable object for pity. The man, however, is. He has lost his life, and if he had not died, he would have continued to live it, and to possess whatever good there is in living. If we apply to death the account suggested for the case of dementia, we shall say that although the spatial and temporal locations of the individual who suffered the loss are clear enough, the misfortune itself cannot be so easily located. One must be content just to state that his life is over and there will never be any more of it. That *fact*, rather than his past or present condition, constitutes his misfortune, if it is one. Nevertheless if there is a loss, someone must suffer it, and *he* must have existence and specific spatial and temporal location even if the loss itself does not. The fact that Beethoven had no children may have been a cause of regret to him, or a sad thing for the world, but it cannot be described as a misfortune for the children that he never had. All of us, I believe, are fortunate to have been born. But unless good and ill can be assigned to an embryo, or even to an unconnected pair of gametes, it cannot be said that not to be born is a misfortune. (That is a factor to be considered in deciding whether abortion and contraception are akin to murder.)

This approach also provides a solution to the problem of temporal asymmetry, pointed out by Lucretius. He observed that no one finds it disturbing to contemplate the eternity preceding his own birth, and he took this to show that it must be irrational to fear death, since death is simply the mirror image of the prior abyss. That is not true, however, and the difference between the two explains why it is reasonable to regard them differently. It is true that both the time before a man's birth and the time after his death are times when he does not exist. But the time after his death is time of which his death deprives him. It is time in which, had he not died then, he would be alive. Therefore any death entails the loss of *some* life that its victim would have led had he not died at that or any earlier point. We know perfectly well what it would be for him to have had it instead of losing it, and there is no difficulty in identifying the loser.

But we cannot say that the time prior to a man's birth is time in which he would have lived had he been born not then but earlier.

For aside from the brief margin permitted by premature labour, he *could* not have been born earlier: anyone born substantially earlier than he was would have been someone else. Therefore the time prior to his birth is not time in which his subsequent birth prevents him from living. His birth, when it occurs, does not entail the loss to him of any life whatever.

The direction of time is crucial in assigning possibilities to people or other individuals. Distinct possible lives of a single person can diverge from a common beginning, but they cannot converge to a common conclusion from diverse beginnings. (The latter would represent not a set of different possible lives of one individual, but a set of distinct possible individuals, whose lives have identical conclusions.) Given an identifiable individual, countless possibilities for his continued existence are imaginable, and we can clearly conceive of what it would be for him to go on existing indefinitely. However inevitable it is that this will not come about, its possibility is still that of the continuation of a good for him, if life is the good we take it to be.[3]

We are left, therefore, with the question whether the non-realization of this possibility is in every case a misfortune, or

---

[3] I confess to being troubled by the above argument, on the ground that it is too sophisticated to explain the simple difference between our attitudes to pre-natal and posthumous non-existence. For this reason I suspect that something essential is omitted from the account of the badness of death by an analysis which treats it as a deprivation of possibilities. My suspicion is supported by the following suggestion of Robert Nozick. We could imagine discovering that people developed from individual spores that had existed indefinitely far in advance of their birth. In this fantasy, birth never occurs naturally more than a hundred years before the permanent end of the spore's existence. But then we discover a way to trigger the premature hatching of these spores, and people are born who have thousands of years of active life before them. Given such a situation, it would be possible to imagine *oneself* having come into existence thousands of years previously. If we put aside the question whether this would really be the same person, even given the identity of the spore, then the consequence appears to be that a person's birth at a given time *could* deprive him of many earlier years of possible life. Now while it would be cause for regret that one had been deprived of all those possible years of life by being born too late, the feeling would differ from that which many people have about death. I conclude that something about the future *prospect* of permanent nothingness is not captured by the analysis in terms of denied possibilities. If so, then Lucretius' argument still awaits an answer. I suspect that it requires a general treatment of the difference between past and future in our attitudes toward our own lives. Our attitudes toward past and future pain are very different, for example. Derek Parfit's unpublished writings on this topic have revealed its difficulty to me.

whether it depends on what can naturally be hoped for. This seems to me the most serious difficulty with the view that death is always an evil. Even if we can dispose of the objections against admitting misfortune that is not experienced, or cannot be assigned to a definite time in the person's life, we still have to set some limits on *how* possible a possibility must be for its non-realization to be a misfortune (or good fortune, should the possibility be a bad one). The death of Keats at 24 is generally regarded as tragic; that of Tolstoy at 82 is not. Although they will both be dead for ever, Keats's death deprived him of many years of life which were allowed to Tolstoy; so in a clear sense Keats's loss was greater (though not in the sense standardly employed in mathematical comparison between infinite quantities). However, this does not prove that Tolstoy's loss was insignificant. Perhaps we record an objection only to evils which are gratuitously added to the inevitable; the fact that it is worse to die at 24 than at 82 does not imply that it is not a terrible thing to die at 82, or even at 806. The question is whether we can regard as a misfortune any limitation, like mortality, that is normal to the species. Blindness or near-blindness is not a misfortune for a mole, nor would it be for a man, if that were the natural condition of the human race.

The trouble is that life familiarizes us with the goods of which death deprives us. We are already able to appreciate them, as a mole is not able to appreciate vision. If we put aside doubts about their status as goods and grant that their quantity is in part a function of their duration, the question remains whether death, no matter when it occurs, can be said to deprive its victim of what is in the relevant sense a possible continuation of life.

The situation is an ambiguous one. Observed from without, human beings obviously have a natural life-span and cannot live much longer than a hundred years. A man's sense of his own experience, on the other hand, does not embody this idea of a natural limit. His existence defines for him an essentially open-ended possible future, containing the usual mixture of goods and evils that he has found so tolerable in the past. Having been gratuitously introduced to the world by a collection of natural, historical, and social accidents, he finds himself the subject of a *life*, with an indeterminate and not essentially limited future. Viewed in this way, death, no matter how inevitable, is an abrupt cancellation of indefinitely extensive possible goods. Normality seems to have nothing to do with it, for the fact that we will all inevitably die in a few score years cannot by itself imply that it would not be good to live longer. Suppose that we were all inevitably going to die in *agony*—physical agony lasting six months. Would inevitability make *that* prospect any less unpleasant? And why should it be different for a deprivation? If the normal life-span were a thousand years, death at 80 would be a tragedy. As things are, it may just be a more widespread tragedy. If there is no limit to the amount of life that it would be good to have, then it may be that a bad end is in store for us all.

II

OF SUICIDE

DAVID HUME

ONE considerable advantage that arises from Philosophy, consists in the sovereign antidote which it affords to superstition and false religion. All other remedies against the pestilent distemper are vain, or at least uncertain. Plain good sense and the practice of the world, which alone serve most purposes of life, are here found ineffectual: History as well as daily experience furnish instances of men endowed with the strongest capacity for business and affairs, who have all their lives crouched under slavery to the grossest superstition. Even gaiety and sweetness of temper, which infuse a balm into every other wound, afford no remedy to so virulent a poison; as we may particularly observe of the fair Sex, who, tho' commonly possest of these rich presents of nature, feel many of their joys blasted by this importunate intruder. But when sound Philosophy has once gained possession of the mind, superstition is effectually excluded; and one may fairly affirm, that her triumph over this enemy is more complete than over most of the vices and imperfections incident to human nature. Love or anger, ambition, or avarice, have their root in the temper and affections, which the soundest reason is scarce ever able fully to correct; but superstition being founded on false opinion, must immediately vanish when true philosophy has inspired juster sentiments of superior powers. The contest is here more equal between the distemper and the medicine, and nothing can hinder the latter from proving effectual, but its being false and sophisticated.

It will here be superfluous to magnify the merits of philosophy, by displaying the pernicious tendency of that vice of which it cures the human mind. The superstitious man, says TULLY,[1] is miserable in

Published posthumously in 1784 and reprinted from *The Philosophical Works of David Hume*, ed. T. H. Green and T. H. Gosse (London, 1874–5).
[1] De Divin. lib. ii. 72, 150.

every scene, in every incident of life; even sleep itself, which banishes all other cares of unhappy mortals, affords to him matter of new terror; while he examines his dreams, and finds in those visions of the night prognostications of future calamities. I may add, that tho' death alone can put a full period to his misery, he dares not fly to this refuge, but still prolongs a miserable existence from a vain fear lest he offend his maker, by using the power, with which that beneficent being has endowed him. The presents of God and nature are ravished from us by his cruel enemy; and notwithstanding that one step would remove us from the regions of pain and sorrow, her menaces still chain us down to a hated being, which she herself chiefly contributes to render miserable.

'Tis observed by such as have been reduced by the calamities of life to the necessity of employing this fatal remedy, that if the unseasonable care of their friends deprive them of that species of Death, which they proposed to themselves, they seldom venture upon any other, or can summon up so much resolution a second time, as to execute their purpose. So great is our horror of death, that when it presents itself, under any form, besides that to which a man has endeavoured to reconcile his imagination, it acquires new terrors and overcomes his feeble courage: But when the menaces of superstition are joined to this natural timidity, no wonder it quite deprives men of all power over their lives, since even many pleasures and enjoyments, to which we are carried by a strong propensity, are torn from us by this inhuman tyrant. Let us here endeavour to restore men to their native liberty by examining all the common arguments against Suicide, and shewing that that action may be free from every imputation of guilt or blame, according to the sentiments of all the antient philosophers.

If Suicide be criminal, it must be a transgression of our duty either to God, our neighbour, or ourselves.—To prove that suicide is no transgression of our duty to God, the following considerations may perhaps suffice. In order to govern the material world, the almighty Creator has established general and immutable laws by which all bodies, from the greatest planet to the smallest particle of matter, are maintained in their proper sphere and function. To govern the animal world, he has endowed all living creatures with bodily and mental powers; with senses, passions, appetites, memory and judgement, by which they are impelled or regulated in that course of life to which they are destined. These two distinct principles of the material and animal world, continually encroach upon each other, and mutually retard or forward each other's operations. The powers of men and of all other animals are restrained and directed by the nature and qualities of the surrounding bodies; and the modifications and actions of these bodies are incessantly altered by the operation of all animals. Man is stopt by rivers in his passage over the surface of the earth; and rivers, when properly directed, lend their force to the motion of machines, which serve to the use of man. But tho' the provinces of the material and animal powers are not kept entirely separate, there results from thence no discord or disorder in the creation; on the contrary, from the mixture, union and contrast of all the various powers of inanimate bodies and living creatures, arises that surprising harmony and proportion which affords the surest argument of supreme wisdom. The providence of the Deity appears not immediately in any operation, but governs everything by those general and immutable laws, which have been established from the beginning of time. All events, in one sense, may be pronounced the action of the Almighty; they all proceed from those powers with which he has endowed his creatures. A house which falls by its own weight is not brought to ruin by his providence more than one destroyed by the hands of men; nor are the human faculties less his workmanship, than the laws of motion and gravitation. When the passions play, when the judgement dictates, when the limbs obey; this is all the operation of God, and upon these animate principles, as well as upon the inanimate, has he established the government of the universe. Every event is alike important in the eyes of that infinite being, who takes in at one glance the most distant regions of space and remotest periods of time. There is no event, however important to us, which he has exempted from the general laws that govern the universe, or which he has peculiarly reserved for his own immediate action and operation. The revolution of states and empires depends upon the smallest caprice or passion of single men; and the lives of men are shortened or extended by the smallest accident of air or diet, sunshine or tempest. Nature still continues her progress and operation; and if general laws be ever broke by particular volitions of the

Deity, 'tis after a manner which entirely escapes human observation. As, on the one hand, the elements and other inanimate parts of the creation carry on their action without regard to the particular interest and situation of men; so men are entrusted to their own judgement and discretion, in the various shocks of matter, and may employ every faculty with which they are endowed, in order to provide for their ease, happiness, or preservation. What is the meaning then of that principle, that a man who, tired of life, and hunted by pain and misery, bravely overcomes all the natural terrors of death and makes his escape from this cruel scene; that such a man, I say, has incurred the indignation of his Creator by encroaching on the office of divine providence, and disturbing the order of the universe? shall we assert that the Almighty has reserved to himself in any peculiar manner the disposal of the lives of men, and has not submitted that event, in common with others, to the general laws by which the universe is governed? This is plainly false; the lives of men depend upon the same laws as the lives of all other animals; and these are subjected to the general laws of matter and motion. The fall of a tower, or the infusion of a poison, will destroy a man equally with the meanest creature; an inundation sweeps away every thing without distinction that comes within the reach of its fury. Since therefore the lives of men are for ever dependent on the general laws of matter and motion, is a man's disposing of his life criminal, because in every case it is criminal to encroach upon these laws, or disturb their operation? But this seems absurd; all animals are entrusted to their own prudence and skill for their conduct in the world, and have full authority, as far as their power extends, to alter all the operations of nature. Without the exercise of this authority they could not subsist a moment; every action, every motion of a man, innovates on the order of some parts of matter, and diverts from their ordinary course the general laws of motion. Putting together, therefore, these conclusions, we find that human life depends upon the general laws of matter and motion, and that it is no encroachment on the office of providence to disturb or alter these general laws: Has not every one, of consequence, the free disposal of his own life? And may he not lawfully employ that power with which nature has endowed him? In order to destroy the evidence of this conclusion, we must shew a reason, why this particular case is excepted; is it because human life is of so great importance, that 'tis a presumption for human prudence to dispose of it? But the life of a man is of no greater importance to the universe than that of an oyster. And were it of ever so great importance, the order of nature has actually submitted it to human prudence, and reduced us to a necessity in every incident of determining concerning it. Were the disposal of human life so much reserved as the peculiar province of the Almighty that it were an encroachment on his right, for men to dispose of their own lives; it would be equally criminal to act for the preservation of life as for its destruction. If I turn aside a stone which is falling upon my head, I disturb the course of nature, and I invade the peculiar province of the Almighty by lengthening out my life beyond the period which by the general laws of matter and motion he had assigned it.

A hair, a fly, an insect is able to destroy this mighty being whose life is of such importance. Is it an absurdity to suppose that human prudence may lawfully dispose of what depends on such insignificant causes? It would be no crime in me to divert the *Nile* or *Danube* from its course, were I able to effect such purposes. Where then is the crime of turning a few ounces of blood from their natural channel?—Do you imagine that I repine at providence or curse my creation, because I go out of life, and put a period to a being, which, were it to continue, would render me miserable? Far be such sentiments from me; I am only convinced of a matter of fact, which you yourself acknowledge possible, that human life may be unhappy, and that my existence, if further prolonged, would become ineligible: but I thank providence, both for the good which I have already enjoyed, and for the power with which I am endowed of escaping the ill that threatens me.[2] To you it belongs to repine at providence, who foolishly imagine that you have no such power, and who must still prolong a hated life, tho' loaded with pain and sickness, with shame and poverty.—Do you not teach, that when any ill befalls me, tho' by the malice of my enemies, I ought to be resigned to providence, and that the actions of men are the operations of the Almighty as much as the actions of inanimate beings? When I fall upon my own sword, therefore, I receive my death equally from the hands of the Deity as if it had proceeded from a

[2] Agamus Deo gratias, quod nemo in vita teneri potest. SEN., Epist. 12.

lion, a precipice, or a fever. The submission which you require to providence, in every calamity that befalls me, excludes not human skill and industry, if possibly by their means I can avoid or escape the calamity: And why may I not employ one remedy as well as another?—If my life be not my own, it were criminal for me to put it in danger, as well as to dispose of it; nor could one man deserve the appellation of *hero* whom glory or friendship transports into the greatest dangers, and another merit the reproach of *wretch* or *miscreant* who puts a period to his life from the same or like motives.—There is no being, which possesses any power or faculty, that it receives not from its Creator, nor is there any one, which by ever so irregular an action can encroach upon the plan of his providence, or disorder the universe. Its operations are his works equally with that chain of events, which it invades, and which ever principle prevails, we may for that very reason conclude it to be most favoured by him. Be it animate, or inanimate, rational, or irrational; 'tis all a case: Its power is still derived from the supreme creator, and is alike comprehended in the order of his providence. When the horror of pain prevails over the love of life; when a voluntary action anticipates the effects of blind causes; 'tis only in consequence of those powers and principles, which he has implanted in his creatures. Divine providence is still inviolate and placed far beyond the reach of human injuries.[3] 'Tis impious, says the old Roman superstition, to divert rivers from their course, or invade the prerogatives of nature. 'Tis impious, says the French superstition, to inoculate for the small-pox, or usurp the business of providence, by voluntarily producing distempers and maladies. 'Tis impious, says the modern *European* superstition, to put a period to our own life, and thereby rebel against our creator; and why not impious, say I, to build houses, cultivate the ground, or sail upon the ocean? In all these actions we employ our powers of mind and body, to produce some innovation in the course of nature; and in none of them do we any more. They are all of them therefore equally innocent, or equally criminal.—*But you are placed by providence, like a centinel in a particular station, and when you desert it without being recalled, you are equally guilty of rebellion against your almighty sovereign, and have incurred his displeasure.*—I ask, why

---

[3] TACIT. Ann lib. i. 79.

do you conclude that providence has placed me in this station? For my part I find that I owe my birth to a long chain of causes, of which many depended upon voluntary actions of men. *But Providence guided all these Causes, and nothing happens in the universe without its consent and Co-operation.* If so, then neither does my death, however voluntary, happen without its consent; and whenever pain or sorrow so far overcome my patience, as to make me tired of life, I may conclude that I am recalled from my station in the clearest and most express terms. 'Tis Providence surely that has placed me at this present moment in this chamber: but may I not leave it when I think proper, without being liable to the imputation of having deserted my post or station? When I shall be dead, the principles of which I am composed will still perform their part in the universe, and will be equally useful in the grand fabric, as when they composed this individual creature. The difference to the whole will be no greater than betwixt my being in a chamber and in the open air. The one change is of more importance to me than the other; but not more so to the universe.

'Tis a kind of blasphemy to imagine that any created being can disturb the order of the world or invade the business of providence! It supposes, that that Being possesses powers and faculties, which it received not from its creator, and which are not subordinate to his government and authority. A man may disturb society no doubt, and thereby incur the displeasure of the Almighty: But the government of the world is placed far beyond his reach and violence. And how does it appear that the Almighty is displeased with those actions that disturb society? By the principles which he has implanted in human nature, and which inspire us with a sentiment of remorse if we ourselves have been guilty of such actions, and with that of blame and disapprobation, if we ever observe them in orders.—Let us now examine, according to the method proposed, whether Suicide be of this kind of actions, and be a breach of our duty to our *neighbour* and to *society*.

A man, who retires from life, does no harm to society: He only ceases to do good; which, if it is an injury, is of the lowest kind.—All our obligations to do good to society seem to imply something reciprocal. I receive the benefits of society and therefore ought to promote its interests, but when I withdraw myself altogether from society, can I be bound any longer? But, allowing that our obligations to do good were perpetual, they have certainly some bounds; I am not obliged to do a small good to society at the expense of a great harm to myself; why then should I prolong a miserable existence, because of some frivolous advantage which the public may perhaps receive from me? If upon account of age and infirmities I may lawfully resign any office, and employ my time altogether in fencing against these calamities, and alleviating as much as possible the miseries of my future life: Why may I not cut short these miseries at once by an action which is no more prejudicial to society?—But suppose that it is no longer in my power to promote the interest of society; suppose that I am a burthen to it; suppose that my life hinders some person from being much more useful to society. In such cases my resignation of life must not only be innocent but laudable. And most people who lie under any temptation to abandon existence, are in some such situation; those, who have health, or power, or authority, have commonly better reason to be in humour with the world.

A man is engaged in a conspiracy for the public interest; is seized upon suspicion; is threatened with the rack; and knows from his own weakness that the secret will be extorted from him: Could such a one consult the public interest better than by putting a quick period to a miserable life? This was the case of the famous and brave *Strozi* of *Florence.*—Again, suppose a malefactor is justly condemned to a shameful death; can any reason be imagined, why he may not anticipate his punishment, and save himself all the anguish of thinking on its dreadful approaches? He invades the business of providence no more than the magistrate did, who ordered his execution; and his voluntary death is equally advantageous to society by ridding it of a pernicious member.

That suicide may often be consistent with interest and with our duty to ourselves, no one can question, who allows that age, sickness, or misfortune may render life a burthen, and make it worse even than annihilation. I believe that no man ever threw away life, while it was worth keeping. For such is our natural horror of death, that small motives will never be able to reconcile us to it; and though perhaps the situation of a man's health or fortune did not seem to require this remedy, we may at least be assured, that any one who, without apparent reason, has had recourse to it, was curst with such an incurable depravity or gloominess of temper as must poison all enjoyment, and render him equally miserable as if he had been loaded with the most grievous misfortunes.—If suicide be supposed a crime, 'tis only cowardice can impel us to it. If it be no crime, both prudence and courage should engage us to rid ourselves at once of existence, when it becomes a burthen. 'Tis the only way that we can then be useful to society, by setting an example, which, if imitated, would preserve to every one his chance for happiness in life and would effectually free him from all danger or misery.[4]

---

[4] It would be easy to prove that Suicide is as lawful under the Christian dispensation as it was to the Heathens. There is not a single text of Scripture which prohibits it. That great and infallible rule of faith and practice which must controul all philosophy and human reasoning, has left us in this particular to our natural liberty. Resignation to Providence is indeed recommended in Scripture; but that implies only submission to ills that are unavoidable, not to such as may be remedied by prudence or courage. *Thou shalt not kill*, is evidently meant to exclude only the killing of others over whose life we have no authority. That this precept, like most of the Scripture precepts, must be modified by reason and common sense, is plain from the practice of magistrates, who punish criminals capitally, notwithstanding the letter of the law. But were this commandment ever so express against suicide, it would now have no authority, for all the law of *Moses* is abolished, except so far as it is established by the law of Nature. And we have already endeavoured to prove, that suicide is not prohibited by that law. In all cases Christians and Heathens are precisely upon the same footing; *Cato* and *Brutus*, *Arria* and *Portia* acted heroically; those who now imitate their example ought to receive the same praises from posterity. The power of committing suicide is regarded by *Pliny* as an advantage which men possess even above the deity himself. 'Deus non sibi potest mortem consciscere si velit, quod homini dedit optimum in tantis vitæ pœnis."—Lib. ii. cap. 5.

III

ACTIVE AND PASSIVE EUTHANASIA

JAMES RACHELS

THE distinction between active and passive euthanasia is thought to be crucial for medical ethics. The idea is that it is permissible, at least in some cases, to withhold treatment and allow a patient to die, but it is never permissible to take any direct action designed to kill the patient. This doctrine seems to be accepted by most doctors, and it is endorsed in a statement adopted by the House of Delegates of the American Medical Association on 4 December 1973:

> The intentional termination of the life of one human being by another—mercy killing—is contrary to that for which the medical profession stands and is contrary to the policy of the American Medical Association.
>
> The cessation of the employment of extraordinary means to prolong the life of the body when there is irrefutable evidence that biological death is imminent is the decision of the patient and/or his immediate family. The advice and judgement of the physician should be freely available to the patient and/or his immediate family.

However, a strong case can be made against this doctrine. In what follows I will set out some of the relevant arguments, and urge doctors to reconsider their views on this matter.

To begin with a familiar type of situation, a patient who is dying of incurable cancer of the throat is in terrible pain, which can no longer be satisfactorily alleviated. He is certain to die within a few days, even if present treatment is continued, but he does not want to go on living for those days since the pain is unbearable. So he asks the doctor for an end to it, and his family joins in the request.

Suppose the doctor agrees to withhold treatment, as the conventional doctrine says he may. The justification for his doing so is that the patient is in terrible agony, and since he is going to die anyway, it

James Rachels, 'Active and Passive Euthanasia', *The New England Journal of Medicine*, Vol. 292, pp. 78–80, 1975. Copyright 1975 Massachusetts Medical Society. Reprinted by permission.

would be wrong to prolong his suffering needlessly. But now notice this. If one simply withholds treatment, it may take the patient longer to die, and so he may suffer more than he would if more direct action were taken and a lethal injection given. This fact provides strong reason for thinking that, once the initial decision not to prolong his agony has been made, active euthanasia is actually preferable to passive euthanasia, rather than the reverse. To say otherwise is to endorse the option that leads to more suffering rather than less, and is contrary to the humanitarian impulse that prompts the decision not to prolong his life in the first place.

Part of my point is that the process of being 'allowed to die' can be relatively slow and painful, whereas being given a lethal injection is relatively quick and painless. Let me give a different sort of example. In the United States about one in 600 babies is born with Down's syndrome. Most of these babies are otherwise healthy— that is, with only the usual pediatric care, they will proceed to an otherwise normal infancy. Some, however, are born with con- genital defects such as intestinal obstructions that require opera- tions if they are to live. Sometimes, the parents and the doctor will decide not to operate, and let the infant die. Anthony Shaw describes what happens then:

When surgery is denied [the doctor] must try to keep the infant from suffering while natural forces sap the baby's life away. As a surgeon whose natural inclination is to use the scalpel to fight off death, standing by and watching a salvageable baby die is the most emotionally exhausting experi- ence I know. It is easy at a conference, in a theoretical discussion to decide that such infants should be allowed to die. It is altogether different to stand by in the nursery and watch as dehydration and infection wither a tiny being over hours and days. This is a terrible ordeal for me and the hospital staff— much more so than for the parents who never set foot in the nursery.[1]

I can understand why some people are opposed to all euthanasia, and insist that such infants must be allowed to live. I think I can also understand why other people favour destroying these babies quickly and painlessly. But why should anyone favour letting 'dehydration and infection wither a tiny being over hours and

[1] Shaw, Anthony, 'Doctor, Do We Have a Choice?' *The New York Times Magazine*, 30 Jan. 1972, p. 54.

days'? The doctrine that says a baby may be allowed to dehydrate and wither, but may not be given an injection that would end its life without suffering, seems so patently cruel as to require no further refutation. The strong language is not intended to offend, but only to put the point in the clearest possible way.

My second argument is that the conventional doctrine leads to decisions concerning life and death made on irrelevant grounds.

Consider again the case of the infants with Down's syndrome who need operations for congenital defects unrelated to the syndrome to live. Sometimes, there is no operation, and the baby dies, but when there is no such defect, the baby lives on. Now, an operation such as that to remove an intestinal obstruction is not prohibitively difficult. The reason why such operations are not performed in these cases is, clearly, that the child has Down's syndrome and the parents and the doctor judge that because of that fact it is better for the child to die.

But notice that this situation is absurd, no matter what view one takes of the lives and potentials of such babies. If the life of such an infant is worth preserving what does it matter if it needs a simple operation? Or, if one thinks it better that such a baby should not live on, what difference does it make that it happens to have an unobstructed intestinal tract? In either case, the matter of life and death is being decided on irrelevant grounds. It is the Down's syndrome, and not the intestines, that is the issue. The matter should be decided, if at all, on that basis, and not be allowed to depend on the essentially irrelevant question of whether the intestinal tract is blocked.

What makes this situation possible, of course, is the idea that when there is an intestinal blockage, one can 'let the baby die', but when there is no such defect there is nothing that can be done, for one must not 'kill' it. The fact that this idea leads to such results as deciding life or death on irrelevant grounds is another good reason why the doctrine would be rejected.

One reason why so many people think that there is an important moral difference between active and passive euthanasia is that they think killing someone is morally worse than letting someone die. But is it? Is killing, in itself, worse than letting die? To investigate this issue, two cases may be considered that are exactly alike except that one involves killing whereas the other involves letting someone die. Then, it can be asked whether this difference makes any difference to the moral assessments. It is important that the cases be exactly alike, except for this one difference, since otherwise one cannot be confident that it is this difference and not some other that accounts for any variation in the assessments of the two cases. So, let us consider this pair of cases:

In the first, Smith stands to gain a large inheritance if anything should happen to his six-year-old cousin. One evening while the child is taking his bath, Smith sneaks into the bathroom and drowns the child, and then arranges things so that it will look like an accident.

In the second, Jones also stands to gain if anything should happen to his six-year-old cousin. Like Smith, Jones sneaks in planning to drown the child in his bath. However, just as he enters the bathroom Jones sees the child slip and hit his head, and fall face down in the water. Jones is delighted; he stands by, ready to push the child's head back under if it is necessary, but it is not necessary. With only a little thrashing about, the child drowns all by himself, 'accidentally', as Jones watches and does nothing.

Now Smith killed the child, whereas Jones 'merely' let the child die. That is the only difference between them. Did either man behave better, from a moral point of view? If the difference between killing and letting die were in itself a morally important matter, one should say that Jones's behaviour was less reprehensible than Smith's. But does one really want to say that? I think not. In the first place, both men acted from the same motive, personal gain, and both had exactly the same end in view when they acted. It may be inferred from Smith's conduct that he is a bad man, although that judgement may be withdrawn or modified if certain further facts are learned about him—for example, that he is mentally deranged. But would not the very same thing be inferred about Jones from his conduct? And would not the same further considerations also be relevant to any modification of this judgement? Moreover, suppose Jones pleaded, in his own defence, 'After all, I didn't do anything except just stand there and watch the child drown. I didn't kill him; I only let him die.' Again, if letting die were in itself less bad than killing, this defence should have at least some weight. But it does not. Such a 'defence' can only be regarded as a grotesque perversion of moral reasoning. Morally speaking, it is no defence at all.

Now, it may be pointed out, quite properly, that the cases of euthanasia with which doctors are concerned are not like this at all. They do not involve personal gain or the destruction of normal healthy children. Doctors are concerned only with cases in which the patient's life is of no further use to him, or in which the patient's life has become or will soon become a terrible burden. However, the point is the same in these cases: the bare difference between killing and letting die does not, in itself, make a moral difference. If a doctor lets a patient die, for humane reasons, he is in the same moral position as if he had given the patient a lethal injection for humane reasons. If his decision was wrong—if, for example, the patient's illness was in fact curable—the decision would be equally regrettable no matter which method was used to carry it out. And if the doctor's decision was the right one, the method used is not in itself important.

The AMA policy statement isolates the crucial issue very well; the crucial issue is 'the intentional termination of the life of one human being by another'. But after identifying this issue, and forbidding 'mercy killing', the statement goes on to deny that the cessation of treatment is the intentional termination of a life. This is where the mistake comes in, for what is the cessation of treatment, in these circumstances, if it is not 'the intentional termination of the life of one human being by another'? Of course it is exactly that, and if it were not, there would be no point to it.

Many people will find this judgement hard to accept. One reason, I think, is that it is very easy to conflate the question of whether killing is, in itself, worse than letting die, with the very different question of whether most actual cases of killing are more reprehensible than most actual cases of letting die. Most actual cases of killing are clearly terrible (think, for example, of all the murders reported in the newspapers), and one hears of such cases every day. On the other hand, one hardly ever hears of a case of letting die, except for the actions of doctors who are motivated by humanitarian reasons. So one learns to think of killing in a much worse light than of letting die. But this does not mean that there is something about killing that makes it in itself worse than letting die, for it is not the bare difference between killing and letting die that makes the difference in these cases. Rather, the other factors—the murderer's motive of personal gain, for example, contrasted with the doctor's humanitarian motivation—account for different reactions to the different cases.

I have argued that killing is not in itself any worse than letting die; if my contention is right, it follows that active euthanasia is not any worse than passive euthanasia. What arguments can be given on the other side? The most common, I believe, is the following:

> The important difference between active and passive euthanasia is that, in passive euthanasia, the doctor does not do anything to bring about the patient's death. The doctor does nothing, and the patient dies of whatever ills already afflict him. In active euthanasia, however, the doctor does something to bring about the patient's death: he kills him. The doctor who gives the patient with cancer a lethal injection has himself caused his patient's death; whereas if he merely ceases treatment, the cancer is the cause of the death.

A number of points need to be made here. The first is that it is not exactly correct to say that in passive euthanasia the doctor does nothing, for he does do one thing that is very important: he lets the patient die. 'Letting someone die' is certainly different, in some respects, from other types of action—mainly in that it is a kind of action that one may perform by way of not performing certain other actions. For example, one may let a patient die by way of not giving medication, just as one may insult someone by way of not shaking his hand. But for any purpose of moral assessment, it is a type of action none the less. The decision to let a patient die is subject to moral appraisal in the same way that a decision to kill him would be subject to moral appraisal: it may be assessed as wise or unwise, compassionate or sadistic, right or wrong. If a doctor deliberately let a patient die who was suffering from a routinely curable illness, the doctor would certainly be to blame for what he had done, just as he would be to blame if he had needlessly killed the patient. Charges against him would then be appropriate. If so, it would be no defence at all for him to insist that he didn't 'do anything'. He would have done something very serious indeed, for he let his patient die.

Fixing the cause of death may be very important from a legal point of view, for it may determine whether criminal charges are brought against the doctor. But I do not think that this notion can be used to show a moral difference between active and passive euthanasia. The reason why it is considered bad to be the cause of someone's death is that death is regarded as a great evil—and so it is. However, if it has been decided that euthanasia—even passive euthanasia—is desirable in a given case, it has also been decided that in this instance death is no greater an evil than the patient's continued existence. And if this is true, the usual reason for not wanting to be the cause of someone's death simply does not apply.

Finally, doctors may think that all of this is only of academic interest—the sort of thing that philosophers may worry about but that has no practical bearing on their own work. After all, doctors must be concerned about the legal consequences of what they do, and active euthanasia is clearly forbidden by the law. But even so, doctors should also be concerned with the fact that the law is forcing upon them a moral doctrine that may be indefensible, and has a considerable effect on their practices. Of course, most doctors are not now in the position of being coerced in this matter, for they do not regard themselves as merely going along with what the law requires. Rather, in statements such as the AMA policy statement that I have quoted, they are endorsing this doctrine as a central point of medical ethics. In that statement, active euthanasia is condemned not merely as illegal but as 'contrary to that for which the medical profession stands', whereas passive euthanasia is approved. However, the preceding considerations suggest that there is really no moral difference between the two, considered in themselves (there may be important moral differences in some cases in their *consequences*, but, as I pointed out, these differences may make active euthanasia, and not passive euthanasia, the morally preferable option). So, whereas doctors may have to discriminate between active and passive euthanasia to satisfy the law, they should not do any more than that. In particular, they should not give the distinction any added authority and weight by writing it into official statements of medical ethics.

IV

A DEFENCE OF ABORTION[1]

JUDITH JARVIS THOMSON

MOST opposition to abortion relies on the premiss that the foetus is a human being, a person, from the moment of conception. The premiss is argued for, but, as I think, not well. Take, for example, the most common argument. We are asked to notice that the development of a human being from conception through birth into childhood is continuous; then it is said that to draw a line, to choose a point in this development and say 'before this point the thing is not a person, after this point it is a person' is to make an arbitrary choice, a choice for which in the nature of things no good reason can be given. It is concluded that the foetus is, or anyway that we had better say it is, a person from the moment of conception. But this conclusion does not follow. Similar things might be said about the development of an acorn into an oak tree, and it does not follow that acorns are oak trees, or that we had better say they are. Arguments of this form are sometimes called 'slippery slope arguments'—the phrase is perhaps self-explanatory—and it is dismaying that opponents of abortion rely on them so heavily and uncritically.

I am inclined to agree, however, that the prospects for 'drawing a line' in the development of the foetus look dim. I am inclined to think also that we shall probably have to agree that the foetus has already become a human person well before birth. Indeed, it comes as a surprise when one first learns how early in its life it begins to acquire human characteristics. By the tenth week, for example, it already has a face, arms and legs, fingers and toes; it has internal organs, and brain activity is detectable.[2] On the other hand, I think

Judith Jarvis Thomson, 'A Defense of Abortion', *Philosophy & Public Affairs* 1, No. 1 (Fall 1971). Copyright © 1971 by Princeton University Press. Reprinted by permission.

[1] I am very much indebted to James Thomson for discussion, criticism, and many helpful suggestions.

[2] Daniel Callahan, *Abortion: Law, Choice and Morality* (New York, 1970),

that the premiss is false, that the foetus is not a person from the moment of conception. A newly fertilized ovum, a newly implanted clump of cells, is no more a person than an acorn is an oak tree. But I shall not discuss any of this. For it seems to me to be of great interest to ask what happens if, for the sake of argument, we allow the premiss. How, precisely, are we supposed to get from there to the conclusion that abortion is morally impermissible? Opponents of abortion commonly spend most of their time establishing that the foetus is a person, and hardly any time explaining the step from there to the impermissibility of abortion. Perhaps they think the step too simple and obvious to require much comment. Or perhaps instead they are simply being economical in argument. Many of those who defend abortion rely on the premiss that the foetus is not a person, but only a bit of tissue that will become a person at birth; and why pay out more arguments than you have to? Whatever the explanation, I suggest that the step they take is neither easy nor obvious, that it calls for closer examination than it is commonly given, and that when we do give it this closer examination we shall feel inclined to reject it.

I propose, then, that we grant that the foetus is a person from the moment of conception. How does the argument go from here? Something like this, I take it. Every person has a right to life. So the foetus has a right to life. No doubt the mother has a right to decide what shall happen in and to her body; everyone would grant that. But surely a person's right to life is stronger and more stringent than the mother's right to decide what happens in and to her body, and so outweighs it. So the foetus may not be killed; an abortion may not be performed.

It sounds plausible. But now let me ask you to imagine this. You wake up in the morning and find yourself back to back in bed with an unconscious violinist. A famous unconscious violinist. He has been found to have a fatal kidney ailment, and the Society of Music Lovers has canvassed all the available medical records and found that you alone have the right blood type to help. They have

p. 373. This book gives a fascinating survey of the available information on abortion. The Jewish tradition is surveyed in David M. Feldman, *Birth Control in Jewish Law* (New York, 1968), Part 5, the Catholic tradition in John T. Noonan, Jr., 'An Almost Absolute Value in History', in *The Morality of Abortion*, ed. John T. Noonan, Jr. (Cambridge, Mass., 1970).

therefore kidnapped you, and last night the violinist's circulatory system was plugged into yours, so that your kidneys can be used to extract poisons from his blood as well as your own. The director of the hospital now tells you, 'Look, we're sorry the Society of Music Lovers did this to you—we would never have permitted it if we had known. But still, they did it, and the violinist now is plugged into you. To unplug you would be to kill him. But never mind, it's only for nine months. By then he will have recovered from his ailment, and can safely be unplugged from you.' Is it morally incumbent on you to accede to this situation? No doubt it would be very nice of you if you did, a great kindness. But do you *have* to accede to it? What if it were not nine months, but nine years? Or longer still? What if the director of the hospital says, 'Tough luck, I agree, but you've now got to stay in bed, with the violinist plugged into you, for the rest of your life. Because remember this. All persons have a right to life, and violinists are persons. Granted you have a right to decide what happens in and to your body, but a person's right to life outweighs your right to decide what happens in and to your body. So you cannot ever be unplugged from him.' I imagine you would regard this as outrageous, which suggests that something really is wrong with that plausible-sounding argument I mentioned a moment ago.

In this case, of course, you were kidnapped; you didn't volunteer for the operation that plugged the violinist into your kidneys. Can those who oppose abortion on the ground I mentioned make an exception for a pregnancy due to rape? Certainly. They can say that persons have a right to life only if they didn't come into existence because of rape; or they can say that all persons have a right to life, but that some have less of a right to life than others, in particular, that those who came into existence because of rape have less. But these statements have a rather unpleasant sound. Surely the question of whether you have a right to life at all, or how much of it you have, shouldn't turn on the question of whether or not you are the product of a rape. And in fact the people who oppose abortion on the ground I mentioned do not make this distinction, and hence do not make an exception in case of rape.

Nor do they make an exception for a case in which the mother has to spend the nine months of her pregnancy in bed. They would agree that would be a great pity, and hard on the mother; but all the same, all persons have a right to life, the foetus is a person, and so on. I suspect, in fact, that they would not make an exception for a case in which, miraculously enough, the pregnancy went on for nine years, or even the rest of the mother's life.

Some won't even make an exception for a case in which continuation of the pregnancy is likely to shorten the mother's life; they regard abortion as impermissible even to save the mother's life. Such cases are nowadays very rare, and many opponents of abortion do not accept this extreme view. All the same, it is a good place to begin: a number of points of interest come out in respect to it.

1. Let us call the view that abortion is impermissible even to save the mother's life 'the extreme view'. I want to suggest first that it does not issue from the argument I mentioned earlier without the addition of some fairly powerful premisses. Suppose a woman has become pregnant, and now learns that she has a cardiac condition such that she will die if she carries the baby to term. What may be done for her? The foetus, being a person, has a right to life, but as the mother is a person too, so has she a right to life. Presumably they have an equal right to life. How is it supposed to come out that an abortion may not be performed? If mother and child have an equal right to life, shouldn't we perhaps flip a coin? Or should we add to the mother's right to life her right to decide what happens in and to her body, which everybody seems to be ready to grant—the sum of her rights now outweighing the foetus's right to life?

The most familiar argument here is the following. We are told that performing the abortion would be directly killing[3] the child, whereas doing nothing would not be killing the mother, but only letting her die. Moreover, in killing the child, one would be killing an innocent person, for the child has committed no crime, and is not aiming at his mother's death. And then there are a variety of ways in which this might be continued. (1) But as directly killing an innocent person is always and absolutely impermissible, an abortion may not be performed. Or, (2) as directly killing an innocent person is

[3] The term 'direct' in the arguments I refer to is a technical one. Roughly, what is meant by 'direct killing' is either killing as an end in itself, or killing as a means to some end, for example, the end of saving someone else's life. See note 6, below, for an example of its use.

murder, and murder is always and absolutely impermissible, an abortion may not be performed.[4] Or, (3) as one's duty to refrain from directly killing an innocent person is more stringent than one's duty to keep a person from dying, an abortion may not be performed. Or, (4) if one's only options are directly killing an innocent person or letting a person die, one must prefer letting the person die, and thus an abortion may not be performed.[5]

Some people seem to have thought that these are not further premises which must be added if the conclusion is to be reached, but that they follow from the very fact that an innocent person has a right to life.[6] But this seems to me to be a mistake, and perhaps the simplest way to show this is to bring out that while we must certainly grant that innocent persons have a right to life, the theses in (1) to (4) are all false. Take (2), for example. If directly killing an innocent person is murder, and thus is impermissible, then the mother's directly killing the innocent person inside her is murder, and thus is impermissible. But it cannot seriously be thought to be murder if the mother performs an abortion on herself to save her life. It cannot seriously be said that she *must* refrain, that she *must* sit passively by and wait for her death. Let us look again at the case of you and the violinist. There you are, in bed with the violinist, and the director of the hospital says to you, 'It's all most distressing, and

---

[4] Cf. *Encyclical Letter of Pope Pius XI on Christian Marriage*, St. Paul Editions (Boston, n.d.), p. 32: 'however much we may pity the mother whose health and even life is gravely imperiled in the performance of the duty allotted to her by nature, nevertheless what could ever be a sufficient reason for excusing in any way the direct murder of the innocent? This is precisely what we are dealing with here.' Noonan (*The Morality of Abortion*, p. 43) reads this as follows: 'What cause can ever avail to excuse in any way the direct killing of the innocent? For it is a question of that.'

[5] The thesis in (4) is in an interesting way weaker than those in (1), (2), and (3): they rule out abortion even in cases in which both mother *and* child will die if the abortion is not performed. By contrast, one who held the view expressed in (4) could consistently say that one needn't prefer letting two persons die to killing one.

[6] Cf. the following passage from Pius XII, *Address to the Italian Catholic Society of Midwives*: 'The baby in the maternal breast has the right to life immediately from God.—Hence there is no man, no human authority, no science, no medical, eugenic, social, economic or moral "indication" which can establish or grant a valid juridical ground for a direct deliberate disposition of an innocent human life, that is a disposition which looks to its destruction either as an end or as a means to another end perhaps in itself not illicit.—The baby, still not born, is a man in the same degree and for the same reason as the mother' (quoted in Noonan, *The Morality of Abortion*, p. 45).

I deeply sympathize, but you see this is putting an additional strain on your kidneys, and you'll be dead within the month. But you *have* to stay where you are all the same. Because unplugging you would be directly killing an innocent violinist, and that's murder, and that's impermissible.' If anything in the world is true, it is that you do not commit murder, you do not do what is impermissible, if you reach around to your back and unplug yourself from that violinist to save your life.

The main focus of attention in writings on abortion has been on what a third party may or may not do in answer to a request from a woman for an abortion. This is in a way understandable. Things being as they are, there isn't much a woman can safely do to abort herself. So the question asked is what a third party may do, and what the mother may do, if it is mentioned at all, is deduced, almost as an afterthought, from what it is concluded that third parties may do. But it seems to me that to treat the matter in this way is to refuse to grant to the mother that very status of person which is so firmly insisted on for the foetus. For we cannot simply read off what a person may do from what a third party may do. Suppose you find yourself trapped in a tiny house with a growing child. I mean a very tiny house, and a rapidly growing child—you are already up against the wall of the house and in a few minutes you'll be crushed to death. The child on the other hand won't be crushed to death; if nothing is done to stop him from growing he'll be hurt, but in the end he'll simply burst open the house and walk out a free man. Now I could well understand it if a bystander were to say, 'There's nothing we can do for you. We cannot choose between your life and his, we cannot be the ones to decide who is to live, we cannot intervene.' But it cannot be concluded that you too can do nothing, that you cannot attack it to save your life. However innocent the child may be, you do not have to wait passively while it crushes you to death. Perhaps a pregnant woman is vaguely felt to have the status of house, to which we don't allow the right of self-defence. But if the woman houses the child, it should be remembered that she is a person who houses it.

I should perhaps stop to say explicitly that I am not claiming that people have a right to do anything whatever to save their lives. I think, rather, that there are drastic limits to the right of self-defence. If someone threatens you with death unless you torture someone else to death, I think you have not the right, even to save your life, to do so. But the case under consideration here is very different. In our case there are only two people involved, one whose life is threatened, and one who threatens it. Both are innocent: the one who is threatened is not threatened because of any fault, the one who threatens does not threaten because of any fault. For this reason we may feel that we bystanders cannot intervene. But the person threatened can.

In sum, a woman surely can defend her life against the threat to it posed by the unborn child, even if doing so involves its death. And this shows not merely that the theses in (1) to (4) are false; it shows also that the extreme view of abortion is false, and so we need not canvass any other possible ways of arriving at it from the argument I mentioned at the outset.

2. The extreme view could of course be weakened to say that while abortion is permissible to save the mother's life, it may not be performed by a third party, but only by the mother herself. But this cannot be right either. For what we have to keep in mind is that the mother and the unborn child are not like two tenants in a small house which has, by an unfortunate mistake, been rented to both: the mother *owns* the house. The fact that she does adds to the offensiveness of deducing that the mother can do nothing from the supposition that third parties can do nothing. But it does more than this: it casts a bright light on the supposition that third parties can do nothing. Certainly it lets us see that a third party who says 'I cannot choose between you' is fooling himself if he thinks this is impartiality. If Jones has found and fastened on a certain coat, which he needs to keep him from freezing, but which Smith also needs to keep him from freezing, then it is not impartiality that says 'I cannot choose between you' when Smith owns the coat. Women have said again and again 'This body is *my* body!' and they have reason to feel angry, reason to feel that it has been like shouting into the wind. Smith, after all, is hardly likely to bless us if we say to him, 'Of course it's your coat, anybody would grant that it is. But no one may choose between you and Jones who is to have it.'

We should really ask what it is that says 'no one may choose' in the face of the fact that the body that houses the child is the mother's body. It may be simply a failure to appreciate this fact. But it may be something more interesting, namely the sense that one has a right to refuse to lay hands on people, even where it would be just and fair to do so, even where justice seems to require that somebody do so. Thus justice might call for somebody to get Smith's coat back from Jones, and yet you have a right to refuse to be the one to lay hands on Jones, a right to refuse to do physical violence to him. This, I think, must be granted. But then what should be said is not 'no one may choose', but only '*I* cannot choose', and indeed not even this, but '*I* will not *act*', leaving it open that somebody else can or should, and in particular that anyone in a position of authority, with the job of securing people's rights, both can and should. So this is no difficulty. I have not been arguing that any given third party must accede to the mother's request that he perform an abortion to save her life, but only that he may.

I suppose that in some views of human life the mother's body is only on loan to her, the loan not being one which gives her any prior claim to it. One who held this view might well think it impartiality to say 'I cannot choose'. But I shall simply ignore this possibility. My own view is that if a human being has any just, prior claim to anything at all, he has a just, prior claim to his own body. And perhaps this needn't be argued for here anyway, since, as I mentioned, the arguments against abortion we are looking at do grant that the woman has a right to decide what happens in and to her body.

But although they do grant it, I have tried to show that they do not take seriously what is done in granting it. I suggest the same thing will reappear even more clearly when we turn away from cases in which the mother's life is at stake, and attend, as I propose we now do, to the vastly more common cases in which a woman wants an abortion for some less weighty reason than preserving her own life.

3. Where the mother's life is not at stake, the argument I mentioned at the outset seems to have a much stronger pull. 'Everyone has a right to life, so the unborn person has a right to life.' And isn't the child's right to life weightier than anything other than the mother's own right to life, which she might put forward as ground for an abortion?

This argument treats the right to life as if it were unproblematic.

It is not, and this seems to me to be precisely the source of the mistake.

For we should now, at long last, ask what it comes to, to have a right to life. In some views having a right to life includes having a right to be given at least the bare minimum one needs for continued life. But suppose that what in fact *is* the bare minimum a man needs for continued life is something he has no right at all to be given? If I am sick unto death, and the only thing that will save my life is the touch of Henry Fonda's cool hand on my fevered brow, then all the same, I have no right to be given the touch of Henry Fonda's cool hand on my fevered brow. It would be frightfully nice of him to fly in from the West Coast to provide it. It would be less nice, though no doubt well meant, if my friends flew out to the West Coast and carried Henry Fonda back with them. But I have no right at all against anybody that he should do this for me. Or again, to return to the story I told earlier, the fact that for continued life that violinist needs the continued use of your kidneys does not establish that he has a right to be given the continued use of your kidneys. He certainly has no right against you that *you* should give him continued use of your kidneys. For nobody has any right to use your kidneys unless you give him such a right; and nobody has the right against you that you shall give him this right—if you do allow him to go on using your kidneys, this is a kindness on your part, and not something he can claim from you as his due. Nor has he any right against anybody else that *they* should give him continued use of your kidneys. Certainly he had no right against the Society of Music Lovers that they should plug him into you in the first place. And if you now start to unplug yourself, having learned that you will otherwise have to spend nine years in bed with him, there is nobody in the world who must try to prevent you, in order to see to it that he is given something he has a right to be given.

Some people are rather stricter about the right to life. In their view, it does not include the right to be given anything, but amounts to, and only to, the right not to be killed by anybody. But here a related difficulty arises. If everybody is to refrain from killing that violinist, then everybody must refrain from doing a great many different sorts of things. Everybody must refrain from slitting his throat, everybody must refrain from shooting him—and everybody must refrain from unplugging you from him. But does he have a right against everybody that they shall refrain from unplugging you from him? To refrain from doing this is to allow him to continue to use your kidneys. It could be argued that he has a right against us that *we* should allow him to continue to use your kidneys. That is, while he had no right against us that we should give him the use of your kidneys, it might be argued that he anyway has a right against us that we shall not now intervene and deprive him of the use of your kidneys. I shall come back to third-party interventions later. But certainly the violinist has no right against you that *you* shall allow him to continue to use your kidneys. As I said, if you do allow him to use them, it is a kindness on your part, and not something you owe him.

The difficulty I point to here is not peculiar to the right to life. It reappears in connection with all the other natural rights; and it is something which an adequate account of rights must deal with. For present purposes it is enough just to draw attention to it. But I would stress that I am not arguing that people do not have a right to life—quite to the contrary, it seems to me that the primary control we must place on the acceptability of an account of rights is that it should turn out in that account to be a truth that all persons have a right to life. I am arguing only that having a right to life does not guarantee having either a right to be given the use of or a right to be allowed continued use of another person's body—even if one needs it for life itself. So the right to life will not serve the opponents of abortion in the very simple and clear way in which they seem to have thought it would.

4. There is another way to bring out the difficulty. In the most ordinary sort of case, to deprive someone of what he has a right to is to treat him unjustly. Suppose a boy and his small brother are jointly given a box of chocolates for Christmas. If the older boy takes the box and refuses to give his brother any of the chocolates, he is unjust to him, for the brother has been given a right to half of them. But suppose that, having learned that otherwise it means nine years in bed with that violinist, you unplug yourself from him. You surely are not being unjust to him, for you gave him no right to use your kidneys, and no one else can have given him any such right. But we have to notice that in unplugging yourself, you are killing

him; and violinists, like everybody else, have a right to life, and thus in the view we were considering just now, the right not to be killed. So here you do what he supposedly has a right you shall not do, but you do not act unjustly to him in doing it.

The emendation which may be made at this point is this: the right to life consists not in the right not to be killed, but rather in the right not to be killed unjustly. This runs a risk of circularity, but never mind: it would enable us to square the fact that the violinist has a right to life with the fact that you do not act unjustly toward him in unplugging yourself, thereby killing him. For if you do not kill him unjustly, you do not violate his right to life, and so it is no wonder you do him no injustice.

But if this emendation is accepted, the gap in the argument against abortion stares us plainly in the face: it is by no means enough to show that the foetus is a person, and to remind us that all persons have a right to life—we need to be shown also that killing the foetus violates its right to life, i.e. that abortion is unjust killing. And is it?

I suppose we may take it as a datum that in a case of pregnancy due to rape the mother has not given the unborn person a right to the use of her body for food and shelter. Indeed, in what pregnancy could it be supposed that the mother has given the unborn person such a right? It is not as if there were unborn persons drifting about the world, to whom a woman who wants a child says 'I invite you in'.

But it might be argued that there are other ways one can have acquired a right to the use of another person's body than by having been invited to use it by that person. Suppose a woman voluntarily indulges in intercourse, knowing of the chance it will issue in pregnancy, and then she does become pregnant; is she not in part responsible for the presence, in fact the very existence, of the unborn person inside her? No doubt she did not invite it in. But doesn't her partial responsibility for its being there itself give it a right to the use of her body?[7] If so, then her aborting it would be more like the boy's taking away the chocolates, and less like your unplugging yourself from the violinist—doing so would be depriv-

---

[7] The need for a discussion of this argument was brought home to me by members of the Society for Ethical and Legal Philosophy, to whom this paper was originally presented.

ing it of what what it does have a right to, and thus would be doing it an injustice.

And then, too, it might be asked whether or not she can kill it even to save her own life: If she voluntarily called it into existence, how can she now kill it, even in self-defence?

The first thing to be said about this is that it is something new. Opponents of abortion have been so concerned to make out the independence of the foetus, in order to establish that it has a right to life, just as its mother does, that they have tended to overlook the possible support they might gain from making out that the foetus is *dependent* on the mother, in order to establish that she has a special kind of responsibility for it, a responsibility that gives it rights against her which are not possessed by any independent person— such as an ailing violinist who is a stranger to her.

On the other hand, this argument would give the unborn person a right to its mother's body only if her pregnancy resulted from a voluntary act, undertaken in full knowledge of the chance a pregnancy might result from it. It would leave out entirely the unborn person whose existence is due to rape. Pending the availability of some further argument, then we would be left with the conclusion that unborn persons whose existence is due to rape have no right to the use of their mothers' bodies, and thus that aborting them is not depriving them of anything they have a right to and hence is not unjust killing.

And we should also notice that it is not at all plain that this argument really does go even as far as it purports to. For there are cases and cases, and the details make a difference. If the room is stuffy, and I therefore open a window to air it, and a burglar climbs in, it would be absurd to say, 'Ah, now he can stay, she's given him a right to the use of her house—for she is partially responsible for his presence there, having voluntarily done what enabled him to get in, in full knowledge that there are such things as burglars, and that burglars burgle.' It would be still more absurd to say this if I had had bars installed outside my windows, precisely to prevent burglars from getting in, and a burglar got in only because of a defect in the bars. It remains equally absurd if we imagine it is not a burglar who climbs in, but an innocent person who blunders or falls in. Again, suppose it were like this: people-seeds drift about in the air like pollen, and if you open your windows, one may drift in and take root in your carpets or upholstery. You don't want children, so you fix up your windows with fine mesh screens, the very best you can buy. As can happen, however, and on very, very rare occasions does happen, one of the screens is defective; and a seed drifts in and takes root. Does the person-plant who now develops have a right to the use of your house? Surely not—despite the fact that you voluntarily opened your windows, you knowingly kept carpets and upholstered furniture, and you knew that screens were sometimes defective. Someone may argue that you are responsible for its rooting, that it does have a right to your house, because after all you *could* have lived out your life with bare floors and furniture, or with sealed windows and doors. But this won't do—for by the same token anyone can avoid a pregnancy due to rape by having a hysterectomy, or anyway by never leaving home without a (reliable!) army.

It seems to me that the argument we are looking at can establish at most that there are *some* cases in which the unborn person has a right to the use of its mother's body, and therefore *some* cases in which abortion is unjust killing. There is room for much discussion and argument as to precisely which, if any. But I think we should side-step this issue and leave it open, for at any rate the argument certainly does not establish that all abortion is unjust killing.

5. There is room for yet another argument here, however. We surely must all grant that there may be cases in which it would be morally indecent to detach a person from your body at the cost of his life. Suppose you learn that what the violinist needs is not nine years of your life, but only one hour: all you need do to save his life is to spend one hour in that bed with him. Suppose also that letting him use your kidneys for that one hour would not affect your health in the slightest. Admittedly you were kidnapped. Admittedly you did not give anyone permission to plug him into you. Nevertheless it seems to me plain you *ought* to allow him to use your kidneys for that hour—it would be indecent to refuse.

Again, suppose pregnancy lasted only an hour, and constituted no threat to life or health. And suppose that a woman becomes pregnant as a result of rape. Admittedly she did not voluntarily do anything to bring about the existence of a child. Admittedly she did nothing at all which would give the unborn person a right to the use of her body. All the same it might well be said, as in the newly emended violinist story, that she *ought* to allow it to remain for that hour—that it would be indecent in her to refuse.

Now some people are inclined to use the term 'right' in such a way that it follows from the fact that you ought to allow a person to use your body for the hour he needs, that he has a right to use your body for the hour he needs, even though he has not been given that right by any person or act. They may say that it follows also that if you refuse, you act unjustly toward him. This use of the term is perhaps so common that it cannot be called wrong; nevertheless it seems to me to be an unfortunate loosening of what we would do better to keep a tight rein on. Suppose that box of chocolates I mentioned earlier had not given given to both boys jointly, but was given only to the older boy. There he sits, stolidly eating his way through the box, his small brother watching enviously. Here we are likely to say 'You ought not to be so mean. You ought to give your brother some of those chocolates.' My own view is that it just does not follow from the truth of this that the brother has any right to any of the chocolates. If the boy refuses to give his brother any, he is greedy, stingy, callous—but not unjust. I suppose that the people I have in mind will say it does follow that the brother has a right to some of the chocolates, and thus that the boy does act unjustly if he refuses to give his brother any. But the effect of saying this is to obscure what we should keep distinct, namely the difference between the boy's refusal in this case and the boy's refusal in the earlier case, in which the box was given to both boys jointly, and in which the small brother thus had what was from any point of view clear title to half.

A further objection to so using the term 'right' that from the fact that A ought to do a thing for B, it follows that B has a right against A that A do it for him, is that it is going to make the question of whether or not a man has a right to a thing turn on how easy it is to provide him with it; and this seems not merely unfortunate, but morally unacceptable. Take the case of Henry Fonda again. I said earlier that I had no right to the touch of his cool hand on my fevered brow, even though I needed it to save my life. I said it would be frightfully nice of him to fly in from the West Coast to provide me with it, but that I had no right against him that he should do so. But suppose he isn't on the West Coast. Suppose he has only to walk across the room, place a hand briefly on my brow—and lo, my life is saved. Then surely he ought to do it, it would be indecent to refuse. Is it to be said 'Ah, well, it follows that in this case she has a right to the touch of his hand on her brow, and so it would be an injustice in him to refuse?' So that I have a right to it when it is easy for him to provide it, though no right when it's hard? It's rather a shocking idea that anyone's rights should fade away and disappear as it gets harder and harder to accord them to him.

So my own view is that even though you ought to let the violinist use your kidneys for the one hour he needs, we should not conclude that he has a right to do so—we should say that if you refuse, you are, like the boy who owns all the chocolates and will give none away, self-centred and callous, indecent in fact, but not unjust. And similarly, that even supposing a case in which a woman pregnant due to rape ought to allow the unborn person to use her body for the hour he needs, we should not conclude that he has a right to do so; we should conclude that she is self-centred, callous, indecent, but not unjust, if she refuses. The complaints are no less grave; they are just different. However, there is no need to insist on this point. If anyone does wish to deduce 'he has a right' from 'you ought', then all the same he must surely grant that there are cases in which it is not morally required of you that you allow that violinist to use your kidneys, and in which he does not have a right to use them, and so also for mother and unborn child. Except in such cases as the unborn person has a right to demand it—and we were leaving open the possibility that there may be such cases—nobody is morally *required* to make large sacrifices, of health, of all other interests and concerns, of all other duties and commitments, for nine years, or even for nine months, in order to keep another person alive.

6. We have in fact to distinguish between two kinds of Samaritan: the Good Samaritan and what we might call the Minimally Decent Samaritan. The story of the Good Samaritan, you will remember, goes like this:

> A certain man went down from Jerusalem to Jericho, and fell among thieves, which stripped him of his raiment, and wounded him, and departed, leaving him half dead.

And by chance there came down a certain priest that way; and when he saw him, he passed by on the other side.

And likewise a Levite, when he was at the place, came and looked on him, and passed by on the other side.

But a certain Samaritan, as he journeyed, came where he was; and when he saw him he had compassion on him.

And went to him, and bound up his wounds, pouring in oil and wine, and set him on his own beast, and brought him to an inn, and took care of him.

And on the morrow, when he departed, he took out two pence, and gave them to the host, and said unto him, 'Take care of him; and whatsoever thou spendest more, when I come again, I will repay thee.'

(Luke 10: 30–5)

The Good Samaritan went out of his way, at some cost to himself, to help one in need of it. We are not told what the options were, that is, whether or not the priest and the Levite could have helped by doing less than the Good Samaritan did, but assuming they could have, then the fact they did nothing at all shows they were not even Minimally Decent Samaritans, not because they were not Samaritans, but because they were not even minimally decent.

These things are a matter of degree, of course, but there is a difference, and it comes out perhaps most clearly in the story of Kitty Genovese, who, as you will remember, was murdered while thirty-eight people watched or listened, and did nothing at all to help her. A Good Samaritan would have rushed out to give direct assistance against the murderer. Or perhaps we had better allow that it would have been a Splendid Samaritan who did this, on the ground that it would have involved a risk of death for himself. But the thirty-eight not only did not do this, they did not even trouble to pick up a phone to call the police. Minimally Decent Samaritanism would call for doing at least that, and their not having done it was monstrous.

After telling the story of the Good Samaritan, Jesus said 'Go, and do thou likewise.' Perhaps he meant that we are morally required to act as the Good Samaritan did. Perhaps he was urging people to do more than is morally required of them. At all events it seems plain that it was not morally required of any of the thirty-eight that he rush out to give direct assistance at the risk of his own life, and that it is not morally required of anyone that he give long stretches of his life—nine years or nine months—to sustaining the life of a person who has no special right (we were leaving open the possibility of this) to demand it.

Indeed, with one rather striking class of exceptions, no one in any country in the world is *legally* required to do anywhere near as much as this for anyone else. The class of exceptions is obvious. My main concern here is not the state of the law in respect to abortion, but it is worth drawing attention to the fact that in no state in this country is any man compelled by law to be even a Minimally Decent Samaritan to any person; there is no law under which charges could be brought against the thirty-eight who stood by while Kitty Genovese died. By contrast, in most states in this country women are compelled by law to be not merely Minimally Decent Samaritans, but Good Samaritans to unborn persons inside them. This doesn't by itself settle anything one way or the other, because it may well be argued that there should be laws in this country—as there are in many European countries—compelling at least Minimally Decent Samaritanism.[8] But it does show that there is a gross injustice in the existing state of the law. And it shows also that the groups currently working against liberalization of abortion laws, in fact working toward having it declared unconstitutional for a state to permit abortion, had better start working for the adoption of Good Samaritan laws generally, or earn the charge that they are acting in bad faith.

I should think, myself, that Minimally Decent Samaritan laws would be one thing, Good Samaritan laws quite another, and in fact highly improper. But we are not here concerned with the law. What we should ask is not whether anybody should be compelled by law to be a Good Samaritan, but whether we must accede to a situation in which somebody is being compelled—by nature, perhaps—to be a Good Samaritan. We have, in other words, to look now at third-party interventions. I have been arguing that no person is morally required to make large sacrifices to sustain the life of another who has no right to demand them, and this even where the sacrifices do not include life itself; we are not morally required to be Good

---

[8] For a discussion of the difficulties involved, and a survey of the European experience with such laws, see *The Good Samaritan and the Law*, ed. James M. Ratcliffe (New York, 1966).

Samaritans or anyway Very Good Samaritans to one another. But what if a man cannot extricate himself from such a situation? What if he appeals to us to extricate him? It seems to me plain that there are cases in which we can, cases in which a Good Samaritan would extricate him. There you are, you were kidnapped, and nine years in bed with that violinist lie ahead of you. You have your own life to lead. You are sorry, but you simply cannot see giving up so much of your life to the sustaining of his. You cannot extricate yourself, and ask us to do so. I should have thought that—in light of his having no right to the use of your body—it was obvious that we do not have to accede to your being forced to give up so much. We can do what you ask. There is no injustice to the violinist in our doing so.

7. Following the lead of the opponents of abortion, I have throughout been speaking of the foetus merely as a person, and what I have been asking is whether or not the argument we began with, which proceeds only from the foetus's being a person, really does establish its conclusion. I have argued that it does not.

But of course there are arguments and arguments, and it may be said that I have simply fastened on the wrong one. It may be said that what is important is not merely the fact that the foetus is a person, but that it is a person for whom the woman has a special kind of responsibility issuing from the fact that she is its mother. And it might be argued that all my analogies are therefore irrelevant—for you do not have that special kind of responsibility for that violinist, Henry Fonda does not have that special kind of responsibility for me. And our attention might be drawn to the fact that men and women both *are* compelled by law to provide support for their children.

I have in effect dealt (briefly) with this argument in section 4 above; but a (still briefer) recapitulation now may be in order. Surely we do not have any such 'special responsibility' for a person unless we have assumed it, explicitly or implicitly. If a set of parents do not try to prevent pregnancy, do not obtain an abortion, and then at the time of birth of the child do not put it out for adoption, but rather take it home with them, then they have assumed responsibility for it, they have given it rights, and they cannot *now* withdraw support from it at the cost of its life because they now find it difficult to go on providing for it. But if they have taken all reasonable precautions against having a child, they do not simply by virtue of their biological relationship to the child who comes into existence have a special responsibility for it. They may wish to assume responsibility for it, or they may not wish to. And I am suggesting that if assuming responsibility for it would require large sacrifices, then they may refuse. A Good Samaritan would not refuse—or anyway, a Splendid Samaritan, if the sacrifices that had to be made were enormous. But then so would a Good Samaritan assume responsibility for that violinist; so would Henry Fonda, if he is a Good Samaritan, fly in from the West Coast and assume responsibility for me.

8. My argument will be found unsatisfactory on two counts by many of those who want to regard abortion as morally permissible. First, while I do argue that abortion is not impermissible, I do not argue that it is always permissible. There may well be cases in which carrying the child to term requires only Minimally Decent Samaritanism of the mother, and this is a standard we must not fall below. I am inclined to think it a merit of my account precisely that it does *not* give a general yes or a general no. It allows for and supports our sense that, for example, a sick and desperately frightened fourteen-year-old schoolgirl, pregnant due to rape, may *of course* choose abortion, and that any law which rules this out is an insane law. And it also allows for and supports our sense that in other cases resort to abortion is even positively indecent. It would be indecent in the woman to request an abortion, and indecent in a doctor to perform it, if she is in her seventh month, and wants the abortion just to avoid the nuisance of postponing a trip abroad. The very fact that the arguments I have been drawing attention to treat all cases of abortion, or even all cases of abortion in which the mother's life is not at stake, as morally on a par ought to have made them suspect at the outset.

Secondly, while I am arguing for the permissibility of abortion in some cases, I am not arguing for the right to secure the death of the unborn child. It is easy to confuse these two things in that up to a certain point in the life of the foetus it is not able to survive outside the mother's body; hence removing it from her body guarantees its death. But they are importantly different. I have argued that you are not morally required to spend nine months in bed, sustaining the life of that violinist; but to say this is by no means to say that if, when you unplug yourself, there is a miracle and he survives, you then have a right to turn round and slit his throat. You may detach yourself even if this costs him his life; you have no right to be guaranteed his death, by some other means, if unplugging yourself does not kill him. There are some people who will feel dissatisfied by this feature of my argument. A woman may be utterly devastated by the thought of a child, a bit of herself, put out for adoption and never seen or heard of again. She may therefore want not merely that the child be detached from her, but more, that it die. Some opponents of abortion are inclined to regard this as beneath contempt—thereby showing insensitivity to what is surely a powerful source of despair. All the same, I agree that the desire for the child's death is not one which anybody may gratify, should it turn out to be possible to detach the child alive.

At this place, however, it should be remembered that we have only been pretending throughout that the foetus is a human being from the moment of conception. A very early abortion is surely not the killing of a person, and so is not dealt with by anything I have said here.

V

ABORTION AND INFANTICIDE[1]

MICHAEL TOOLEY

THIS essay deals with the question of the morality of abortion and infanticide. The fundamental ethical objection traditionally advanced against these practices rests on the contention that human foetuses and infants have a right to life. It is this claim which will be the focus of attention here. The basic issue to be discussed, then, is what properties a thing must possess in order to have a serious right to life. My approach will be to set out and defend a basic moral principle specifying a condition an organism must satisfy if it is to have a serious right to life. It will be seen that this condition is not satisfied by human foetuses and infants, and thus that they do not have a right to life. So unless there are other substantial objections to abortion and infanticide, one is forced to conclude that these practices are morally acceptable ones. In contrast, it may turn out that our treatment of adult members of other species—cats, dogs, polar bears—is morally indefensible. For it is quite possible that such animals do possess properties that endow them with a right to life.

I. ABORTION AND INFANTICIDE

One reason the question of the morality of infanticide is worth examining is that it seems very difficult to formulate a completely satisfactory liberal position on abortion without coming to grips with the infanticide issue. The problem the liberal encounters is essentially that of specifying a cut-off point which is not arbitrary: at what stage in the development of a human being does it cease to be

Michael Tooley, 'Abortion and Infanticide', *Philosophy & Public Affairs* 2, No. 1 (Fall, 1972). Copyright © 1972 by Princeton University Press. Reprinted with permission.

[1] I am grateful to a number of people, particularly the Editors of *Philosophy and Public Affairs*, Rodelia Hapke, and Walter Kaufmann, for their helpful comments. It should not, of course, be inferred that they share the views expressed in this paper.

MICHAEL TOOLEY

morally permissible to destroy it? It is important to be clear about the difficulty here. The conservative's objection is not that since there is a continuous line of development from a zygote to a newborn baby, one must conclude that if it is seriously wrong to destroy a newborn baby it is also seriously wrong to destroy a zygote or any intermediate stage in the development of a human being. His point is rather that if one says it is wrong to destroy a newborn baby but not a zygote or some intermediate stage in the development of a human being, one should be prepared to point to a *morally relevant* difference between a newborn baby and the earlier stage in the development of a human being.

Precisely the same difficulty can, of course, be raised for a person who holds that infanticide is morally permissible. The conservative will ask what morally relevant differences there are between an adult human being and a newborn baby. What makes it morally permissible to destroy a baby, but wrong to kill an adult? So the challenge remains. But I will argue that in this case there is an extremely plausible answer.

Reflecting on the morality of infanticide forces one to face up to this challenge. In the case of abortion a number of events—quickening or viability, for instance—might be taken as cut-off points, and it is easy to overlook the fact that none of these events involves any morally significant change in the developing human. In contrast, if one is going to defend infanticide, one has to get very clear about what makes something a person, what gives something a right to life.

One of the interesting ways in which the abortion issue differs from most other moral issues is that the plausible positions on abortions appear to be extreme positions. For if a human foetus is a person, one is inclined to say that, in general, one would be justified in killing it only to save the life of the mother.[2] Such is the extreme conservative position.[3] On the other hand, if the foetus is not a

---

[2] Judith Jarvis Thomas, pp. 37–56, above, argues with great force and ingenuity that this conclusion is mistaken. I will comment on her argument later in this paper.

[3] While this is the position conservatives tend to hold, it is not clear that it is the position they ought to hold. For if the foetus is a person it is far from clear that it is permissible to destroy it to save the mother. Two moral principles lend support to the view that it is the foetus which should live. First, other things being equal, should not one give something to a person who has had less rather than to a person who has had more? The mother has had a chance to live, while the foetus has not. The choice is

person, how can it be seriously wrong to destroy it? Why would one need to point to special circumstances to justify such action? The upshot is that there is no room for a moderate position on the issue of abortion such as one finds, for example, in the Model Penal Code recommendations.[4]

Aside from the light it may shed on the abortion question, the issue of infanticide is both interesting and important in its own right. The theoretical interest has been mentioned: it forces one to face up to the question of what makes something a person. The practical importance need not be laboured. Most people would prefer to raise children who do not suffer from gross deformities or from severe physical, emotional, or intellectual handicaps. If it could be shown that there is no moral objection to infanticide the happiness of society could be significantly and justifiably increased.

Infanticide is also of interest because of the strong emotions it arouses. The typical reaction to infanticide is like the reaction to incest or cannibalism, or the reaction of previous generations to masturbation or oral sex. The response, rather than appealing to carefully formulated moral principles, is primarily visceral. When philosophers themselves respond in this way, offering no arguments, and dismissing infanticide out of hand, it is reasonable to suspect that one is dealing with a taboo rather than with a rational prohibition.[5] I shall attempt to show that this is in fact the case.

thus between the giving the mother more of an opportunity to live while giving the foetus none at all and giving the foetus an opportunity to enjoy life while not giving the mother a further opportunity to do so. Surely fairness requires the latter. Secondly, since the foetus has a greater life expectancy than the mother, one is in effect distributing more goods by choosing the life of the foetus over the life of the mother.

The position I am here recommending to the conservative should not be confused with the official Catholic position. The Catholic Church holds that it is seriously wrong to kill a foetus directly even if failure to do so will result in the death of *both* the mother and the foetus. This perverse value judgement is not part of the conservative's position.

[4] Section 230.3 of the American Law Institute's *Model Penal Code* (Philadelphia, 1962). There is some interesting, though at time confused, discussion of the proposed code in *Model Penal Code—Tentative Draft No. 9* (Philadelphia, 1959), pp. 146–62.

[5] A clear example of such an unwillingness to entertain seriously the possibility that moral judgements widely accepted in one's own society may nevertheless be incorrect is provided by Roger Wertheimer's superficial dismissal of infanticide on pages 69–70 of his article 'Understanding the Abortion Argument', *Philosophy and Public Affairs* 1, no. 1 (Fall, 1971): 67–95.

II. TERMINOLOGY: 'PERSON' VERSUS 'HUMAN BEING'

How is the term 'person' to be interpreted? I shall treat the concept of a person as a purely moral concept, free of all descriptive content. Specifically, in my usage the sentence 'X is a person' will be synonymous with the sentence 'X has a (serious) moral right to life.'

This usage diverges slightly from what is perhaps the more common way of interpreting the term 'person' when it is employed as a purely moral term, where to say that X is a person is to say that X has rights. If everything that had rights had a right to life, these interpretations would be extensionally equivalent. But I am inclined to think that it does not follow from acceptable moral principles that whatever has any rights at all has a right to life. My reason is this. Given the choice between being killed and being tortured for an hour, most adult humans would surely choose the latter. So it seems plausible to say it is worse to kill an adult human being than it is to torture him for an hour. In contrast, it seems to me that while it is not seriously wrong to kill a newborn kitten, it is seriously wrong to torture one for an hour. This *suggests* that newborn kittens may have a right not to be tortured without having a serious right to life. For it seems to be true that an individual has a right to something whenever it is the case that, if he wants that thing, it would be wrong for others to deprive him of it. Then if it is wrong to inflict a certain sensation upon a kitten if it doesn't want to experience that sensation, it will folllow that the kitten has a right not to have sensation inflicted upon it.[6] I shall return to this example later. My point here is merely that it provides some reason for holding that it does not follow from acceptable moral principles that if something has any rights at all, it has a serious right to life.

There has been a tendency in recent discussions of abortion to use expressions such as 'person' and 'human being' interchangeably. B. A. Brody, for example, refers to the difficulty of determining 'whether destroying the foetus constitutes the taking of a human

[6] Compare the discussion of the concept of a right offered by Richard B. Brandt in his *Ethical Theory* (Englewood Cliffs, N.J., 1959), pp. 434–41. As Brandt points out, some philosophers have maintained that only things that can *claim* rights can have rights. I agree with Brandt's view that 'inability to claim does not destroy the right' (p. 440).

life', and suggests it is very plausible that 'the taking of a human life is an action that has bad consequences for him whose life is being taken'.[7] When Brody refers to something as a human life he apparently construes this as entailing that the thing is a person. For if every living organism belonging to the species *Homo sapiens* counted as a human life, there would be no difficulty in determining whether a foetus inside a human mother was a human life.

The same tendency is found in Judith Jarvis Thomson's article, which opens with the statement: 'Most opposition to abortion relies on the premiss that the foetus is a human being, a person, from the moment of conception.'[8] The same is true of Roger Wertheimer, who explicitly says: 'First off I should note that the expressions "a human life", "a human being", "a person" are virtually interchangeable in this context.'[9]

The tendency to use expressions like 'person' and 'human being' interchangeably is an unfortunate one. For one thing, it tends to lend covert support to anti-abortionist positions. Given such usage, one who holds a liberal view of abortion is put in the position of maintaining that foetuses, at least up to a certain point, are not human beings. Even philosophers are led astray by this usage. Thus Wertheimer says that 'except for monstrosities, every member of our species is indubitably a person, a human being, at the very latest at birth'.[10] Is it really *indubitable* that newborn babies are persons? Surely this is a wild contention. Wertheimer is falling prey to the confusion naturally engendered by the practice of using 'person' and 'human being' interchangeably. Another example of this is provided by Thomson: 'I am inclined to think also that we shall probably have to agree that the foetus has already become a human person well before birth. Indeed, it comes as a surprise when one first learns how early in its life it begins to acquire human characteristics. By the tenth week, for example, it already has a face, arms and legs, fingers and toes; it has internal organs, and brain activity is detectable.'[11] But what do such physiological

[7] B. A. Brody, 'Abortion and the Law', *Journal of Philosophy*, LXVIII, no. 12 (17 June 1971): 357–69. See pp. 357–8.
[8] Thomson, 'A Defence of Abortion', p. 47.
[9] Wertheimer, 'Understanding the Abortion Argument', p. 69.
[10] Ibid.
[11] Thomson, 'A Defence of Abortion', pp. 47–8.

characteristics have to do with the question of whether the organism is a person? Thomson, partly, I think, because of the unfortunate use of terminology, does not even raise this question. As a result she virtually takes it for granted that there are some cases in which abortion is 'positively indecent'.[12]

There is a second reason why using 'person' and 'human being' interchangeably is unhappy philosophically. If one says that the dispute between pro- and anti-abortionists centres on whether the foetus is a human, it is natural to conclude that it is essentially a disagreement about certain facts, a disagreement about what properties a foetus possesses. Thus Wertheimer says that 'if one insists on using the raggy fact-value distinction, then one ought to say that the dispute is over a matter of fact in the sense in which it is a fact that the Negro slaves were human beings'.[13] I shall argue that the two cases are not parallel, and that in the case of abortion what is primarily at stake is what moral principles one should accept. If one says that the central issue between conservatives and liberals in the abortion question is whether the foetus is a person, it is clear that the dispute may be either about what properties a thing must have in order to be a person, in order to have a right to life—a moral question—or about whether a foetus at a given stage of development as a matter of fact possesses the properties in question. The temptation to suppose that the disagreement must be a factual one is removed.

It should now be clear why the common practice of using expressions such as 'person' and 'human being' interchangeably in discussions of abortion is unfortunate. It would perhaps be best to avoid the term 'human' altogether, employing instead some expression that is more naturally interpreted as referring to a certain type of biological organism characterized in physiological terms, such as 'member of the species *Homo sapiens*'. My own approach will be to use the term 'human' only in contexts where it is not philosophically dangerous.

---

[12] Ibid., p. 65.
[13] Wertheimer, 'Understanding the Abortion Argument', p. 78.

III. THE BASIC ISSUE: WHEN IS A MEMBER OF THE SPECIES *HOMO SAPIENS* A PERSON?

Settling the issue of the morality of abortion and infanticide will involve answering the following questions: What properties must something have to be a person, i.e. to have a serious right to life? At what point in the development of a member of the species *Homo sapiens* does the organism possess the properties that make it a person? The first question raises a moral issue. To answer it is to decide what basic[14] moral principles involving the ascription of a right to life one ought to accept. The second question raises a purely factual issue, since the properties in question are properties of a purely descriptive sort.

Some writers seem quite pessimistic about the possibility of resolving the question of the morality of abortion. Indeed, some have gone so far as to suggest that the question of whether the foetus is a person is in principle unanswerable: 'we seem to be stuck with the indeterminateness of the foetus's humanity'.[15] An understanding of some of the sources of this pessimism will, I think, help us to tackle the problem. Let us begin by considering the similarity a number of people have noted between the issue of abortion and the issue of Negro slavery. The question here is why it should be more difficult to decide whether abortion and infanticide are acceptable than it was to decide whether slavery was acceptable. The answer seems to be that in the case of slavery there are moral principles of a quite uncontroversial sort that settle the issue. Thus most people would agree to some such principle as the following: No organism that has experiences, that is capable of thought and of using language, and that has harmed no one, should be made a slave. In the case of abortion, on the other hand, conditions that are generally agreed to be sufficient grounds for ascribing a right to life to something do not suffice to settle the issue. It is easy to specify other, purportedly sufficient conditions that will settle the issue, but no one has been successful in putting forward considerations that

---

[14] A moral principle accepted by a person is *basic for him* if and only if his acceptance of it is not dependent upon any of his (non-moral) factual beliefs. That is, no change in his factual beliefs would cause him to abandon the principle in question.

[15] Wertheimer, 'Understanding the Abortion Argument', p. 88.

will convince others to accept those additional moral principles.

i do not share the general pessimism about the possibility of resolving the issue of abortion and infanticide because I believe it is possible to point to a very plausible moral principle dealing with the question of *necessary* conditions for something's having a right to life, where the conditions in question will provide an answer to the question of the permissibility of abortion and infanticide.

There is a second cause of pessimism that should be noted before proceeding. It is tied up with the fact that the development of an organism is one of gradual and continuous change. Given this continuity, how is one to draw a line at one point and declare it permissible to destroy a member of *Homo sapiens* up to, but not beyond, that point? Won't there be an arbitrariness about any point that is chosen? I will return to this worry shortly. It does not present a serious difficulty once the basic moral principles relevant to the ascription of a right to life to an individual are established.

Let us turn now to the first and most fundamental question: What properties must something have in order to be a person, i.e. to have a serious right to life? The claim I wish to defend is this: An organism possesses a serious right to life only if it possesses the concept of a self as a continuing subject of experiences and other mental states, and believes that it is itself such a continuing entity.

My basic argument in support of this claim, which I will call the self-consciousness requirement, will be clearest, I think, if I first offer a simplified version of the argument, and then consider a modification that seems desirable. The simplified version of my argument is this. To ascribe a right to an individual is to assert something about the prima-facie obligations of other individuals to act, or to refrain from acting, in certain ways. However, the obligations in question are conditional ones, being dependent upon the existence of certain desires of the individual to whom the right is ascribed. Thus if an individual asks one to destroy something to which he has a right, one does not violate his right to that thing if one proceeds to destroy it. This suggests the following analysis: 'A has a right to X' is roughly synonymous with 'If A desires X, then others are under a prima-facie obligation to refrain from actions that would deprive him of it.'[16]

---

[16] Again, compare the analysis defended by Brandt in *Ethical Theory*, pp. 434–41.

Although this analysis is initially plausible, there are reasons for thinking it not entirely correct. I will consider these later. Even here, however, some expansion is necessary, since there are features of the concept of a right that are important in the present context, and that ought to be dealt with more explicitly. In particular, it seems to be a conceptual truth that things that lack consciousness, such as ordinary machines, cannot have rights. Does this conceptual truth follow from the above analysis of the concept of a right? The answer depends on how the term 'desire' is interpreted. If one adopts a completely behaviouristic interpretation of 'desire', so that a machine that searches for an electrical outlet in order to get its batteries recharged is described as having a desire to be recharged, then it will not follow from this analysis that objects that lack consciousness cannot have rights. On the other hand, if 'desire' is interpreted in such a way that desires are states necessarily standing in some sort of relationship to states of consciousness, it will follow from the analysis that a machine that is not capable of being conscious, and consequently of having desires, cannot have any rights. I think those who defend analyses of the concept of a right along the lines of this one do have in mind an interpretation of the term 'desire' that involves reference to something more than behavioural dispositions. However, rather than relying on this, it seems preferable to make such an interpretation explicit. The following analysis is a natural way of doing that: 'A has a right to X' is roughly synonymous with 'A is the sort of thing that is a subject of experiences and other mental states, A is capable of desiring X, and if A does desire X, then others are under a prima-facie obligation to refrain from actions that would deprive him of it.'

The next step in the argument is basically a matter of applying this analysis to the concept of a right to life. Unfortunately the expression 'right to life' is not entirely a happy one, since it suggests that the right in question concerns the continued existence of a biological organism. That this is incorrect can be brought out by considering possible ways of violating an individual's right to life. Suppose, for example, that by some technology of the future the brain of an adult human were to be completely reprogrammed, so that the organism wound up with memories (or rather, apparent memories), beliefs, attitudes, and personality traits completely different from those associated with it before it was subjected to reprogramming. In such a case one would surely say that an individual had been destroyed, that an adult human's right to life had been violated, even though no biological organism had been killed. This example shows that the expression 'right to life' is misleading, since what one is really concerned about is not just the continued existence of a biological organism, but the right of a subject of experiences and other mental states to continue to exist.

Given this more precise description of the right with which we are here concerned, we are now in a position to apply the analysis of the concept of a right stated above. When we do so we find that the statement 'A has a right to continue to exist as a subject of experiences and other mental states' is roughly synonymous with the statement 'A is a subject of experiences and other mental states, A is capable of desiring to continue to exist as a subject of experiences and other mental states, and if A does desire to continue to exist as such an entity, then others are under a prima-facie obligation not to prevent him from doing so.'

The final stage in the argument is simply a matter of asking what must be the case if something is to be capable of having a desire to continue existing as a subject of experiences and other mental states. The basic point here is that the desires a thing can have are limited by the concepts it possesses. For the fundamental way of describing a given desire is as a desire that a certain proposition be true.[17] Then, since one cannot desire that a certain proposition be true unless one understands it, and since one cannot understand it without possessing the concepts involved in it, it follows that the desires one can have are limited by the concepts one possesses. Applying this to the previous case results in the conclusion that an

---

[17] In everyday life one often speaks of desiring things, such as an apple or a newspaper. Such talk is elliptical, the context together with one's ordinary beliefs serving to make it clear that one wants to eat the apple and read the newspaper. To say that what one desires is that a certain proposition be true should not be construed as involving any particular ontological commitment. The point is merely that it is sentences such as 'John wants it to be the case that he is eating an apple in the next few minutes' that provide a completely explicit description of a person's desires. If one fails to use such sentences, one can be badly misled about what concepts are presupposed by a particular desire.

entity cannot be the sort of thing that can desire that a subject of experiences and other mental states exist unless it possesses the concept of such a subject. Moreover, an entity cannot desire that it itself *continue* existing as a subject of experiences and other mental states unless it believes that it is now such a subject. This completes the justification of the claim that it is a necessary condition of something's having a serious right to life that it possess the concept of a self as a continuing subject of experiences, and that it believe that it is itself such an entity.

Let us now consider a modification in the above argument that seems desirable. This modification concerns the crucial conceptual claim advanced about the relationship between ascription of rights and ascription of the corresponding desires. Certain situations suggest that there may be exceptions to the claim that if a person doesn't desire something, one cannot violate his right to it. There are types of situations that call this claim into question: (i) situations in which an individual's desires reflect a state of emotional disturbance; (ii) situations in which a previously conscious individual is temporarily unconscious; (iii) situations in which an individual's desires have been distorted by conditioning or by indoctrination.

As an example of the first, consider a case in which an adult human falls into a state of depression which his psychiatrist recognizes as temporary. While in the state he tells people he wishes he were dead. His psychiatrist, accepting the view that there can be no violation of an individual's right to life unless the individual has a desire to live, decides to let his patient have his way and kills him. Or consider a related case in which one person gives another a drug that produces a state of temporary depression; the recipient expresses a wish that he were dead. The person who administered the drug then kills him. Doesn't one want to say in both these cases that the agent did something seriously wrong in killing the other person? And isn't the reason the action was seriously wrong in each case the fact that it violated the individual's right to life? If so, the right to life cannot be linked with a desire to live in the way claimed above.

The second set of situations are ones in which an individual is unconscious for some reason—that is, he is sleeping, or drugged, or in a temporary coma. Does an individual in such a state have any desires? People do sometimes say that an unconscious individual wants something, but it might be argued that if such talk is not to be simply false it must be interpreted as actually referring to the desires the individual *would* have if he were now conscious. Consequently, if the analysis of the concept of a right proposed above were correct, it would follow that one does not violate an individual's right if one takes his car, or kills him, while he is asleep.

Finally, consider situations in which an individual's desires have been distorted, either by inculcation of irrational beliefs or by direct conditioning. Thus an individual may permit someone to kill him because he has been convinced that if he allows himself to be sacrificed to the gods he will be gloriously rewarded in a life to come. Or an individual may be enslaved after first having been conditioned to desire a life of slavery. Doesn't one want to say that in the former case an individual's right to life has been violated, and in the latter his right to freedom?

Situations such as these strongly suggest that even if an individual doesn't want something, it is still possible to violate his right to it. Some modification of the earlier account of the concept of a right thus seems in order. The analysis given covers, I believe, the paradigmatic cases of violation of an individual's rights, but there are other, secondary cases where one also wants to say that someone's right has been violated which are not included.

Precisely how the revised analysis should be formulated is unclear. Here it will be sufficient merely to say that, in view of the above, an individual's right to X can be violated not only when he desires X, but also when he *would* now desire X were it not for one of the following: (i) he is in an emotionally unbalanced state; (ii) he is temporarily unconscious; (iii) he has been conditioned to desire the absence of X.

The critical point now is that, even given this extension of the conditions under which an individual's right to something can be violated, it is still true that one's right to something can be violated only when one has the conceptual capability of desiring the thing in question. For example, an individual who would now desire not to be a slave if he weren't emotionally unbalanced, or if he weren't temporarily unconscious, or if he hadn't previously been conditioned to want to be a slave, must possess the concepts involved in the desire not to be a slave. Since it is really only the conceptual capability presupposed by the desire to continue existing as a subject of experiences and other mental states, and not the desire itself, that enters into the above argument, the modification required in the account of the conditions under which an individual's rights can be violated does not undercut my defence of the self-consciousness requirement.[18]

To sum up, my argument has been that having a right to life presupposes that one is capable of desiring to continue existing as a subject of experiences and other mental states. This in turn presupposes both that one has the concept of such a continuing entity and that one believes that one is oneself such an entity. So an entity that lacks such a consciousness of itself as a continuing subject of mental states does not have a right to life.

It would be natural to ask at this point whether satisfaction of this requirement is not only necessary but also sufficient to ensure that a thing has a right to life. I am inclined to an affirmative answer. However, the issue is not urgent in the present context, since as long as the requirement is in fact a necessary one we have the basis of an adequate defence of abortion and infanticide. If an organism must satisfy some other condition before it has a serious right to life, the result will merely be that the interval during which infanticide is morally permissible may be somewhat longer. Although the point at which an organism first achieves self-consciousness and hence the capacity of desiring to continue existing as a subject of experiences and other mental states may be a theoretically incorrect cut-off point, it is at least a morally safe one: any error it involves is on the side of caution.

---

[18] There are, however, situations other than those discussed here which might seem to count against the claim that a person cannot have a right unless he is conceptually capable of having the corresponding desire. Can't a young child, for example, have a right to an estate, even though he may not be conceptually capable of wanting the estate? It is clear that such situations have to be carefully considered if one is to arrive at a satisfactory account of the concept of a right. My inclination is to say that the correct description is not that the child now has a right to the estate, but that he will come to have such a right when he is mature, and that in the meantime no one else has a right to the estate. My reason for saying that the child does not now have a right to the estate is that he cannot now do things with the estate, such as selling it or giving it away, that he will be able to do later on.

IV. SOME CRITICAL COMMENTS ON ALTERNATIVE
PROPOSALS

I now want to compare the line of demarcation I am proposing with the cut-off points traditionally advanced in discussions of abortion. My fundamental claim will be that none of these cut-off points can be defended by appeal to plausible, basic moral principles. The main suggestions as to the point past which it is seriously wrong to destroy something that will develop into an adult member of the species *Homo sapiens* are these: (a) conception; (b) the attainment of human form; (c) the achievement of the ability to move about spontaneously; (d) viability; (e) birth.[19] The corresponding moral principles suggested by these cut-off points are as follows: (1) It is seriously wrong to kill an organism, from a zygote on, that belongs to the species *Homo sapiens*. (2) It is seriously wrong to kill an organism that belongs to *Homo sapiens* and that has achieved human form. (3) It is seriously wrong to kill an organism that is a member of *Homo sapiens* and that is capable of spontaneous movement. (4) It is seriously wrong to kill an organism that belongs to *Homo sapiens* and that is capable of existing outside the womb. (5) It is seriously wrong to kill an organism that is a member of *Homo sapiens* that is no longer in the womb.

My first comment is that it would not do *simply* to omit the reference to membership in the species *Homo sapiens* from the above principles, with the exception of principle (2). For then the principles would be applicable to animals in general, and one would be forced to conclude that it was seriously wrong to abort a cat foetus, or that it was seriously wrong to abort a motile cat foetus, and so on.

The second and crucial comment is that none of the five principles given above can plausibly be viewed as a *basic* moral principle. To accept any of them as such would be akin to accepting as a basic moral principle the proposition that it is morally permissible to enslave black members of the species *Homo sapiens* but not white

---

[19] Another frequent suggestion as to the cut-off point not listed here is quickening. I omit it because it seems clear that if abortion after quickening is wrong, its wrongness must be tied up with the motility of the foetus, not with the mother's awareness of the foetus's ability to move about.

members. Why should it be seriously wrong to kill an unborn member of the species *Homo sapiens* but not seriously wrong to kill an unborn kitten? Difference in species is not *per se* a morally relevant difference. If one holds that it is seriously wrong to kill an unborn member of the species *Homo sapiens* but not an unborn kitten, one should be prepared to point to some property that is morally significant and that is possessed by unborn members of *Homo sapiens* but not by unborn kittens. Similarly, such a property must be identified if one believes it seriously wrong to kill unborn members of *Homo sapiens* that have achieved viability but not seriously wrong to kill unborn kittens that have achieved that state.

What property might account for such a difference? That is to say, what *basic* moral principles might a person who accepts one of these five principles appeal to in support of his secondary moral judgement? Why should events such as the achievement of human form, or the achievement of the ability to move about, or the achievement of viability, or birth serve to endow something with a right to life? What the liberal must do is to show that these events involve changes, or are associated with changes, that are morally relevant.

Let us now consider reasons why the events involved in cut-off points (b) to (e) are not morally relevant, beginning with the last two: viability and birth. The fact that an organism is not physiologically dependent upon another organism, or is capable of such physiological independence, is surely irrelevant to whether the organism has a right to life. In defence of this contention, consider a speculative case where a foetus is able to learn a language while in the womb. One would surely not say that the foetus had no right to life until it emerged from the womb, or until it was capable of existing outside the womb. A less speculative example is the case of Siamese twins who have learned to speak. One doesn't want to say that since one of the twins would die were the two to be separated, it therefore has no right to life. Consequently it seems difficult to disagree with the conservative's claim that an organism which lacks a right to life before birth or before becoming viable cannot acquire this right immediately upon birth or upon becoming viable.

This does not, however, completely rule out viability as a line of demarcation. For instead of defending viability as a cut-off point on the ground that only then does a foetus acquire a right to life, it is possible to argue rather that when one organism is physiologically dependent upon another, the former's right to life may conflict with the latter's right to use its body as it will, and moreover, that the latter's right to do what it wants with its body may often take precedence over the other organism's right to life. Thomson has defended this view: 'I am arguing only that having a right to life does not guarantee having either a right to the use of or a right to be allowed continued use of another person's body—even if one needs it for life itself. So the right to life will not serve the opponents of abortion in the very simple and clear way in which they seem to have thought it would.'[20] I believe that Thomson is right in contending that philosophers have been altogether too casual in assuming that if one grants the foetus a serious right to life, one must accept a conservative position on abortion.[21] I also think the only defence of viability as a cut-off point which has any hope of success at all is one based on the considerations she advances. I doubt very much, however, that this defence of abortion is ultimately tenable. I think that one can grant even stronger assumptions than those made by Thomson and still argue persuasively for a semi-conservative view. What I have in mind is this. Let it be granted, for the sake of argument, that a woman's right to free her body of parasites which will inhibit her freedom of action and possibly impair her health is stronger than the parasite's right to life, and is so even if the parasite has as much right to life as an adult human. One can still argue that abortion ought not to be permitted. For if A's right is stronger than B's, and it is impossible to satisfy both, it does not follow that A's should be satisfied rather than B's. It may be possible to compensate A if his right isn't satisfied, but impossible to compensate B if his right isn't satisfied. In such a case the best thing to do may be to satisfy B's claim and to compensate A. Abortion may be a case in point. If the foetus has a right to life and the right is not satisfied, there is certainly no way the foetus can be compensated. On the other hand, if the woman's right to rid her body of harmful and annoying parasites is not satisfied, she can be

[20] See p. 46, above.
[21] A good example of a failure to probe this issue is provided by Brody's 'Abortion and the Law'.

compensated. Thus it would seem that the just thing to do would be to prohibit abortion, but to compensate women for the burden of carrying a parasite to term. Then, however, we are back at a (modified) conservative position.[22] Our conclusion must be that it appears unlikely there is any satisfactory defence either of viability or of birth as cut-off points.

Let us now consider the third suggested line of demarcation, the achievement of the power to move about spontaneously. It might be argued that acquiring this power is a morally relevant event on the ground that there is a connection between the concept of an agent and the concept of a person, and being motile is an indication that a thing is an agent.[23]

It is difficult to respond to this suggestion unless it is made more specific. Given that one's interest here is in defending a certain cut-off point, it is natural to interpret the proposal as suggesting that motility is a necessary condition of an organism's having a right to life. But this won't do, because one certainly wants to ascribe a right to life to adult humans who are completely paralysed. Maybe the suggestion is rather that motility is a sufficient condition of something's having a right to life. However, it is clear that motility alone is not sufficient, since this would imply that all animals, and also certain machines, have a right to life. Perhaps, then, the most reasonable interpretation of the claim is that motility together with some other property is a sufficient condition of something's having a right to life, where the other property will have to be a property possessed by unborn members of the species *Homo sapiens* but not by unborn members of other familiar species.

The central question, then, is what this other property is. Until one is told, it is very difficult to evaluate either the moral claim that motility together with that property is a sufficient basis for ascribing to an organism a right to life or the factual claim that a motile human foetus possesses that property while a motile foetus belonging to some other species does not. A conservative would presumably reject motility as a cut-off point by arguing that whether an

[22] Admittedly the modification is a substantial one, since given a society that refused to compensate women, a woman who had an abortion would not be doing anything wrong.

[23] Compare Wertheimer's remarks, 'Understanding the Abortion Argument', p. 79.

organism has a right to life depends only upon its potentialities, which are of course not changed by its becoming motile. If, on the other hand, one favours a liberal view of abortion, I think that one can attack this third suggested cut-off point, in its unspecified form, only by determining what properties are necessary, or what properties sufficient, for an individual to have a right to life. Thus I would base my rejection of motility as a cut-off point on my claim, defended above, that a necessary condition of an organism's possessing a right to life is that it conceive of itself as a continuing subject of experiences and other mental states.

The second suggested cut-off point—the development of a recognizably human form—can be dismissed fairly quickly. I have already remarked that membership in a particular species is not itself a morally relevant property. For it is obvious that if we encountered other 'rational animals', such as Martians, the fact that their physiological make-up was very different from our own would not be grounds for denying them a right to life.[24] Similarly, it is clear that the development of human form is not in itself a morally relevant event. Nor do there seem to be any grounds for holding that there is some other change, associated with this event, that is morally relevant. The appeal of this second cut-off point is, I think, purely emotional.

The overall conclusion seems to be that it is very difficult to defend the cut-off points traditionally advanced by those who advocate either a moderate or a liberal position on abortion. The reason is that there do not seem to be any basic moral principles one can appeal to in support of the cut-off points in question. We must now consider whether the conservative is any better off.

V. REFUTATION OF THE CONSERVATIVE POSITION

Many have felt that the conservative's position is more defensible than the liberal's because the conservative can point to the gradual and continuous development of an organism as it changes from a

[24] This requires qualification. If their central nervous systems were radically different from ours, it might be thought that one would not be justified in ascribing to them mental states of an experiential sort. And then, since it seems to be a conceptual truth that only things having experiential states can have rights, one would be forced to conclude that one was not justified in ascribing any rights to them.

zygote to an adult human being. He is then in a position to argue that it is morally arbitrary for the liberal to draw a line at some point in this continuous process and to say that abortion is permissible before, but not after, that particular point. The liberal's reply would presumably be that the emphasis upon the continuity of the process is misleading. What the conservative is really doing is simply challenging the liberal to specify the properties a thing must have in order to be a person, and to show that the developing organism does acquire the properties at the point selected by the liberal. The liberal may then reply that the difficulty he has meeting this challenge should not be taken as grounds for rejecting his position. For the conservative cannot meet this challenge either; the conservative is equally unable to say what properties something must have if it is to have a right to life.

Although this rejoinder does not dispose of the conservative's argument, it is not without bite. For defenders of the view that abortion is always wrong have failed to face up to the question of the basic moral principles on which their position rests. They have been content to assert the wrongness of killing any organism, from a zygote on, if that organism is a member of the species *Homo sapiens*. But they have overlooked the point that this cannot be an acceptable *basic* moral principle, since difference in species is not in itself a morally relevant difference. The conservative can reply, however, that it is possible to defend his position—but not the liberal's—*without* getting clear about the properties a thing must possess if it is to have a right to life. The conservative's defence will rest upon the following two claims: first, that there is a property, even if one is unable to specify what it is, that (i) is possessed by adult humans, and (ii) endows any organism possessing it with a serious right to life. Second, that if there are properties which satisfy (i) and (ii) above, at least one of those properties will be such that any organism potentially possessing that property has a serious right to life even now, simply by virtue of that potentiality, where an organism possesses a property potentially if it will come to have that property in the normal course of its development. The second claim—which I shall refer to as the potentiality principle—is critical to the conservative's defence. Because of it he is able to defend his position without deciding what properties a thing must possess in order to have a right to life. It is enough to know that adult members of *Homo sapiens* do have such a right. For then one can conclude that any organism which belongs to the species *Homo sapiens*, from a zygote on, must also have a right to life by virtue of the potentiality principle.

The liberal, by contrast, cannot mount a comparable argument. He cannot defend his position without offering at least a partial answer to the question of what properties a thing must possess in order to have a right to life.

The importance of the potentiality principle, however, goes beyond the fact that it provides support for the conservative's position. If the principle is unacceptable, then so is his position. For if the conservative cannot defend the view that an organism's having certain potentialities is sufficient grounds for ascribing to it a right to life, his claim that a foetus which is a member of *Homo sapiens* has a right to life can be attacked as follows. The reason an adult member of *Homo sapiens* has a right to life, but an infant ape does not, is that there are certain psychological properties which the former possesses and the latter lacks. Now, even if one is unsure exactly what these psychological properties are, it is clear that an organism in the early stages of development from a zygote into an adult member of *Homo sapiens* does not possess these properties. One need merely compare a human foetus with an ape foetus. What mental states does the former enjoy that the latter does not? Surely it is reasonable to hold that there are no significant differences in their respective mental lives—assuming that one wishes to ascribe any mental states at all to such organisms. (Does a zygote have a mental life? Does it have experiences? Or beliefs? Or desires?) There are, of course, physiological differences, but these are not in themselves morally significant. *If* one held that potentialities were relevant to the ascription of a right to life, one could argue that the physiological differences, though not morally significant in themselves, are morally significant by virtue of their causal consequences: they will lead to later psychological differences that are morally relevant, and for this reason the physiological differences are themselves morally significant. But if the potentiality principle is not available, this line of argument cannot be used, and there will then be no differences between a human foetus and an ape foetus that the conservative can use as grounds for ascribing a serious right to life to the former but not to the latter.

It is therefore tempting to conclude that the conservative view of abortion is acceptable if and only if the potentiality principle is acceptable. But to say that the conservative position can be defended if the potentiality principle is acceptable is to assume that the argument is over once it is granted that the foetus has a right to life, and, as was noted above, Thomson has shown that there are serious grounds for questioning this assumption. In any case, the important point here is that the conservative position on abortion is acceptable *only if* the potentiality principle is sound.

One way to attack the potentiality principle is simply to argue in support of the self-consciousness requirement—the claim that only an organism that conceives of itself as a continuing subject of experiences has a right to life. For this requirement, when taken together with the claim that there is at least one property, possessed by adult humans, such that any organism possessing it has a serious right to life, entails the denial of the potentiality principle. Or at least this is so if we add the uncontroversial empirical claim that an organism that will in the normal course of events develop into an adult human does not from the very beginning of its existence possess a concept of a continuing subject of experiences together with a belief that it is itself such an entity.

I think it best, however, to scrutinize the potentiality principle itself, and not to base one's case against it simply on the self-consciousness requirement. Perhaps the first point to note is that the potentiality principle should not be confused with principles such as the following: the value of an object is related to the value of the things into which it can develop. This 'valuation principle' is rather vague. There are ways of making it more precise, but we need not consider these here. Suppose now that one were to speak not of a right to life, but of the value of life. It would then be easy to make the mistake of thinking that the valuation principle was relevant to the potentiality principle—indeed, that it entailed it. But an individual's right to life is not based on the value of his life. To say that the world would be better off if it contained fewer people is not to say that it would be right to achieve such a better world by killing some of the present inhabitants. *If* having a right to life were a matter of a thing's value, then a thing's potentialities, being connected with its expected value, would clearly be relevant to the question of what rights it had. Conversely, once one realizes that a thing's rights are not a matter of its value, I think it becomes clear that an organism's potentialities are irrelevant to the question of whether it has a right to life.

But let us now turn to the task of finding a direct refutation of the potentiality principle. The basic issue is this. Is there any property J which satisfies the following conditions: (1) There is a property K such that any individual possessing property K has a right to life, and there is a scientific law L to the effect that any organism possessing property J will in the normal course of events come to possess property K at some later time. (2) Given the relationship between property J and property K just described, anything possessing property J has a right to life. (3) If property J were not related to property K in the way indicated, it would not be the case that anything possessing property J thereby had a right to life. In short, the question is whether there is a property J that bestows a right to life on an organism *only because* J stands in a certain causal relationship to a second property K, which is such that anything possessing that property *ipso facto* has a right to life.

My argument turns upon the following critical principle: Let C be a causal process that normally leads to outcome E. Let A be an action that initiates process C, and B be an action involving a minimal expenditure of energy that stops process C before outcome E occurs. Assume further that actions A and B do not have any other consequences, and that E is the only morally significant outcome of process C. Then there is no moral difference between intentionally performing action B and intentionally refraining from performing action A, assuming identical motivation in both cases. This principle, which I shall refer to as the moral symmetry principle with respect to action and inaction, would be rejected by some philosophers. They would argue that there is an important distinction to be drawn between 'what we owe people in the form of aid and what we owe them in the way of non-interference',[25] and that the latter, 'negative duties', are duties that it is more serious to neglect

[25] Philippa Foot, 'The Problem of Abortion and the Doctrine of the Double Effect', *The Oxford Review* 5 (1967): 5–15. See the discussion on pp. 11 ff.

than the former, 'positive' ones. This view arises from an intuitive response to examples such as the following. Even if it is wrong not to send food to starving people in other parts of the world, it is more wrong still to kill someone. And isn't the conclusion, then, that one's obligation to refrain from killing someone is a more serious obligation than one's obligation to save lives?

I want to argue that this is not the correct conclusion. I think it is tempting to draw this conclusion if one fails to consider the motivation that is likely to be associated with the respective actions. If someone performs an action he knows will kill someone else, this will usually be grounds for concluding that he wanted to kill the person in question. In contrast, failing to help someone may indicate only apathy, laziness, selfishness, or an amoral outlook: the fact that a person knowingly allows another to die will not normally be grounds for concluding that he desired that person's death. Someone who knowingly kills another is more likely to be seriously defective from a moral point of view than someone who fails to save another's life.

If we are not to be led to false conclusions by our intuitions about certain cases, we must explicitly assume identical motivations in the two situations. Compare, for example, the following: (1) Jones sees that Smith will be killed by a bomb unless he warns him. Jones's reaction is: 'How lucky, it will save me the trouble of killing Smith myself.' So Jones allows Smith to be killed by the bomb, even though he could easily have warned him. (2) Jones wants Smith dead, and therefore shoots him. Is one to say there is a significant difference between the wrongness of Jones's behaviour in these two cases? Surely not. This shows the mistake of drawing a distinction between positive duties and negative duties and holding that the latter impose stricter obligations than the former. The difference in our intuitions about situations that involve giving aid to others and corresponding situations that involve not interfering with others is to be explained by reference to probable differences in the motivations operating in the two situations, and not by reference to a distinction between positive and negative duties. For once it is specified that the motivation is the same in the two situations, we realize that inaction is as wrong in the one case as action is in the other.

There is another point that may be relevant. Action involves effort, while inaction usually does not. It usually does not require any effort on my part to refrain from killing someone, but saving someone's life will require an expenditure of energy. One must then ask how large a sacrifice a person is morally required to make to save the life of another. If the sacrifice of time and energy is quite large it may be that one is not morally obliged to save the life of another in that situation. Superficial reflection upon such cases might easily lead us to introduce the distinction between positive and negative duties, but again it is clear that this would be a mistake. The point is not that one has a greater duty to refrain from killing others than to perform positive actions that will save them. It is rather that positive actions require effort, and this means that in deciding what to do a person has to take into account his own right to do what he wants with his life, and not only the other person's right to life. To avoid this confusion, we should confine ourselves to comparisons between situations in which the positive action involves minimal effort.

The moral symmetry principle, as formulated above, explicitly takes these two factors into account. It applies only to pairs of situations in which the motivations are identical and the positive action involves minimal effort. Without these restrictions, the principle would be open to serious objection; with them, it seems perfectly acceptable. For the central objection to it rests on the claim that we must distinguish positive from negative duties and recognize that negative duties impose stronger obligations than positive ones. I have tried to show how this claim derives from an unsound account of our moral intuitions about certain situations.

My argument against the potentiality principle can now be stated. Suppose at some future time a chemical were to be discovered which when injected into the brain of a kitten would cause the kitten to develop into a cat possessing a brain of the sort possessed by humans, and consequently into a cat having all the psychological capabilities characteristic of adult humans. Such cats would be able to think, to use language, and so on. Now it would surely be morally indefensible in such a situation to ascribe a serious right to life to members of the species *Homo sapiens* without also ascribing it to cats that have undergone such a process of development: there would be no morally significant differences.

Secondly, it would not be seriously wrong to refrain from injecting a newborn kitten with the special chemical, and to kill it instead. The fact that one could initiate a causal process that would transform a kitten into an entity that would eventually possess properties such that anything possessing them *ipso facto* has a serious right to life does not mean that the kitten has a serious right to life even before it has been subjected to the process of injection and transformation. The possibility of transforming kittens into persons will not make it any more wrong to kill newborn kittens than it is now.

Thirdly, in view of the symmetry principle, if it is not seriously wrong to refrain from initiating such a causal process, neither is it seriously wrong to interfere with such a process. Suppose a kitten is accidentally injected with the chemical. As long as it has not yet developed those properties that in themselves endow something with a right to life, there cannot be anything wrong with interfering with the causal process and preventing the development of the properties in question. Such interference might be accomplished either by injecting the kitten with some 'neutralizing' chemical or simply by killing it.

But if it is not seriously wrong to destroy an injected kitten which will naturally develop the properties that bestow a right to life, neither can it be seriously wrong to destroy a member of *Homo sapiens* which lacks such properties, but will naturally come to have them. The potentialities are the same in both cases. The only difference is that in the case of a human foetus the potentialities have been present from the beginning of the organism's development, while in the case of the kitten they have been present only from the time it was injected with the special chemical. This difference in the time at which the potentialities were acquired is a morally irrelevant difference.

It should be emphasized that I am not here assuming that a human foetus does not possess properties which in themselves, and irrespective of their causal relationships to other properties, provide grounds for ascribing a right to life to whatever possesses them. The point is merely that if it is seriously wrong to kill something, the reason cannot be that the thing will later acquire properties that in themselves provide something with a right to life.

Finally, it is reasonable to believe that there are properties possessed by adult members of *Homo sapiens* which establish their right to life, and also that any normal human foetus will come to possess those properties shared by adult humans. But it has just been shown that if it is wrong to kill a human foetus, it cannot be because of its potentialities. One is therefore forced to conclude that the conservative's potentiality principle is false.

In short, anyone who wants to defend the potentiality principle must either argue against the moral symmetry principle or hold that in a world in which kittens could be transformed into 'rational animals' it would be seriously wrong to kill newborn kittens. It is hard to believe there is much to be said for the latter moral claim. Consequently one expects the conservative's rejoinder to be directed against the symmetry principle. While I have not attempted to provide a thorough defense of that principle, I have tried to show that what seems to be the most important objection to it—the one that appeals to a distinction between positive and negative duties—is based on a superficial analysis of our moral intuitions. I believe that a more thorough examination of the symmetry principle would show it to be sound. If so, we should reject the potentiality principle, and the conservative position on abortion as well.

VI. SUMMARY AND CONCLUSIONS

Let us return now to my basic claim, the self-consciousness requirement: An organism possesses a serious right to life only if it possesses the concept of a self as a continuing subject of experiences and other mental states, and believes that it is itself such a continuing entity. My defence of this claim has been twofold. I have offered a direct argument in support of it, and I have tried to show that traditional conservative and liberal views on abortion and infanticide, which involve a rejection of it, are unsound. I now want to mention one final reason why my claim should be accepted. Consider the example mentioned in section II—that of killing, as opposed to torturing, newborn kittens. I suggested there that while in the case of adult humans most people would consider it worse to kill an individual than to torture him for an hour, we do not usually view the killing of a newborn kitten as morally outrageous, although we would regard someone who tortured a newborn kitten for an hour as heinously evil. I pointed out that a possible conclusion that might be drawn from this is that newborn kittens have a right not to be tortured, but do not have a serious right to life. If this is the correct conclusion, how is one to explain it? One merit of the self-consciousness requirement is that it provides an explanation of this situation. The reason a newborn kitten does not have a right to life is explained by the fact that it does not possess the concept of a self. But how is one to explain the kitten's having a right not to be tortured? The answer is that a desire not to suffer pain can be ascribed to something without assuming that it has any concept of a continuing self. For while something that lacks the concept of a self cannot desire that a self not suffer, it can desire that a given sensation not exist. The state desired—the absence of a particular sensation, or of sensations of a certain sort—can be described in a purely phenomenalistic language, and hence without the concept of a continuing self. So long as the newborn kitten possesses the relevant phenomenal concepts, it can truly be said to desire that a certain sensation not exist. So we can ascribe to it a right not to be tortured even though, since it lacks the concept of a continuing self, we cannot ascribe to it a right to life.

This completes my discussion of the basic moral principles involved in the issue of abortion and infanticide. But I want to comment upon an important factual question, namely, at what point an organism comes to possess the concept of a self as a continuing subject of experiences and other mental states, together with the belief that it is itself such a continuing entity. This is obviously a matter for detailed psychological investigation, but everyday observation makes it perfectly clear, I believe, that a newborn baby does not possess the concept of a continuing self, any more than a newborn kitten possesses such a concept. If so, infanticide during a time interval shortly after birth must be morally acceptable.

But where is the line to be drawn? What is the cut-off point? If one maintained, as some philosophers have, that an individual possesses concepts only if he can express these concepts in language, it would be a matter of everyday observation whether or not a given organism possessed the concept of a continuing self. Infanticide would then be permissible up to the time an organism learned how to use certain expressions. However, I think the claim that acquisition of concepts is dependent on acquisition of language is mistaken. For example, one wants to ascribe mental states of a conceptual sort—such as beliefs and desires—to organisms that are incapable of learning a language. The issue of prelinguistic understanding is clearly outside the scope of this discussion. My point is simply that *if* an organism can acquire concepts without thereby acquiring a way of expressing those concepts linguistically, the question of whether a given organism possesses the concept of a self as a continuing subject of experiences and other mental states, together with the belief that it is itself such a continuing entity, may be a question that requires fairly subtle experimental techniques to answer.

If this view of the matter is roughly correct, there are two worries one is left with at the level of practical moral decisions, one of which may turn out to be deeply disturbing. The lesser worry is where the line is to be drawn in the case of infanticide. It is not troubling because there is no serious need to know the exact point at which a human infant acquires a right to life. For in the vast majority of cases in which infanticide is desirable, its desirability will be apparent within a short time after birth. Since it is virtually certain that an infant at such a stage of its development does not possess the concept of a continuing self, and thus does not possess a serious right to life, there is excellent reason to believe that infanticide is morally permissible in most cases where it is otherwise desirable. The practical moral problem can thus be satisfactorily handled by choosing some period of time, such as a week after birth, as the interval during which infanticide will be permitted. This interval could then be modified once psychologists have established the point at which a human organism comes to believe that it is a continuing subject of experiences and other mental states.

The troubling worry is whether adult animals belonging to species other than *Homo sapiens* may not also possess a serious right to life. For once one says that an organism can possess the concept of a continuing self, together with the belief that it is itself such an entity, without having any way of expressing that concept and that belief linguistically, one has to face up to the question of whether animals may not possess properties that bestow a serious right to life upon them. The suggestion itself is a familiar one, and one that most of us are accustomed to dismiss very casually. The line of thought advanced here suggests that this attitude may turn out to be tragically mistaken. Once one reflects upon the question of the *basic* moral principles involved in the ascription of a right to life to organisms, one may find himself driven to conclude that our everyday treatment of animals is morally indefensible, and that we are in fact murdering innocent persons.

VI

THE SURVIVAL LOTTERY

JOHN HARRIS

LET us suppose that organ transplant procedures have been perfected; in such circumstances if two dying patients could be saved by organ transplants then, if surgeons have the requisite organs in stock and no other needy patients, but nevertheless allow their patients to die, we would be inclined to say, and be justified in saying, that the patients died because the doctors refused to save them. But if there are no spare organs in stock and none otherwise available, the doctors have no choice, they cannot save their patients and so must let them die. In this case we would be disinclined to say that the doctors are in any sense the cause of their patients' deaths. But let us further suppose that the two dying patients, Y and Z, are not happy about being left to die. They might argue that it is not strictly true that there are no organs which could be used to save them. Y needs a new heart and Z new lungs. They point out that if just one healthy person were to be killed his organs could be removed and both of them be saved. We and the doctors would probably be alike in thinking that such a step, while technically possible, would be out of the question. We would not say that the doctors were killing their patients if they refused to prey upon the healthy to save the sick. And because this sort of surgical Robin Hoodery is out of the question we can tell Y and Z that they cannot be saved, and that when they die they will have died of natural causes and not of the neglect of their doctors. Y and Z do not agree, however, they insist that if the doctors fail to kill a healthy man and use his organs to save them, then the doctors will be responsible for their deaths.

Many philosophers have for various reasons believed that we must not kill even if by doing so we could save life. They believe that

John Harris, 'The Survival Lottery', *Philosophy* 50, (1975), pp. 81–7. Reprinted by permission of Cambridge University Press and the author.

there is a moral difference between killing and letting die. On this view, to kill A so that Y and Z might live is ruled out because we have a strict obligation not to kill but a duty of some lesser kind to save life. A. H. Clough's dictum 'Thou shalt not kill but need'st not strive officiously to keep alive' expresses bluntly this point of view. The dying Y and Z may be excused for not being much impressed by Clough's dictum. They agree that it is wrong to kill the innocent and are prepared to agree to an absolute prohibition against so doing. They do not agree, however, that A is more innocent than they are. Y and Z might go on to point out that the currently acknowledged right of the innocent not to be killed, even where their deaths might give life to others, is just a decision to prefer the lives of the fortunate to those of the unfortunate. A is innocent in the sense that he has done nothing to deserve death, but Y and Z are also innocent in this sense. Why should they be the ones to die simply because they are so unlucky as to have diseased organs? Why, they might argue, should their living or dying be left to chance when in so many other areas of human life we believe that we have an obligation to ensure the survival of the maximum number of lives possible?

Y and Z argue that if a doctor refuses to treat a patient, with the result that the patient dies, he has killed that patient as sure as shooting, and that, in exactly the same way, if the doctors refuse Y and Z the transplants that they need, then their refusal will kill Y and Z, again as sure as shooting. The doctors, and indeed the society which supports their inaction, cannot defend themselves by arguing that they are neither expected, nor required by law or convention, to kill so that lives may be saved (indeed, quite the reverse) since this is just an appeal to custom or authority. A man who does his own moral thinking must decide whether, in these circumstances, he ought to save two lives at the cost of one, or one life at the cost of two. The fact that so called 'third parties' have never before been brought into such calculations, have never before been thought of as being involved, is not an argument against their now becoming so. There are, of course, good arguments against allowing doctors simply to haul passers-by off the streets whenever they have a couple of patients in need of new organs. And the harmful side-effects of such a practice in terms of terror and distress to the victims, the witnesses and society generally, would give us further reasons for dismissing the idea. Y and Z realize this and have a proposal, which they will shortly produce, which would largely meet objections to placing such power in the hands of doctors and eliminate at least some of the harmful side-effects.

In the unlikely event of their feeling obliged to reply to the reproaches of Y and Z, the doctors might offer the following argument: they might maintain that a man is only responsible for the death of someone whose life he might have saved, if, in all the circumstances of the case, he ought to have saved the man by the means available. This is why a doctor might be a murderer if he simply refused or neglected to treat a patient who would die without treatment, but not if he could only save the patient by doing something he ought in no circumstances to do—kill the innocent. Y and Z readily agree that a man ought not to do what he ought not to do, but they point out that if the doctors, and for that matter society at large, ought on balance to kill one man if two can thereby be saved, then failure to do so will involve responsibility for the consequent deaths. The fact that Y's and Z's proposal involves killing the innocent cannot be a reason for refusing to consider their proposal, for this would just be a refusal to face the question at issue and so avoid having to make a decision as to what ought to be done in circumstances like these. It is Y's and Z's claim that failure to adopt their plan will also involve killing the innocent, rather more of the innocent than the proposed alternative.

To back up this last point, to remove the arbitrariness of permitting doctors to select their donors from among the chance passers-by outside hospitals, and the tremendous power this would place in doctors' hands, to mitigate worries about side-effects and lastly to appease those who wonder why poor old A should be singled out for sacrifice, Y and Z put forward the following scheme: they propose that everyone be given a sort of lottery number. Whenever doctors have two or more dying patients who could be saved by transplants, and no suitable organs have come to hand through 'natural' deaths, they can ask a central computer to supply a suitable donor. The computer will then pick the number of a suitable donor at random and he will be killed so that the lives of two or more others may be saved. No doubt if the scheme were ever to be implemented a suitable euphemism for 'killed' would be employed. Perhaps we would begin to talk about citizens being called upon to 'give life' to others. With the refinement of transplant procedures such a scheme could offer the chance of saving large numbers of lives that are now lost. Indeed, even taking into account the loss of the lives of donors, the numbers of untimely deaths each year might be dramatically reduced, so much so that everyone's chance of living to a ripe old age might be increased. If this were to be the consequence of the adoption of such a scheme, and it might well be, it could not be dismissed lightly. It might of course be objected that it is likely that more old people will need transplants to prolong their lives than will the young, and so the scheme would inevitably lead to a society dominated by the old. But if such a society is thought objectionable, there is no reason to suppose that a program could not be designed for the computer that would ensure the maintenance of whatever is considered to be an optimum age distribution throughout the population.

Suppose that inter-planetary travel revealed a world of people like ourselves, but who organized their society according to this scheme. No one was considered to have an absolute right to life or freedom from interference, but everything was always done to ensure that as many people as possible would enjoy long and happy lives. In such a world a man who attempted to escape when his number was up or who resisted on the grounds that no one had a right to take his life, might well be regarded as a murderer. We might or might not prefer to live in such a world, but the morality of its inhabitants would surely be one that we could respect. It would not be obviously more barbaric or cruel or immoral than our own.

Y and Z are willing to concede one exception to the universal application of their scheme. They realize that it would be unfair to allow people who have brought their misfortune on themselves to benefit from the lottery. There would clearly be something unjust about killing the abstemious B so that W (whose heavy smoking has given him lung cancer) and X (whose drinking has destroyed his liver) should be preserved to over-indulge again.

What objections could be made to the lottery scheme? A first straw to clutch at would be the desire for security. Under such a scheme we would never know when we would hear *them* knocking at the door. Every post might bring a sentence of death, every sound in the night might be the sound of boots on the stairs. But, as we have seen, the chances of actually being called upon to make the ultimate sacrifice might be slimmer than is the present risk of being killed on the roads, and most of us do not lie trembling a-bed, appalled at the prospect of being dispatched on the morrow. The truth is that lives might well be more secure under such a scheme.

If we respect individuality and see every human being as unique in his own way, we might want to reject a society in which it appeared that individuals were seen merely as interchangeable units in a structure, the value of which lies in its having as many healthy units as possible. But of course Y and Z would want to know why A's individuality was more worthy of respect than theirs.

Another plausible objection is the natural reluctance to play God with men's lives, the feeling that it is wrong to make any attempt to re-allot the life opportunities that fate has determined, that the deaths of Y and Z would be 'natural', whereas the death of anyone killed to save them would have been perpetrated by men. But if we are able to change things, then to elect not to do so is also to determine what will happen in the world.

Neither does the alleged moral difference between killing and letting die afford a respectable way of rejecting the claims of Y and Z. For if we really want to counter proponents of the lottery, if we really want to answer Y and Z and not just put them off, we cannot do so by saying that the lottery involves killing and object to it for that reason, because to do so would, as we have seen, just beg the question as to whether the failure to save as many people as possible might not also amount to killing.

To opt for the society which Y and Z propose would be then to adopt a society in which saintliness would be mandatory. Each of us would have to recognize a binding obligation to give up his own life for others when called upon to do so. In such a society anyone who reneged upon this duty would be a murderer. The most promising objection to such a society, and indeed to any principle which required us to kill A in order to save Y and Z, is, I suspect, that we are committed to the right of self-defence. If I can kill A to save Y and Z then he can kill me to save P and Q, and it is only if I am prepared to agree to this that I will opt for the lottery or be prepared to agree to a man's being killed if doing so would save the lives of more than one other man. Of course, there is something paradoxical about basing objections to the lottery scheme on the right of self-defence since, *ex hypothesi*, each person would have a better chance of living to a ripe old age if the lottery scheme were to be implemented. None the less, the feeling that no man should be required to lay down his life for others makes many people shy away from such a scheme, even though it might be rational to accept it on prudential grounds, and perhaps even mandatory on utilitarian grounds. Again, Y and Z would reply that the right of self-defence must extend to them as much as to anyone else, and while it is true that they can only live if another man is killed, they would claim that it is also true that if they are left to die, then someone who lives on does so over their dead bodies.

It might be argued that the institution of the survival lottery has not gone far to mitigate the harmful side-effects in terms of terror and distress to victims, witnesses, and society generally, that would be occasioned by doctors simply snatching passers-by off the streets and disorganizing them for the benefit of the unfortunate. Donors would after all still have to be procured, and this process, however it was carried out, would still be likely to prove distressing to all concerned. The lottery scheme would eliminate the arbitrariness of leaving the life and death decisions to the doctors, and remove the possibility of such terrible power falling into the hands of any individuals, but the terror and distress would remain. The effect of having to apprehend presumably unwilling victims would give us pause. Perhaps only a long period of education or propaganda could remove our abhorrence. What this abhorrence reveals about the rights and wrongs of the situation is, however, more difficult to assess. We might be inclined to say that only monsters could ignore the promptings of conscience so far as to operate the lottery scheme. But the promptings of conscience are not necessarily the most reliable guide. In the present case Y and Z would argue that such promptings are mere squeamishness, an over-nice self-indulgence that costs lives. Death, Y and Z would remind us, is a distressing experience whenever and to whomever it occurs, so the less it occurs the better. Fewer victims and witnesses will be distressed as part of the side-effects of the lottery scheme than would suffer as part of the side-effects of not instituting it.

Lastly, a more limited objection might be made, not to the idea of killing to save lives, but to the involvement of 'third parties'. Why, so the objection goes, should we not give X's heart to Y or Y's lungs to X, the same number of lives being thereby preserved and no one else's life set at risk? Y's and Z's reply to this objection differs from their previous line of argument. To amend their plan so that the involvement of so called 'third parties' is ruled out would, Y and Z claim, violate their right to equal concern and respect with the rest of society. They argue that such a proposal would amount to treating the unfortunate who need new organs as a class within society whose lives are considered to be of less value than those of its more fortunate members. What possible justification could there be for singling out one group of people whom we would be justified in using as donors but not another? The idea in the mind of those who would propose such a step must be something like the following: since Y and Z cannot survive, since they are going to die in any event, there is no harm in putting their names into the lottery, for the chances of their dying cannot thereby be increased and will in fact almost certainly be reduced. But this is just to ignore everything that Y and Z have been saying. For if their lottery scheme is adopted they are not going to die anyway—their chances of dying are no greater and no less than those of any other participant in the lottery whose number may come up. This ground for confining selection of donors to the unfortunate therefore disappears. Any other ground must discriminate against Y and Z as members of a class whose lives are less worthy of respect than those of the rest of society.

It might more plausibly be argued that the dying who cannot themselves be saved by transplants, or by any other means at all, should be the priority selection group for the computer program. But how far off must death be for a man to be classified as 'dying'? Those so classified might argue that their last few days or weeks of life are as valuable to them (if not more valuable) than the possibly longer span remaining to others. The problem of narrowing down the class of possible donors without discriminating unfairly against some sub-class of society is, I suspect, insoluble.

Such is the case for the survival lottery. Utilitarians ought to be in favour of it, and absolutists cannot object to it on the ground that it involves killing the innocent, for it is Y's and Z's case that any alternative must also involve killing the innocent. If the absolutist wishes to maintain his objection he must point to some morally relevant difference between positive and negative killing. This challenge opens the door to a large topic with a whole library of literature, but Y and Z are dying and do not have time to explore it exhaustively. In their own case the most likely candidate for some feature which might make this moral difference is the malevolent intent of Y and Z themselves. An absolutist might well argue that while no one intends the deaths of Y and Z, no one necessarily wishes them dead, or aims at their demise for any reason, they do mean to kill A (or have him killed). But Y and Z can reply that the death of A is no part of their plan, they merely wish to use a couple of his organs, and if he cannot live without them . . . *tant pis*! None would be more delighted than Y and Z if artificial organs would do as well, and so render the lottery scheme otiose.

One form of absolutist argument perhaps remains. This involves taking an Orwellian stand on some principle of common decency. The argument would then be that even to enter into the sort of 'macabre' calculations that Y and Z propose displays a blunted sensibility, a corrupted and vitiated mind. Forms of this argument have recently been advanced by Noam Chomsky (*American Power and the New Mandarins*) and Stuart Hampshire (*Morality and Pessimism*). The indefatigable Y and Z would of course deny that their calculations are in any sense 'macabre', and would present them as the most humane course available in the circumstances. Moreover they would claim that the Orwellian stand on decency is the product of a closed mind, and not susceptible to rational argument. Any reasoned defence of such a principle must appeal to notions like respect for human life, as Hampshire's argument in fact does, and these Y and Z could make conformable to their own position.

Can Y and Z be answered? Perhaps only by relying on moral intuition, on the insistence that we do feel there is something wrong with the survival lottery and our confidence that this feeling is prompted by some morally relevant difference between our bringing about the death of A and our bringing about the deaths of Y and Z. Whether we could retain this confidence in our intuitions if we were to be confronted by a society in which the survival lottery operated, was accepted by all, and was seen to save many lives that would otherwise have been lost, it would be interesting to know.

There would of course be great practical difficulties in the way of implementing the lottery. In so many cases it would be agonizingly difficult to decide whether or not a person had brought his misfortune on himself. There are numerous ways in which a person may contribute to his predicament, and the task of deciding how far, or how decisively, a person is himself responsible for his fate would be formidable. And in those cases where we can be confident that a person is innocent of responsibility for his predicament, can we acquire this confidence in time to save him? The lottery scheme would be a powerful weapon in the hands of someone willing and able to misuse it. Could we ever feel certain that the lottery was safe from unscrupulous computer programmers? Perhaps we should be thankful that such practical difficulties make the survival lottery an unlikely consequence of the perfection of transplants. Or perhaps we should be appalled.

It may be that we would want to tell Y and Z that the difficulties and dangers of their scheme would be too great a price to pay for its benefits. It is as well to be clear, however, that there is also a high, perhaps an even higher, price to be paid for the rejection of the scheme. That price is the lives of Y and Z and many like them, and we delude ourselves if we suppose that the reason why we reject their plan is that we accept the sixth commandment.[1]

Balliol College Oxford

[1] Thanks are due to Ronald Dworkin, Jonathan Glover, M. J. Inwood, and Anne Seller for helpful comments.

VII

SPEECH IN FAVOUR OF CAPITAL PUNISHMENT (1868)

JOHN STUART MILL

. . . IT would be a great satisfaction to me if I were able to support this Motion. It is always a matter of regret to me to find myself, on a public question, opposed to those who are called—sometimes in the way of honour, and sometimes in what is intended for ridicule—the philanthropists. Of all persons who take part in public affairs, they are those for whom, on the whole, I feel the greatest amount of respect; for their characteristic is, that they devote their time, their labour, and much of their money to objects purely public, with a less admixture of either personal or class selfishness, than any other class of politicians whatever. On almost all the great questions, scarcely any politicians are so steadily and almost uniformly to be found on the side of right; and they seldom err, but by an exaggerated application of some just and highly important principle. On the very subject that is now occupying us we all know what signal service they have rendered. It is through their efforts that our criminal laws—which within my memory hanged people for stealing in a dwelling house to the value of 40s.—laws by virtue of which rows of human beings might be seen suspended in front of Newgate by those who ascended or descended Ludgate Hill—have so greatly relaxed their most revolting and most impolitic ferocity, that aggravated murder is now practically the only crime which is punished with death by any of our lawful tribunals; and we are even now deliberating whether the extreme penalty should be retained in that solitary case. This vast gain, not only to humanity, but to the ends of penal justice, we owe to the philanthropists; and if they are mistaken, as I cannot but think they are, in the present instance, it is

Reprinted from *Hansard's Parliamentary Debates*, 3rd Series, 21 Apr. 1868 (London, 1868).

only in not perceiving the right time and place for stopping in a career hitherto so eminently beneficial. Sir, there is a point at which, I conceive, that career ought to stop. When there has been brought home to any one, by conclusive evidence, the greatest crime known to the law; and when the attendant circumstances suggest no palliation of the guilt, no hope that the culprit may even yet not be unworthy to live among mankind, nothing to make it probable that the crime was an exception to his general character rather than a consequence of it, then I confess it appears to me that to deprive the criminal of the life of which he has proved himself to be unworthy—solemnly to blot him out from the fellowship of mankind and from the catalogue of the living—is the most appropriate, as it is certainly the most impressive, mode in which society can attach to so great a crime the penal consequences which for the security of life it is indispensable to annex to it. I defend this penalty, when confined to atrocious cases, on the very ground on which it is commonly attacked—on that of humanity to the criminal; as beyond comparison the least cruel mode in which it is possible adequately to deter from the crime. If, in our horror of inflicting death, we endeavour to devise some punishment for the living criminal which shall act on the human mind with a deterrent force at all comparable to that of death, we are driven to inflictions less severe indeed in appearance, and therefore less efficacious, but far more cruel in reality. Few, I think, would venture to propose, as a punishment for aggravated murder, less than imprisonment with hard labour for life; that is the fate to which a murderer would be consigned by the mercy which shrinks from putting him to death. But has it been sufficiently considered what sort of a mercy this is, and what kind of life it leaves to him? If, indeed, the punishment is not really inflicted—if it becomes the sham which a few years ago such punishments were rapidly becoming—then, indeed, its adoption would be almost tantamount to giving up the attempt to repress murder altogether. But if it really is what it professes to be, and if it is realized in all its rigour by the popular imagination, as it very probably would not be, but as it must be if it is to be efficacious, it will be so shocking that when the memory of the crime is no longer fresh, there will be almost insuperable difficulty in executing it. What comparison can there really be, in point of severity, between consigning a man to the short pang of a rapid death, and immuring him in a living tomb, there to linger out what may be a long life in the hardest and most monotonous toil, without any of its alleviations or rewards—debarred from all pleasant sights and sounds, and cut off from all earthly hope, except a slight mitigation of bodily restraint, or a small improvement of diet? Yet even such a lot as this, because there is no one moment at which the suffering is of terrifying intensity, and, above all, because it does not contain the element, so imposing to the imagination, of the unknown, is universally reputed a milder punishment than death—stands in all codes as a mitigation of the capital penalty, and is thankfully accepted as such. For it is characteristic of all punishments which depend on duration for their efficacy—all, therefore, which are not corporal or pecuniary—that they are more rigorous than they seem; while it is, on the contrary, one of the strongest recommendations a punishment can have, that it should seem more rigorous than it is; for its practical power depends far less on what it is than on what it seems. There is not, I should think, any human infliction which makes an impression on the imagination so entirely out of proportion to its real severity as the punishment of death. The punishment must be mild indeed which does not add more to the sum of human misery than is necessarily or directly added by the execution of a criminal. As my hon. Friend the Member for Northampton (Mr Gilpin) has himself remarked, the most that human laws can do to anyone in the matter of death is to hasten it; the man would have died at any rate; not so very much later, and on the average, I fear, with a considerably greater amount of bodily suffering. Society is asked, then, to denude itself of an instrument of punishment which, in the grave cases to which alone it is suitable, effects its purposes at a less cost of human suffering than any other; which, while it inspires more terror, is less cruel in actual fact than any punishment that we should think of substituting for it. My hon. Friend says that it does not inspire terror, and that experience proves it to be a failure. But the influence of a punishment is not to be estimated by its effect on hardened criminals. Those whose habitual way of life keeps them, so to speak, at all times within sight of the gallows, do grow to care less about it; as, to compare good things with bad, an old soldier is not much affected by the chance of dying in battle. I can afford to admit all that is often said about the indifference of professional criminals to the gallows. Though of that indifference one-third is probably bravado and another third confidence that they shall have the luck to escape, it is quite probable that the remaining third is real. But the efficacy of a punishment which acts principally through the imagination, is chiefly to be measured by the impression it makes on those who are still innocent; by the horror with which it surrounds the first promptings of guilt; the restraining influence it exercises over the beginning of the thought which, if indulged, would become a temptation; the check which it exerts over the graded declension towards the state—never suddenly attained—in which crime no longer revolts, and punishment no longer terrifies. As for what is called the failure of death punishment, who is able to judge of that? We partly know who those are whom it has not deterred; but who is there who knows whom it has deterred, or how many human beings it has saved who would have lived to be murderers if that awful association had not been thrown round the idea of murder from their earliest infancy? Let us not forget that the most imposing fact loses its power over the imagination if it is made too cheap. When a punishment fit only for the most atrocious crimes is lavished on small offences until human feeling recoils from it, then, indeed, it ceases to intimidate, because it ceases to be believed in. The failure of capital punishment in cases of theft is easily accounted for; the thief did not believe that it would be inflicted. He had learnt by experience that jurors would perjure themselves rather than find him guilty; that Judges would seize any excuse for not sentencing him to death, or for recommending him to mercy; and that if neither jurors nor Judges were merciful, there were still hopes from an authority above both. When things had come to this pass it was high time to give up the vain attempt. When it is impossible to inflict a punishment, or when its infliction becomes a public scandal, the idle threat cannot too soon disappear from the statute book. And in the case of the host of offences which were formerly capital, I heartily rejoice that it did become impracticable to execute the law. If the same state of public feeling comes to exist in the case of murder; if the time comes when jurors refuse to find a murderer guilty; when Judges will not sentence him to death, or will recommend him to mercy; or when, if juries and Judges do not

flinch from their duty, Home Secretaries, under pressure of deputa-
tions and memorials, shrink from theirs, and the threat becomes, as
it became in the other cases, a mere *brutum fulmen*; then, indeed, it
may become necessary to do in this case what has been done in
those—to abrogate the penalty. That time may come—my hon.
Friend thinks that it has nearly come. I hardly know whether he
lamented it or boasted of it; but he and his Friends are entitled to the
boast; for if it comes it will be their doing, and they will have gained
what I cannot but call a fatal victory, for they will have achieved it by
bringing about, if they will forgive me for saying so, an enervation,
an effeminancy, in the general mind of the country. For what else
than effeminancy is it to be so much more shocked by taking a man's
life than by depriving him of all that makes life desirable or
valuable? Is death, then, the greatest of all earthly ills? *Usque
adeone mori miserum est?* Is it, indeed, so dreadful a thing to die?
Has it not been from of old one chief part of a manly education to
make us despise death—teaching us to account it, if an evil at all, by
no means high in the list of evils; at all events, as an inevitable one,
and to hold, as it were, our lives in our hands, ready to be given or
risked at any moment, for a sufficiently worthy object? I am sure
that my hon. Friends know all this as well, and have as much of all
these feelings as any of the rest of us; possibly more. But I cannot
think that this is likely to be the effect of their teaching on the
general mind. I cannot think that the cultivating of a peculiar
sensitiveness of conscience on this one point, over and above what
results from the general cultivation of the moral sentiments, is
permanently consistent with assigning in our own minds to the fact
of death no more than the degree of relative importance which
belongs to it among the other incidents of our humanity. The men of
old cared too little about death, and gave their own lives or took
those of others with equal recklessness. Our danger is of the
opposite kind, lest we should be so much shocked by death, in
general and in the abstract, as to care too much about it in individual
cases, both those of other people and our own, which call for its
being risked. And I am not putting things at the worst, for it is
proved by the experience of other countries that horror of the
executioner by no means necessarily implies horror of the assassin.
The stronghold, as we all know, of hired assassination in the 18th

century was Italy; yet it is said that in some of the Italian populations the infliction of death by sentence of law was in the highest degree offensive and revolting to popular feeling. Much has been said of the sanctity of human life, and the absurdity of supposing that we can teach respect for life by ourselves destroying it. But I am surprised at the employment of this argument, for it is one which might be brought against any punishment whatever. It is not human life only, not human life as such, that ought to be sacred to us, but human feelings. The human capacity of suffering is what we should cause to be respected, not the mere capacity of existing. And we may imagine somebody asking how we can teach people not to inflict suffering by ourselves inflicting it? But to this I should answer—all of us would answer—that to deter by suffering from inflicting suffering is not only possible, but the very purpose of penal justice. Does fining a criminal show want of respect for property, or imprisoning him, for personal freedom? Just as unreasonable is it to think that to take the life of a man who has taken that of another is to show want of regard for human life. We show, on the contrary, most emphatically our regard for it, by the adoption of a rule that he who violates that right in another forfeits it for himself, and that while no other crime that he can commit deprives him of his right to live, this shall. There is one argument against capital punishment, even in extreme cases, which I cannot deny to have weight—on which my hon. Friend justly laid great stress, and which never can be entirely got rid of. It is this—that if by an error of justice an innocent person is put to death, the mistake can never be corrected; all compensation, all reparation for the wrong is impossible. This would be indeed a serious objection if these miserable mistakes—among the most tragical occurrences in the whole round of human affairs—could not be made extremely rare. The argument is invincible where the mode of criminal procedure is dangerous to the innocent, or where the Courts of Justice are not trusted. And this probably is the reason why the objection to an irreparable punishment began (as I believe it did) earlier, and is more intense and more widely diffused, in some parts of the Continent of Europe than it is here. There are on the Continent great and enlightened countries, in which the criminal procedure is not so favourable to innocence, does not afford the same security against erroneous conviction, as it does among us;

countries where the Courts of Justice seem to think they fail in their duty unless they find somebody guilty; and in their really laudable desire to hunt guilt from its hiding places, expose themselves to a serious danger of condemning the innocent. If our own procedure and Courts of Justice afforded ground for similar apprehension, I should be the first to join in withdrawing the power of inflicting irreparable punishment from such tribunals. But we all know that the defects of our procedure are the very opposite. Our rules of evidence are even too favourable to the prisoner; and juries and Judges carry out the maxim, 'It is better that ten guilty should escape than that one innocent person should suffer', not only to the letter, but beyond the letter. Judges are most anxious to point out, and juries to allow for, the barest possibility of the prisoner's innocence. No human judgement is infallible; such sad cases as my hon. Friend cited will sometimes occur; but in so grave a case as that of murder, the accused, in our system, has always the benefit of the merest shadow of a doubt. And this suggests another consideration very germane to the question. The very fact that death punishment is more shocking than any other to the imagination, necessarily renders the Courts of Justice more scrupulous in requiring the fullest evidence of guilt. Even that which is the greatest objection to capital punishment, the impossibility of correcting an error once committed, must make, and does make, juries and Judges more careful in forming their opinion, and more jealous in their scrutiny of the evidence. If the substitution of penal servitude for death in cases of murder should cause any declaration in this conscientious scrupulosity, there would be a great evil to set against the real, but I hope rare, advantage of being able to make reparation to a condemned person who was afterwards discovered to be innocent. In order that the possibility of correction may be kept open wherever the chance of this sad contingency is more than infinitesimal, it is quite right that the Judge should recommend to the Crown a commutation of the sentence, not solely when the proof of guilt is open to the smallest suspicion, but whenever there remains anything unexplained and mysterious in the case, raising a desire for more light, or making it likely that further information may at some future time be obtained. I would also suggest that whenever the sentence is commuted the grounds of the commutation should, in some authentic form, be made known to the public. Thus much I willingly concede to my hon. Friend; but on the question of total abolition I am inclined to hope that the feeling of the country is not with him, and that the limitation of death punishment to the cases referred to in the Bill of last year will be generally considered sufficient. The mania which existed a short time ago for paring down all our punishments seems to have reached its limits, and not before it was time. We were in danger of being left without any effectual punishment, except for small offences. What was formerly our chief secondary punishment—transportation—before it was abolished, had become almost a reward. Penal servitude, the substitute for it, was becoming, to the classes who were principally subject to it, almost nominal, so comfortable did we make our prisons, and so easy had it become to get quickly out of them. Flogging—a most objectionable punishment in ordinary cases, but a particularly appropriate ones for crimes of brutality, especially crimes against women—we would not hear of, except, to be sure, in the case of garrotters, for whose peculiar benefit we re-established it in a hurry, immediately after a Member of Parliament had been garrotted. With this exception, offences, even of an atrocious kind, against the person, as my hon. and learned Friend the Member for Oxford (Mr Neate) well remarked, not only were, but still are, visited with penalties so ludicrously inadequate, as to be almost an encouragement to the crime. I think, Sir, that in the case of most offences, except those against property, there is more need of strengthening our punishments than of weakening them; and that severer sentences, with an apportionment of them to the different kinds of offences which shall approve itself better than at present to the moral sentiments of the community, are the kind of reform of which our penal system now stands in need. I shall therefore vote against the Amendment.

VIII

JUDGEMENT DAY

LOUIS PASCAL

JUDGEMENT DAY OR THE HANDWRITING ON THE WALL*
(Transcript of a speech on overpopulation)

GOOD evening. This is the first time I've spoken before a college audience, and therefore I would like to take advantage of your presence to ask you a few questions before I begin on my prepared speech. Principally I'm interested in asking these questions for my own enlightenment, but I hope many of you will find your answers interesting also. Basically I want to know how morally committed the students at a typical 'good' school are, and while I know an audience of several hundred from one school is neither large enough nor diverse enough to give an especially accurate picture, still the results should provide a rough indication of where the real truth lies. That's sort of an interesting juxtaposition of words. 'Truth lies' I mean.

Anyway, as I said, I'm interested in knowing how morally committed you are. The reasons for my curiosity are surely evident: in today's world of racial prejudice, Vietnam, and above all, the miseries of overpopulation, it will take an uncommonly dedicated and selfless generation to grapple with these issues successfully. I must say at the outset, I am pessimistic. At any rate, primarily what I want to find out tonight is how important it is to you for you to act

Louis Pascal, 'Judgement Day or The Handwriting on the Wall' first appeared as part of a longer article in *Inquiry* 1980, Vol. 23, pp. 242–51; 'On Goodness, Badness and Indifference' and Postscript are © 1986 Louis Pascal. Reprinted by permission of the author.

* This section is the transcript and the next section a discussion of a speech on overpopulation by Walter Bradford Ellis, a too-little-known pioneer in the field of overpopulation. It was delivered before an audience of about 300 at Columbia University on 20 Oct. 1970. I was among the audience and made a recording. (It is reprinted here with his permission.) Some of the numbers have changed in the intervening years, but his ideas have not aged.

according to your own definition of right and wrong. In other words I'm not interested in knowing what sort of behaviour you think is right or wrong but merely how committed you are to living up to whatever standards of right and wrong you possess.

I was trying to think a few minutes ago what questions I could ask you to find out this information, and it is very difficult to come up with anything satisfactory simply because individual standards of right and wrong vary so markedly. I had to pick a situation which seems perhaps a little silly because it is so improbable, but that is because I wanted as pure a case as possible—one which is in no way connected with any existing world situation—so that your prejudices and preconceived notions about a particular situation will play no part in your answers.

I needed to find a situation in which every one of you would agree as to the proper course of action and then ask: but which of you would do it even if it hurt you personally? Probably no situation exists which would elicit your total agreement, but the one which I have picked I think will come as close as possible. My hypothetical circumstances are concerned with a person who murders innocent people, and I suspect that nearly every one of you will agree that that is wrong. So please now imagine yourself to be in an ancient country which is ruled over by an evil king who has absolute power of life or death over all his subjects—including yourself. Now this king is very bored, and so for his amusement he picks 10 of his subjects, men, women, and children, at random as well as an eleventh man who is separate from the rest. Now the king gives the eleventh man a choice: he will either hang the 10 people picked at random and let the eleventh go free, or he will hang the eleventh man and let the other 10 go free. And the eleventh man must decide which it is to be.

Now if death is bad, then on an average 10 deaths must be 10 times as bad as one. So hopefully nearly all of you will agree that the eleventh man should give up his life in order that the other 10 might live. But that is not the question I am asking you. I'm asking whether you would in fact make that sacrifice if you were the eleventh man—if you really did have to decide whether you or they would die. And you knew the king meant business because he did this every year and sometimes killed the 10 people and other times the eleventh depending wholly upon what the eleventh had decided.

Now I am about to ask you for a show of hands, but of course I realize that few of you know yourselves so well that you can be certain of the correctness of your answer—especially if your answer is yes. So I simply will ask you to hold up your hand and answer yes if you are any more than 50 per cent certain that you would make that sacrifice. Understand?

All right, all yes answers, please raise your hands. Let me see, that must be about a third of you. That's more than I would have guessed.

Now let me ask only those who are reasonably certain—say 95 per cent certain—that they would make the sacrifice to please raise their hands.

Yes. That's more like what I expected. That's at most a tenth of you. I have a feeling that most of that tenth of you are kidding yourselves, but perhaps human beings aren't as selfish as I have always thought.

Now just two more quick questions. Same situation except that the king says he will let his 10 hostages go free if you will go to prison for 20 years, otherwise he kills them. That's an easier question to be sure of your answer about than the previous one, so this time answer yes only if you are quite certain—95 per cent or better. All right, everybody hold up his hand if he is at least 95 per cent sure he would go to prison for 20 years in order to save 10 people's lives.

Well that looks like about three-quarters of you. Again I think you have overly high opinions of yourselves, or maybe some of you are too embarrassed to tell the truth, but I sincerely hope you are correct in your self-assessments.

Just one question more now. The king says he will let his people go if you will agree to give him all the money you have and all the money you will make in the future, except of course enough for you to feed and house yourself and take care of all the absolute necessities. In other words he's asking you to be poor, but not so poor that it impairs your health in any way. Again I'm asking for at least 95 per cent certainty. All in that category please hold up your hands.

Well that's nearly every one of you! I'm very pleased; I hope you mean it. Perhaps in fact you do this time. After all, since you have the power to decide whether 10 people die or whether you give up your money, if you made the other decision, you would be killing 10 people in order to keep money for yourself, and surely that is murder.

I see some head-shaking—it looks as though a few of you disagree. The king has said, kill these 10 people or I'll take your money. If you kill them, that is murder.

Look at it another way. If you are poor and kill 10 people in order to steal their money, that is surely murder. But morally speaking, that situation is exactly the same as this one. In both situations if the people die, you will be rich; if they live, you will be poor, and it is within your power to decide which it is to be. In either situation if you decide that they should die in order that you can be rich, you have put your happiness, or not actually even that, you have put material riches for yourself above 10 people's lives. That is the moral error you have made and it is exactly the same for both cases. One is as bad as the other and if one is murder so is the other.

Anyway, those are all the questions I wanted to ask you. I didn't mean to spend as much time on them as I did, but at least from my point of view it was well worth the time. Thanks for your indulgence, and also for your soul-searching—I guess those weren't easy questions to answer if you answered them honestly. Just be happy it was a make-believe situation and none of you is likely ever to really be forced to make any of those rather unpleasant decisions.

And now I'll get on to what is supposed to be my topic: overpopulation.

In 1650 the population of the world was 500 million (500m.). Within the next 50 years an absolute minimum of 500m. people will starve to death. Dr Paul Ehrlich, a Stanford University biologist and leader in the population movement, says between 10m. and 20m. people starve to death every year right now. If you take the smaller figure and make the ridiculous assumption that it will not get any larger in the near future, then you get the figure of 500m. deaths in the next 50 years. But it *will* get larger because in 35 years there will be twice as many people trying to find food in a world which today is so overpopulated that half of all human beings are hungry.

Perhaps that figure of 500m. is too large for you to grasp in abstract terms. Let me translate it into something more concrete: if those 500m. people were all to join hands, then figuring at about 1,000 people per mile, they would form a line long enough to stretch to the moon and back—with enough left over to reach across the United States 6 times. Or if you prefer keeping things more down to earth, they would reach 20 times around the world.

The US Army's M-16 machine-gun fires 700 rounds per minute, or about 12 rounds per second. If you drove a car past this line of people at a little over 40 miles per hour, you would pass 700 people every minute. If you used poisoned bullets or some such deadly concoction, you might be able to kill 1 person with every shot as you drove past. If you kept your finger on the trigger for 10 hours a day, 7 days a week, killing 1 person with each shot, it would take you 3 years and 4 months to kill them all.

It is a rather gruesome picture, and yet all these people—and probably many more—are absolutely doomed to die in the next 25 to 50 years. And it won't be the quick, easy death of a bullet, but the slow, pitiful, wasting death of starvation.

There is one bright spot in all this, however—the legions of the doomed will not really reach quite 20 times around the world. Perhaps they'll reach only 12 or 15 times around, for most of them are children and their arms are short.

Just one more statistic along these lines and then I'll move on. There are 3½ billion (3½b.) or 3,500m. people in the world today.[1] As I have said, somewhere between 10 and 20m. starve to death each year. Thus in a group of 350 average human beings, somewhere between 1 and 2 will starve to death *each year*.

Opposed to these ravaged peoples of the world are the gluttons of America. You yourselves are good examples. As future graduates of a good college, it is surely within the grasp of most of you to be making a salary, after taxes, of $10,000 or more within a few years. How much money is that? Well, you could easily take care of all the true necessities of life for $2,000, thus leaving you $8,000 for the luxuries. In America, anyone can stay healthy spending a dollar a day for food. It is not even hard to do. If one really skimps, he can stay alive and well for 50 cents—for I have done it. If it can be done

[1] The population of the world stood at about 3.6b. in 1970 when this speech was written. It surpassed 4.6b. in 1982.

in America for 50 cents a day, it can surely be done for that in the countries where people are starving. In fact, UNICEF can supply milk to the hungry children of the world at a rate of 5 cups per penny donated. Thus your $8,000 of luxury money could be providing 44 people with 50 cents worth of food a day—people who otherwise might starve. Remember that out of 44 *average* people, 1 will starve to death every 4 to 8 years (since 44 is ⅛ of 350 and 1 to 2 out of 350 starve each year). That's as things now stand. Since in the next 40 years, things will get considerably worse, and since presumably if your $8,000 were donated to UNICEF, they would take care to pick out poorer than average people, I think it not unreasonable to state that $8,000 per year over a period of 40 years is enough to keep healthy 10 people who would otherwise starve to death—plus a good many more who would otherwise be malnourished.

So you see, I lied to you a little while ago when I said none of you would ever have to make any of those three unpleasant decisions. You will never have to make the first or the second—the two hardest choices—but you are this moment confronted with the third: for the 10 who would otherwise starve are the 10 hostages, you are the eleventh man, and hunger is the king. Thus if you decide to go on with the life you were probably planning to lead, you will be letting 10 people die rather than give up your colour television and your cocktail parties. And that is more than gluttony, it is murder.

But don't think of yourselves as murderers, for when I asked a little while ago, nearly all of you said you would make the proper choice. However, before you go out and donate all your money to UNICEF, stop and think for a few minutes. So long as the world remains overpopulated, people will starve. Instead of giving your money to an organization which is trying to stamp out hunger, contribute to one which is trying to stamp out overpopulation—the cause of hunger. For what good does it do to keep 44 people alive enough and well enough to have 80 or 100 children who must then go hungry because you only have sufficient money to feed their parents? Instead of solving the hunger problem, you may in fact be making it even worse.

Of course, there are fairly simple ways to get around this detrimental effect of feeding the hungry. For example, you could feed only sterile people. That is not hard to do, since nearly every woman over age 50 is sterile. But I repeat: so long as the world remains overpopulated, people will starve. It is better in the long run to direct our effort toward eliminating this basic cause of hunger.

That's really all I have to say. I'll close by stating my rather pessimistic outlook. I have a terribly low opinion of human beings and think it extremely unlikely that more than a couple of you will make that decision you said you'd make. As I think I have shown, the world of today is a place of stark horror, and the world of tomorrow bleaker still. While you go your merry way, closing your eyes and holding your nose as you step over the wasted bodies, I am struck—and sometimes almost comforted—by the knowledge that in not too many years you yourselves will be in that same sad state. For the United States—indeed the whole earth—is fast running out of the resources it depends on for its existence. Well before the last of the world's supplies of oil and natural gas are exhausted early in the next century, shortages of these and other substances will have brought about the collapse of our whole economy and, indeed, of our whole technology. And without the wonders of modern technology, America will be left a grossly overpopulated, utterly impoverished, helpless, dying land. Thus I foresee a whole world full of wretched, starving people with no hope of escape, for the only countries which could have aided them will soon be no better off than the rest. And thus unless we are saved from this future by the blessing of a nuclear war or a truly lethal pestilence, I see stretching off into eternity a world of indescribable suffering and hopelessness. It is a vision of truly unspeakable horror mitigated only by the fact that try as I might I could not possibly concoct a creature more deserving of such a fate. Good evening.

ON GOODNESS, BADNESS, AND INDIFFERENCE

I mentioned in a note at the beginning of Ellis's speech on overpopulation that it would be followed by a chapter in which I elaborated on some of his ideas. Before beginning with that task, I have a confession to make. As some of you may have already suspected, I wrote that speech myself. It has never been given before an audience. For the audience's responses I merely guessed at what I thought a real audience might have answered. There is no Walter Bradford Ellis. I used this subterfuge because it seemed by far the best way to make the reader an active participant in answering *personally* the questions I was putting to the audience. This personal involvement was essential if I was to stand any chance of breaking through the many barriers which serve to shield us from such dangerous thoughts.

There were several important ideas compressed into the few paragraphs of that speech, and I would like now to discuss them at greater length to make certain they have been understood. The most important of these ideas, and perhaps the most important idea in this essay, is the notion that one is responsible for the choices one makes, and that choices which do not involve action are as real as those which do. For it is simply a fact that any of you who are making a good salary have it within your power to relieve an enormous amount of misery merely by deciding to spend your money for that purpose rather than on yourselves. The misery is there; the money is there; and you have the power to decide how the money will be spent—to relieve their misery or to store up luxuries and status symbols for yourself.

In the speech I showed that the choice facing the average American was the same as the easiest of the three choices offered to our audience. Now I would like to liken it to a somewhat different situation.

The Paymaster

Although I have no facts or figures, still I find it reasonable to suppose that the average citizen of the typical underdeveloped country works as hard as the average American. Quite possibly he works harder. At any rate it seems a little unlikely that the average American (or perhaps I had better say the average reader of this book) actually believes he is more important or worthy or whatever than the average Asian, African, or Latin American, and still more unlikely that he could be correct in so believing. Surely the typical American, at least if he would stop to think about it, would admit that he was no better a person and no harder a worker than the average Asian, and that their extreme difference in station sprung wholly and simply from the accident of the one's being born in

America and the other's in Asia. So why should one get all the money while the other starves?

Imagine a factory-owner who hires 45 people to work for him. All the employees work equally hard, but when time comes to pay them, the owner entrusts all their salaries to 1 of them and (for some strange reason) leaves it totally up to this 1 worker how much each of the others shall be paid. What would you think of that worker if he kept all or so nearly all the money for himself that the other 44 were always in dire poverty and 10 of them eventually died of starvation? Is he not guilty (morally if not legally) of stealing the others' money; and if he knew some would die because of his theft, is he not also guilty of murder? And is not this the situation of the average American—by an odd quirk of fate entrusted with the salaries of 45 human beings and empowered to dispense the money at his whim? And keeping all of it for himself,[2] leaving them to starve? Killing them in order to steal their money? If he does not want to be guilty of these charges, then let him give them back their money, or else explain how by keeping it nearly all for himself, he has distributed it fairly—why he deserves to bask while they grovel.

Thus we have, I think, a rather complete refutation of those strange people who think that life is nice. In the first place, life is clearly not nice for that substantial proportion of mankind (soon to be a majority)[3] who must live from day to day from hand to mouth for ever on the verge or over the verge of starvation. Ask some of the thousands who starve each day how much they enjoy the beautiful birds and flowers and trees. Ask them their opinion of God's love and His tender mercy. Or if perchance you don't believe in God, then ask them their opinion of the love and tender mercy of their fellow human beings, the rich gods across the sea who couldn't care less about their sufferings—at any rate not enough to go out of

---

[2] Actually not quite all the money was given to him originally—he keeps all he is physically able to keep. Which of course raises the question: if absolutely all of it *had* been given to him, how much would he then return to the others? Exactly as much as was actually not given to him to begin with?

[3] Note that it needn't be anywhere near a majority to support my case: the greatest sorrows in life are many times as intense and, except when followed by death, many times as lasting as the greatest joys. And while the supremely miserable people are so plentiful, I have never met a supremely happy person. The happiest people of all enjoy only very moderate degrees of happiness.

their way to help them. Ask *them* those questions. They count too.

What does a beautiful bird mean beside a starving child?

And as though this were not sufficient, recall the material a couple of paragraphs above. If you are part of that small portion of humanity who are to a significant degree happy, and if your happiness is to any extent at all dependent upon material goods or leisure time, then your happiness is bought at the expense of the misery, degradation, and the very lives of your fellow human beings. How many people had to die and how many people had to suffer in order for you to enjoy that wealth and that leisure? How many people could you have saved had you not preferred your comfort to their lives?

There is so very little happiness; and even what there is, is not a beautiful thing—it is the happiness of successful murderers and rapists. This is not a pretty world.

I think we have arrived now at a point where we are able to formulate a general statement of moral principle, sort of analogous to the Golden Rule: By the various actions a person may take at any given moment, he has the power to bring about various consequences. The action which he should take is the one which in the long run in his opinion will result in the least total 'bad' and the most total 'good'. (By 'bad' we mean certainly unhappiness, perhaps death. By 'good' we mean happiness, at least for the present.) Any other act is morally wrong, and the degree of wrongness depends on the degree to which the rule is violated.[4] There must be noted one possible exception to the rule: it may well be that a person has the right to cause as much unhappiness to himself as he wishes.

---

[4] In order to keep the statement of the principle relatively simple, I have somewhat blurred the distinction between wrongness in an act and wrongness in the person performing the act. Thus, if we had wanted to speak of good and bad *acts*, we should have omitted all reference to the protagonist's opinion and inserted in our parenthesis defining good and bad: 'or whatever the *true* definitions of good and bad are'. Had we wanted to speak only of good and bad *people*, we should have inserted: 'or whatever the protagonist sincerely believes to be the true definitions of good and bad'. This latter case is greatly complicated, however, by a notable tendency for people's 'sincere' beliefs to suit their own best interests and even to change, when circumstances change, so that both interests and conscience may still be served. Despite these difficulties and my blurring, the distinction is an important one and must be kept always in mind.

Written in this way, we can see clearly why the sins of omission are as serious as those of commission: there is really no such thing as omission. There are always choices to be made; it is impossible not to choose. If the passage in the speech comparing a person who lets 10 people die rather than give the king his money with a person who kills 10 people to steal their money wasn't clear before, it should be now.

Offhand, I can think of only three ways in which the rule is commonly violated. People sometimes violate the rule to favour themselves, sometimes they violate it to favour their friends, families, countries, churches, and other people or institutions they are loyal to, and sometimes they violate it to hurt those they dislike. All these practices are totally indefensible, and in fact all the objections I can think of which might be raised are extremely simple-minded.[5]

A long time ago I used to think that if I could get through life without doing any harm, I at least would not be a bad person. If the world ended up being no worse off for my having been born, I would be satisfied. We can now see, however, that that is an extremely erroneous, albeit very seductive, way of thinking. The 'statement of moral principle' makes it clear that this way of thinking is incorrect, but I will give a quick example none the less to make sure this misconception is thoroughly debunked.

Imagine you are walking along a river bank when you come upon a man drowning just a few feet off shore. There is a rope lying on the bank, but you do not throw it to him because you want to watch him drown. In my book, you are as much a murderer as if he had by valiantly struggling made it to the bank, and you had pushed him back in. And yet you have done no harm if you look at it from a

---

[5] For instance one might say, 'But it's insane not to violate the rule to favour your friends. If people didn't, no one would have any friends; no one would care very much about anyone else; and everyone would be miserable!' But this objection to the principle is the very principle itself. They're objecting because treating everyone alike does not provide for the greatest happiness! But the principle doesn't say to treat everyone alike. If everyone would be happier if a certain degree of favouritism were shown to his friends, then let there be favouritism. It may actually be true that a slight amount of favouritism is a good thing. I will not argue against it. Still I think it is obvious that the proper amount is *much* less than the amount people generally show. However, even if one ought to show one's friends some slight degree of favouritism, it is difficult to see how any amount of favouritism at all can be justified for oneself.

viewpoint of what would have happened if you had never passed by. Clearly this is an improper viewpoint. Instead you should see that you have come upon a situation in which you have two choices, neither of which is difficult to execute, but one of which will result in a person's death and the other will not. Someone who makes the choice which will kill the person, simply because he wants him to die, is a murderer.

Now let us consider a flank attack which might be made upon our principle. A friend of mine who had devoted a considerable amount of time toward fighting overpopulation once told me he was quitting his volunteer work because he wanted more time to himself, and besides he had done his share. That is the question I wish now to explore: had he done his share? From the point of view of our principle, he clearly was not justified in stopping his work, since by continuing he would alleviate much more suffering in others than he would cause in himself. And yet he was indeed justified according to the way he applied his principle of 'doing your share'. Since one principle says he should continue and the other says that's not so, we know that (at least) one of the principles must be wrong—or else was incorrectly used. Since we're assuming our principle to be correct, and since the problem is clearly not that our principle was misapplied, we must look for a mistake in my friend's principle or in the way he made use of it. There is, in fact, an obvious mistake in the way he applied his principle; consequently we will be content with pointing that out and leave open the question of whether the principle itself is in error.

Presumably my friend thought he'd done his part because if everyone would do as much as he, the problem would be solved. How does one determine what one's share of a particular job is? Does one take the sum total of what has to be done and divide it by the total number of people in the world? Of course not. Some people are only two years old; you can't count them. Some people are severely mentally retarded. Some people have no arms or legs. A great many other people must be eliminated because, for one reason or another, they are not able to help. But there is another group which must be eliminated as well: those who are not *willing* to help. And when this last category is discounted, there are left few people indeed to share in solving a truly immense problem. The shares, in fact, come out to be so large that it is not humanly possible for a person to do his full share even if he spends his every waking moment in the effort. (This is tantamount to saying the problem will not be satisfactorily solved.) One cannot ever sit back and relax because he has done his share.

There is still one idea in my speech which needs to be better developed: that feeding and supplying medical care to sick, hungry people actually causes more pain than it alleviates. Because of the complexities of the real world, I will have to make several simplifying assumptions, but hopefully the burden will have been placed on those who disagree to show why these simplifications cause the results to be invalid.

Imagine an isolated island in the middle of the ocean which has enough arable land and resources to keep alive 1,000 people. The inhabitants of this land, believing birth control to be immoral and a bother, have filled up their island to capacity, and for several hundred years the population has remained at almost precisely 1,000 miserable, nearly starving people. Under better conditions their growth rate would be 2 per cent (approximately the 1970 world growth rate), but because of the limited carrying capacity of the land, an average of 20 people starve to death yearly, thus keeping their growth rate at zero and their population constant.

Thus in the 70 years from 1900 to 1970, 1,400 people died of starvation. Imagine then in 1970 the United States of America discovered the island, and in a great outpouring of national conscience over the plight of the wretched masses, sent stores of food sufficient to keep alive all the starving. Thus their population began to grow, doubling every 35 years, until in another 70 years there were 4,000 people on the island. But in the meantime the population of the US had doubled once to over 400m. people; much of America's best agricultural land was paved over with highways or covered with urban sprawl or made infertile with air pollution or had had the best topsoil washed away; oil, natural gas, and many other important resources were either exhausted or in critically short supply; and now America herself was facing an imminent crisis.[6] So in the year 2040 the American president summarily

[6] The world growth rate was about 2 per cent in 1971 when this chapter was originally written. Since then it has declined slightly, and the 1986 figure is about 1.7

suspended all food shipments to our hapless island, and in consequence 3,000 people promptly and on cue starved to death. Thus in the 70 years before aid arrived, there were 1,400 deaths from starvation compared to 3,000 in the 70 years after the aid began.

I would like to take now a short quote from *The Population Bomb*, by Dr Paul R. Ehrlich. Compared with 1965

in 1966 each person on Earth had 2% less to eat, the reduction, of course not being uniformly distributed. Only ten countries grew more food than they consumed: the United States, Canada, Australia, Argentina, France, New Zealand, Burma, Thailand, Rumania, and South Africa. The United States produced more than half of the surplus, with Canada and Australia contributing most of the balance.[7]

I think it should be clear from these data that most of the world is

per cent, which represents a doubling time of 41 years. The 1986 US doubling time is still about 70 years, though the figure is only approximate because of large uncertainties about the extent of immigration.

[7] Ehrlich, Dr Paul R., *The Population Bomb* (New York, 1971, p. 19 (revised edn.)). Unfortunately, Ehrlich does not give the source for his data. A more recent paper by David Pimentel *et al.* ('Land Degradation: Effects on Food and Energy Resources', *Science*, vol. 194, p. 154, 1976) reports, 'All nations except the U.S., Canada, Australia, New Zealand, Argentina, and Thailand are consistent net food importers.' He does give a source (*Yearbook of International Trade Statistics* (UN, 1974, vol. 1)). But it is not clear to me how one would use that source to draw his conclusion, because weights of foods are often not given, only the monetary value. It appears one would first have to estimate the weight from the value, as monetary value bears very little relation to food value, and then one would have to translate the weight into different food values for different foods: a country which imports 1,000 tons of wheat and exports 1,500 tons of lettuce is a net food importer.

A number of countries, such as England and Morocco, must import substantial proportions of their total food supply. For instance, 'The Netherlands ... imports about 50% of its wheat, 100% of its rice, 75% of its other cereals, *all* of its steel, antimony, bauxite, chromium, copper, gold, lead, magnesite, manganese, mercury, molybdenum, nickel, silver, tin, tungsten, vanadium, zinc, phosphate rock (fertilizer), potash (fertilizer), asbestos, and diamonds. It produces the energy equivalent of some 20 million metric tons of coal and consumes the equivalent of over 47 million metric tons.' (Paul R. Ehrlich and Richard L. Harriman, *How to Be a Survivor: A Plan to Save Spaceship Earth* (New York, 1971, p. 37).) On the other hand, many other countries are only small-scale importers and, at least for the present, could probably produce all their food and other essentials if really forced to do so. But there are no other countries who are likely ever to become large-scale exporters of food. Thus these statistics are misleading, and not even correct, if interpreted to mean that all countries besides these few would face starvation if their food imports were cut off. But if they are viewed from a perspective of where the rapidly growing food deficit of the rest of the world is going to come from, there is very little room for error: it will come from these countries or not at all.

already grossly overpopulated and that America and the few other food surplus countries are likely not to be able to supply food even to all the rich countries (England, Japan, Russia, The Netherlands, etc.) with money to buy it for much longer, to say nothing of giving it away to the poor countries with their exploding populations.

So the point I am making is this. It should be clear to everybody with even a rudimentary understanding of the population crisis that even if America manages to provide well for herself indefinitely into the future (most unlikely), she cannot possibly continue for very long to provide food to very many other countries. Soon aid must cease or be drastically reduced to any country we are helping now or undertake to help in the future. The point of the example was to show that when that aid finally stops, the resulting disaster will be far more hellish than anything that would have happened had aid never been sent at all. Thus aid in the form of food or medical technology (with the all-important exception of birth control devices) should never be sent to needy countries; and any countries which are now receiving aid should be cut off—and the sooner the better.

There is one clear-cut error which has been introduced by the simplifications I made. Obviously a country which is on the verge of achieving population stabilization and food self-sufficiency should be fed until it has got over the hump. Thus a policy of blanket refusal of aid could be improved upon, though what the criteria for aid should be, I have no idea. None the less I will state without proof my opinion that a policy of blanket refusal of aid would in the long run cause less suffering than either a policy of blanket granting of as much aid as is possible or the present policy (whatever that is). Thus we have reality's consummate and heart-breaking final irony: even those few, those very few people of the rich countries who are not dead to the plight of their fellow human beings, are by and large engaged in food or medical relief projects which in the long run will probably cause much more misery than they cure.

Before ending this chapter, I would like to develop one last statistic whose derivation was too unwieldy to include in the speech. One may be curious as to what fraction of human beings will starve to death. No one can accurately predict the magnitude of the coming cataclysm or what percentage of humanity will perish in it, but we may set a minimum by exploring the question of what fraction will die if things remain as they are. That is, we will assume a constant rate of population increase and assume that the fraction of people dying from starvation remains in the future what it is today.

If our population were stable, things would be quite simple. Then the fraction of people who would eventually die of starvation, or in other words, a newborn baby's chances of eventually starving (call it 'F'), would simply be the deaths due to starvation in any given year divided by the total deaths in that year. But with a constantly increasing population that relation no longer holds true.

Let us call the total number of deaths by starvation which occurred in 1986, 'D_S', and the total number of deaths from all causes, 'D'. Thus

$$F \neq \frac{D_S}{D}$$

though this would be true if the population were stable. Call the total number of births in 1986, 'B'. As we said, the fraction of all people born in 1986 who will eventually starve is F. Therefore the actual number of people born in 1986 who will eventually starve is FB. But this number of deaths is greater than the number who actually did starve to death in 1986 (D_S) because starvation deaths must increase from year to year at the same rate as the population, since F is constant. Thus we may write $FB > D_S$ (where '>' means 'is greater than') or

$$F > \frac{D_S}{B}$$

Thus the fraction of people born in 1986 who will eventually die of starvation is greater than the starvation deaths of 1986 divided by the total *births* for 1986. Putting in actual numbers and using the smaller of Dr Ehrlich's estimates, we get $F > 10,000,000/133,000,000$ or $F > 1/13.3$. Putting in Dr Ehrlich's larger number, we get $F > 1/6.7$. Thus if you are a human being born in 1986, your chances of eventually starving are considerably greater than 1 in 14 and possibly greater than 1 in 7—and those figures are obtained by projecting *today*'s level of misery into the future, ignoring the absolute certainty that the level of misery will soon drastically increase. In fact if you look back through this section and the preceding one, you will find that virtually all the statistics I made use of reflected conditions as they are today.[8]

POSTSCRIPT

Much has happened on the population front since 1970–1 when this essay was first written. A brief comparison of the world situation then and now (1986) is in order. The rate of growth apparently peaked at about 2.0 per cent per year (35-year doubling time) in the early 1970s. It fell slightly during the mid-1970s, reaching approximately 1.7 per cent in 1978. It has remained virtually unchanged since 1978—eight of the last nine growth rate estimates given by the Population Reference Bureau have been 1.7 per cent, the exception coming in 1983 with 1.8 per cent. The corresponding doubling times have oscillated between 40 and 41 years (39 in 1983). These were 9 lost years we were wholly unable to afford, comprising quite possibly more than 25 per cent of the time remaining before nature takes its revenge and quite certainly more than 25 per cent of the time in which to find a solution. Compared to 1970, we are significantly worse off today in the three ways which matter most. First and second: our population is larger by 1.3b., and the number added per year is considerably greater now. Population increase has carried us backward much further than the tiny reduction in *per cent* growth rate has taken us forward. A 1970 world population of 3,632m. growing by 2.0 per cent was adding 73m. people per year;

---

[8] The 'Speech' was originally published in *Inquiry* (vol. 23, 1980, pp. 242–51), along with a few pages of related material. There I estimated a 10 per cent chance of starvation, assuming 10m. deaths per year. There is a great deal of uncertainty over the actual numbers, but I now suspect Ehrlich's larger figure of 20m. is too high. A fairly conservative estimate of 10m. is accepted as 'a pretty good figure to use' by Nick Eberstadt (personal communication, 24 June 1985; see also p. 40 of his 'Hunger and Ideology', *Commentary*, vol. 72, July 1981), an anti-Malthusian writer who has gone to a lot of effort to show that certain hunger figures have been exaggerated. (Unfortunately he has sometimes gone too far in this regard, his well-known statistic that only 2 per cent of the human race are 'critically hungry' at a given time being a fact without any clear meaning, perfectly consistent with *any* fraction of humans starving to death, including 100 per cent.) In 'The Decline in Hunger-Related Deaths' (*Hunger Project Papers*, no. 1, May 1984) Roy L. Prosterman gives a rough procedure that produces a figure of 13m.–18m.

1986's 4,942m. at a little over 1.7 per cent is growing by 85m. Both overpopulation and population growth are substantially greater today.

Under the current circumstances the third area of deterioration may be the most important of all. We have consumed another 16 years' worth of our dwindling resources. Up to the end of 1970 the world had used approximately 244b. barrels of the estimated 2,000b. barrels of crude oil which will ever be recovered. (This includes an estimate for oil as yet undiscovered. At least eight recent studies have come close to this figure, most being slightly below.) Thus at the end of 1970 there were about 478 barrels of oil for every person then alive. In the following 12 years we consumed almost exactly as much oil as we had used from the beginning of the industrial era to the end of 1970, so that by the end of 1982 there were only an estimated 327 barrels of oil remaining per person, a drop of almost one-third in 12 years. Americans, at their 1980 rate of consumption of 26.4 barrels a year apiece, even if the rate does not rise and their population ceases to grow, will consume their 327 barrels in 12.4 years and thereafter will be consuming other countries' shares. Even if other countries consume all their 327 barrels, at their 1980 rate of 3.95 barrels per person per year, it will still be gone in 83 years even if their per capita usage remains at its current low level and their populations grow no larger. But at current rates of growth these countries' populations will more than quintuple in 83 years. Not only is virtually all of modern industry vitally dependent on oil, but American agriculture in 1970 used nine times more energy in producing food than the food contained. And the increased yields of the 'Green Revolution' are paid for through greatly increased energy requirements. We are consuming our oil in quite a literal sense.

One-quarter of the world's people are dependent on wood for their chief source of fuel, yet they are cutting down their forests so rapidly that by the year 2020 (only 34 years away) 'virtually all the physically accessible forest in the Less Developed Countries is expected to have been cut'. (*The Global 2000 Report to the President*, US Govt. Printing Office, 1980, vol. 1, p. 26.) And many other mineral and biological resources will be exhausted or nearing exhaustion by this time.

The world is rushing toward a precipice at dizzying speed. If we are not already beyond the point of no return, it is staring us in the face and we show no sign of turning back. It was 13 years ago (unpublished) and again 5 years later (*Inquiry*, vol. 21, p. 452, Winter 1978) when I predicted that not only would we lose the battle against overpopulation, but that we would not even make any serious attempt to save ourselves. The contest would not even be close. It now looks as if that is going to be even more true than I realized. Complacency has been growing even faster than overpopulation.

Despite all this pessimism, I do not mean to leave the impression nothing can be done. I do not think a catastrophe can be averted, but actions we take or fail to take now will greatly affect the ultimate magnitude of the catastrophe. Uncertain, but potentially of almost unimaginable importance, is the impact we can have on the nature of the post-crash world. The events which are about to unfold will profoundly affect our world for a very long time, and the numbers of people involved over that span may potentially be many times the current world population. It is not outside the realm of possibility that much of the future of sentient life on our planet will be determined by the events of the next twenty or so years.

Much less uncertain, we can probably still today vary the magnitude of the immediate catastrophe by a factor of two, and possibly more. Two catastrophes are twice as bad as one, and the hundreds of millions—if not billions—of people whose lives hang in the balance will be as saved if we save them or as lost if we don't as they would be if theirs were the only lives involved. Indeed, with so few people interested and so much still to be determined, it is likely that never before and never again in human history will the actions of the average individual who *does* take it upon himself to get involved, mean so much.

IX

'IT MAKES NO DIFFERENCE
WHETHER OR NOT I DO IT'

JONATHAN GLOVER

THERE are some arguments used to justify people doing things, otherwise admitted to be wrong, which are puzzling. They are claims that, while a certain act will be bad in its outcome, so that it would be better if it were not performed at all, it makes only an insignificant difference, or even no difference at all, if *I* am the person to do it. One such argument is that used by a scientist who takes a job developing means of chemical and biological warfare, and who admits that it would be better if his country did not sponsor such research, but who says (correctly) 'If I don't do it, someone else will.' This type of argument also appears as an attempted justification of Britain selling arms to South Africa. If we accept this as a justification, it is hard to see what acts, however otherwise wicked, could not be defended in the same way. The job of hired assassin, or controller of the gas supply at Belsen, or chief torturer for the South African Police, will surely be filled by someone, so it seems to make no difference to the total outcome whether *I* accept or refuse such a job. When we think of these cases, most of us are probably reluctant to allow weight to this defence. Yet it is hard for those of us who think that moral choices between courses of action ought to be determined, either largely or entirely, by their different outcomes, to explain what is wrong with such a defence.

'If I don't do it, someone else will' is only one member of a family of arguments relating to the insignificance of a single person's act or omission. It is necessary to distinguish between some of these related defences in order to examine them separately.

Jonathan Glover, 'It makes no difference whether or not I do it', *Proceedings of the Aristotelian Society*, Supp. Vol. XLIX, pp. 171–90. © The Aristotelian Society, 1975. Reprinted by courtesy of the Editor.

A. MY DOING IT MAKES AN INSIGNIFICANT DIFFERENCE

Here, the argument is that, given the size of a problem, the best I can do in the way of acting or refraining will make only an insignificant difference, and so it does not matter what I do. This argument is found in discussions of the population problem or of world poverty. The suggestion is that the problem of over-population is so vast that my refraining from having another child will not make a significant impact. It can similarly be argued that problems of poverty and hunger are so vast that my sending money to relief agencies is a drop in the ocean, and pointless.

B. MY DOING IT MAKES NO DIFFERENCE

At least two sorts of claim are made here:

   (i) 'If I don't do it, someone else will.' (Chemical warfare research; arms to South Africa.)
   (ii) 'One person makes no difference.' This can be used in support of not bothering to vote in any election, except in the extremely rare case where there is a significant chance of one vote tipping the scale.

I shall look first at the argument from the insignificant difference, and then at the argument from no difference.

A

1. *The argument from the insignificant difference: context illusions*

In many of the cases where it is used, the argument from the insignificant difference can be dismissed at once. If I can rescue a single person from death or misery, the fact that there are many others I cannot rescue is irrelevant to the moral worth of doing this. Huge problems sometimes produce an irrational paralysis of the imagination. It is so terrible to think of the poverty and starvation that will still exist in the world whatever I do, that it is tempting to despair and do nothing. But the difference that is small compared to the size of the whole problem may be one that in other contexts we would think worth taking very seriously: when we are not thinking in terms of millions of people, we think it important to save a single life.

But there are other cases where the argument from the insignificant difference is used, and where the harm a single person does seems small in a way that is independent of the size illusions generated by a context of catastrophe. These other cases are best introduced by distinguishing between different kinds of threshold.

2. *Two kinds of threshold*

An *Absolute Threshold* is found where there is a sharp boundary between two different outcomes. The clearest case is that of voting. If there are two candidates, and a thousand votes are cast for one of them, the other will lose if he gets only 999 votes and will win if he gets 1,001 votes. Winning or losing is an all-or-none matter: victory by one vote is still a complete victory. If, for simplicity, we imagine a voter who is fully informed about how everyone else will vote, we see that, except for side effects, there is no point in his voting, except where doing so will lead to either a draw or to the victory of his candidate by one vote. For, in all other cases, his vote will leave the outcome unchanged.

In contrast to an absolute threshold is a *Discrimination Threshold*. This is where a single person's act will push a situation slightly further in a certain direction, but where his contribution, although real, may be too small to be detected when its effects are spread through the community. Here it is not, as with voting, that there is an absolute threshold in reality. In these cases the reality is a gentle slope, and the threshold is defined by the distance apart on the slope two points have to be in order to be seen as separate by us. If there is an electricity shortage, and I keep the heater on when we are asked to economize, the result may be that everyone in the community has a power cut lasting one-hundredth of a second longer than it would have done. This is negligible, but the whole thing is a matter of degree, and things get worse as more people do the same as I do.

In cases with an absolute threshold and where my act (say, of voting) does not result in the threshold being crossed, I have contributed nothing to the outcome. Someone who takes the view that moral grounds for choosing one course of action rather than another must depend on some difference in total outcome will think that, apart from side effects, it does not matter whether or not I vote. There will be a case for my voting to the extent that the outcome of the election is uncertain, but if I know that my vote will not be decisive the argument for voting will have to appeal to considerations other than the desirability of my party or candidate winning.

3. The principle of divisibility

It may be thought that there is no difference in this respect between absolute thresholds and discrimination thresholds. Some people are tempted to assimilate the case of the electricity shortage to the voting case. In the electricity case, the harm I do when spread over the community is below the discrimination threshold. Consequentialists who treat the two kinds of threshold in the same way conclude that, apart from side effects, it does not matter whether I use the electricity or not. The suggestion is that the harm done counts as zero.

But against this I want to argue that the harm done in such cases should be assessed as a fraction of a discriminable unit, rather than as zero. Let us call this the *Principle of Divisibility*. It says that, in cases where harm is a matter of degree, sub-threshold actions are wrong to the extent that they cause harm, and where a hundred acts like mine are necessary to cause a detectable difference I have caused one-hundredth of that detectable harm.

Anyone who doubts this principle should consider the consequences of assigning zero harm to sub-threshold acts.

Suppose a village contains 100 unarmed tribesmen. As they eat their lunch 100 hungry armed bandits descend on the village and each bandit at gunpoint takes one tribesman's lunch and eats it. The bandits then go off, each one having done a discriminable amount of harm to a single tribesman. Next week, the bandits are tempted to do the same thing again, but are troubled by new-found doubts about the morality of such a raid. Their doubts are put to rest by one of their number who does not believe in the principle of divisibility. They then raid the village, tie up the tribesmen, and look at their lunch. As expected, each bowl of food contains 100 baked beans.

The pleasure derived from one baked bean is below the discrimination threshold. Instead of each bandit eating a single plateful as last week, each takes one bean from each plate. They leave after eating all the beans, pleased to have done no harm, as each has done no more than sub-threshold harm to each person. Those who reject the principle of divisibility have to agree.

If we accept that the principle of divisibility applies when a discrimination threshold is reached, a mildly scholastic further question arises. What should we say about a case where a sub-threshold increment is not 'topped up' by other sub-threshold increments to produce a discriminable unit? (Suppose I am the only person in the country to use electricity when economy is asked for.) Should we, appealing to the divisibility principle, assign some disutility to this? The case for answering 'yes' is that it seems incoherent to weight each such act at zero before the threshold is reached, but, if the threshold is reached, then to say that together the acts add up to a detectable disutility.

But there is also a case for saying 'no'. Ignoring side effects, it seems absurd for a consequentialist who is certain the threshold will not be reached to refrain from using electricity although he knows that this will in no way avoid any detectable discomfort or inconvenience to anyone. My inclination to say 'no' makes me want to explain away the supposed paradox in saying 'yes'. Why should we not say that acts which do not contribute to the discrimination threshold being reached have zero disutility, but that they do have disutility where they do so contribute? This should only seem paradoxical to someone who thinks that the utility of an act must be independent of the behaviour of others.

4. *Evaluation of the argument from the insignificant difference*

The argument that my doing something makes only an insignificant difference is in many cases not an acceptable defence. It is not acceptable where the supposed insignificance is a size illusion created by a special context. Nor is it acceptable where its plausibility depends on a tacit denial of the principle of divisibility.

It is only acceptable in cases where sub-threshold increments do not combine to produce discriminable harm, or where it is part of a larger argument, which includes countervailing reasons out-weighing the harm that *is* done.

I turn now to the argument from no difference.

B

5. *The generalization test*

Sometimes it is said that the only reason why the scientist's claim, that if he does not work on chemical warfare someone else will, seems plausible as a defence is a mistaken concentration on the consequences of the act of a single person. It is suggested that we should not ask 'what difference will it make if I do this?', but 'what difference would it make if everyone did this?'

But David Lyons has cast doubt on this by his argument that the second question, when adequately formulated, always gives the same answer as the first question. When the generalization test is applied, everything hangs on how the act is described. We would probably give different answers to the crude question 'what if everyone broke his promises?' and to the slightly more subtle question 'what if everyone broke his promises when this was necessary to save someone's life?' Lyons argues that utilitarians applying the generalization test have to include in the description of the act all those features that affect the utility of the outcome. So, in the case of the scientist and chemical warfare, we have to ask, not the odd question, 'what would happen if all scientists worked on chemical warfare?', but some such complicated question as 'what would happen if all those biologists who had these special skills, and who were offered jobs in chemical warfare, accepted the jobs in those cases where, if they refused, someone else equally able would accept?' This question is itself no doubt over-simplified, but it seems that the more complete in the relevant respects the description becomes, the closer the generalization test comes to giving the same answer that one gets to the question 'what will happen if *I* do this?'

Sometimes the Lyons argument is resisted, as it is by Gertrude Ezorsky, and by J. H. Sobel, by proposing restrictions on those features of other people's behaviour that can be included in the description of the act when applying the generalization test. Sobel uses Prisoner's Dilemma type cases to show that such restrictions can result in the generalization test sometimes giving different answers from those obtained by the simple question about the consequences of a single person's act.

But the difficulty for those versions of the generalization test that do differ in outcome from the simple consequence question is that using them threatens to produce results that differ by being worse. This is because the features of other people's behaviour that we are debarred from considering often do in fact alter the desirability of the outcome. If I am not allowed to take into account how many other people are voting, the generalization test is likely to tell me to vote at some inconvenience to myself, even where my vote will not influence the outcome. If a nation in a balance of terror situation is not allowed to take into account the predictable response of other nations, the generalization test may tell it to disarm in a situation where the outcome will be that, as the only disarmed nation, it is obliterated. Such acts may be noble, but in opting for them we have abandoned consequentialism.

The generalization test could only help us if there were a version of it that would give answers that sometimes differed from those given to the simple test, and which in such cases would not generate a worse total outcome. Until such a version has been found it would be nice to hear no more of the generalization test.

6. *Side effects*

A more promising way of arguing against the scientist taking the chemical warfare job is to examine all the side effects of taking it, together with the alternatives. For the claim that 'if I don't do it, someone else will' is not sufficient to show that the total consequences of *my* taking the job will be no worse than the total consequences of my not taking it.

One factor is the possibility of my doing some socially useful research instead. The probability is that the other people wanting the job are not guided much in their choice of work by considerations of social usefulness. If one of the others gets it, there is only an average chance that the work he would otherwise have done would have been beneficial. But if I refuse the job, it is in my power to look for the most useful project I stand a good chance of completing.

There is also the question of the influence I have on others. If I take the job, this makes a small contribution to making such work respectable among those of my fellow scientists who know me and give any weight to my views. It may be said that the same contribution to an amoral climate of scientific research will be made by whoever takes the job. But this objection ignores the positive influence a refusal on principle can have. If I get the job, the other applicants will probably just grumble about the shortage of scientific jobs and make no contribution to discrediting chemical warfare as a field of research. If I refuse the job on moral grounds, this may itself make a good, if small, impact on the moral climate of science. It also leaves me free to campaign against others taking such jobs. It is true that if I accept the job (perhaps for some very subtle utilitarian reason) I can still campaign against others taking similar jobs. But my campaign would be weakened by the impression of hypocrisy this would create on unsubtle people.

There is also the effect on myself of doing, for good but subtle reasons, something that in crude terms I disapprove of. Suppose I take the job, while thinking it would be better if such research were not done, partly because I need the money more than the other applicants, and partly because I know that (by inefficient work not quite bad enough to get me sacked) I can ensure that the work is less productive. I may find I have underestimated the effects of this bad faith, and when deception gets a permanent foothold in that part of my life, I may find it hard to prevent contamination of other relationships. Consequentialists can justify some acts of lying. But an enormously greater case has to be made out for any policy requiring constant deception, just because of the psychological difficulty of keeping one part of one's mind sufficiently cordoned off from the other parts.

And, even if I can keep my mind compartmentalized in this manner, I may be corrupted in a more oblique way. Our emotional responses are not always governed by our beliefs. An atheist who was strongly conditioned to church-going in childhood may still feel guilty when he lies in bed on Sundays. Similarly, the utilitarian scientist working on chemical warfare may from time to time be filled with self-loathing and disgust, which may not be dispelled even when he rehearses to himself the complex reasons which he thinks justify his having the job. This may not in itself matter very much. But it can be important not to be subjected to too much tension of this kind, not only because it is unpleasant, but also because some constancy of self-esteem may be necessary for going on trying to be moral at all. If among the burdens of being moral there is a heavy weight of self-disgust, the whole policy is likely to break under the load.

But these appeals to side effects although powerful in the chemical warfare case, are not always sufficient to nullify the force of the claim 'if I don't do it, someone else will'. This is because it is always possible to construct a case where the arguments on the other side are even more powerful. Suppose I am very uninfluential in the scientific community and so my example either way carries very little weight. (The effects of a Bertrand Russell not following a multitude to do evil may be immense, but most other people command less attention.) Also suppose that I have a huge family; that we are very poor; and that there is very little chance of my finding any other job at all, let alone doing any useful research. It is plausible that, in the chemical warfare problem, appeals to side effects will in the normal case provide very good reasons against taking the job, even where it is certain that if I do not take it someone else will. But, as with all such arguments, it cannot be guaranteed that this result will be generated in all instances of the dilemma.

7. A special class of side effects: spirals

There are some very important classes of side effects which are often underrated. These are side effects where the *numbers* of actions of a certain type will have an influence on people. If this influence is repeated, we have a spiral.

To illustrate the idea of a spiral, we can again consider the voting problem. At first sight, there seems virtually no consequentialist case for voting in a general election in Britain. The chance of my vote being decisive between governments can be ruled out: the likelihood of a government coming to power with a majority of one MP, where that one MP gets in by a single vote, is laughably small. And even if I care about the size of the governing party's majority, it is still highly unlikely that a single person will be decisive in my own constituency. When this is recognized, it is common for people to produce a quite different argument for voting. My vote will help keep up the morale of my party, or else it will help to support the system of democratic elections.

People will in future be less inclined to vote for my party if it seems to stand very little chance of winning, so the total votes now cast for it matter. And people will start to feel disillusioned with the democratic system if the percentage using their votes becomes alarmingly small. The danger is of a downward spiral, like a flight from a currency, where having few participants leads to loss of confidence, which in turn leads to fewer participants. Small political parties are similarly concerned to generate an upward spiral, where larger numbers of votes lead potential supporters to think they stand a chance of winning, and so their votes increase further.

As so often when the argument from no difference is countered by appeals to side effects, we are back here with problems involving discrimination thresholds. Even where the existence of spiral is recognized, someone may claim that his vote makes an insignificant difference. Potential supporters would have to be *very* sensitive to feel differently about voting for a party which last time scored 8,341,692 votes from how they would feel about one which had scored 8,343,691. We can accept that one vote is below the discrimination threshold, but resist the view that it therefore does not matter at all. Such a view would lead to the baked beans paradox, so we should instead invoke the principle of divisibility. And a spiral magnifies the utilities and disutilities to be divided, sometimes enormously, as when the disutilities of a price increase are turned into the disutilities of the collapse of a currency.

The difficulty with spirals is our uncertainty about their onset and their rate of acceleration or slowing down. A specific number of votes is needed to win an election. It is not certain that there is a specific number marking the point where a small party starts to benefit from an upward spiral, or the point where it starts to be hurt by a downward spiral. We are often unable to identify even the broad region of onset, and equally unable to predict the shape of the upward or downward curve.

Because utilities and disutilities are magnified by spirals, a rational consequentialist would give weight to this wherever it seemed plausible that they would occur. It is this feature of consequentialism that is fatal to D. H. Hodgson's ingenious argument in support of the view that act utilitarianism is self-defeating. His claim that some overriding important utilities depend on expectations that act utilitarians are incapable of generating. For example, communication depends on people expecting to be told the truth. Act utilitarians will only tell the truth where it is useful to do so, i.e. where people expect it. But the expectation can only be generated by the practice, which in turns depends on the expectation. Hodgson claims that act utilitarians are on a downward spiral that they cannot stop. But, as Peter Singer has pointed out, the very danger of the downward spiral gives them a good reason for telling the truth, and the fact that they have this good reason should generate the right expectations in those they talk to.

When the importance of spirals is understood, it is less hard to see how act utilitarians (and others concerned with the contribution that their particular act makes to total outcome) can manage to generate the many benefits that flow from co-operative social practices. But, as with side effects in general, there is no guarantee that these effects will *always* generate a sufficient case for giving support to a co-operative practice. Even where the question of a spiral arises, there may be countervailing side effects that override such a factor.

8. *The appeal to justice*

Suppose I do not vote because I have something else I want to do instead. I know my party will get in anyway, and there are no spirals or other side effects which outweigh the case for my not voting. Some people object here on grounds of justice. My argument for not voting depends on my belief that the other members of my party will mostly turn out to vote. It has been said by Colin Strang and by Lyons that there is something unfair in my allowing others to do the work and not making a contribution myself.

Lyons thinks that the claims of fairness are such that I have a prima-facie obligation to co-operate in social practices from which I benefit even where the threshold would be reached without my doing so. But this derives part of its plausibility in the case of voting from Lyons's assimilation of the voting case to a car-pushing case. In the context of discussing surplus votes for a winning candidate, Lyons asks, 'If it takes six men to push a car up a hill and, not

knowing this, eight lend a hand to do the job, what are we to say?'
But to assimilate these cases is to ignore the distinction between
absolute thresholds and discrimination thresholds. Having made
this distinction, we are free to accept the argument from injustice in
the car-pushing case without accepting it in the voting case. If I do
not push the car, the others will have to push a bit harder. Many of
us are against the kind of injustice that involves giving benefits to
some at the cost of additional hardship to others. But no one has to
vote harder because I do not vote. It seems a dog-in-the-manger
version of justice that objects to one person benefiting because
others are left unchanged.

9. *Ritual*

Appeals to side effects (including spirals) will often not be powerful
enough to generate an adequate consequentialist argument for
voting, and the direct appeal to the question of who will win the
election will carry weight only on very rare occasions. This is
something a consequentialist may just accept, but many others find
this rather shocking. Perhaps this is because, for many people in our
society, voting is a kind of sacred ritual. There are emotional
satisfactions in ritual professions of belief, and people who experience these satisfactions are disturbed by other people taking them
lightly. This is a very minor factor to take into account, and it
cuts both ways. It is a pity to cause minor disturbance to believers,
but it is often beneficial to encourage people to question their
rituals.

10. *Absolute prohibitions*

In considering the argument from no difference, it has so far been
claimed that neither the generalization test nor the appeal to justice
·will defeat the argument. But it has also been suggested that, in very
many cases, the act which apparently has no upshot will turn out to
have side effects too important to dismiss.

Many people will object to the contingency of such a line of
defence against the argument from no difference. To them it will
seem wrong that the question of working on chemical warfare, or of
selling arms to South Africa, should be decided by calculating
consequences, however likely the result is to fit in with their prior

disapproval. They may be tempted to invoke absolute prohibitions, independent of the total outcome of those actions.

The difficulty with absolute prohibitions is that the exclusion of appeals to outcome seems to rule out attempts to justify them, except either by direct appeal to intuitive responses or by appeal to some authority. Appeals to authority are not worth discussing here, so let us look at the alternative: the intuitive acceptability of absolute prohibitions.

The acts that can be defended by the argument from no difference are so varied that, at first sight, the list of absolute prohibitions needed to defeat the argument seems enormous. It ranges from 'Never work on chemical warfare projects' through 'Never sell arms to countries with evil governments' to 'Never fail to vote in a general election where you care about the outcome'. A long list of absolute prohibitions of this kind should appal us. This is not merely because of the aesthetic preference most of us have for economy of principles, the preference for ethical systems in the style of the Bauhaus rather than Baroque. It is partly because we cannot see how to select our long list of absolute prohibited acts or omissions. And it is partly because we are rightly alarmed about what disasters we may be letting ourselves in for, where all escape routes are blocked by our having so many absolute prohibitions.

An alternative is to produce a coherent system of manageable size, where there is a small number of prohibitions stated in very general terms, together with priority rules where prohibitions conflict. Prohibitions would no longer refer to chemical warfare, but to some such act as indiscriminate killing. In recent philosophy such a system is sometimes gestured at, especially in discussions of war or abortion, where the prohibition on killing the innocent is mentioned. But we have not been presented by those sympathetic to this kind of outlook with even the outlines of a properly worked out system. For this reason, we are still justified in any scepticism we feel. In the absence of a whole system to scrutinize, we still do not know what disasters such systems might make inescapable. And we still do not know what principle of selection is supposed to operate when we make up our list of forbidden acts.

11. *The Solzhenitsyn principle*

Bernard Williams has recently argued that it is desirable to find some middle way between a morality of absolute prohibitions and a morality where total outcome is decisive. Such a morality would have to leave more room, he argues, than a consequentialist morality can, for considerations of personal integrity. In such a morality, outcome is not all that matters. It is also important what role my decision or action plays in bringing it about.

Considerations of this sort seem central to people's resistance to consequentialist morality. In Solzhenitsyn's Nobel lecture, he says (echoing one of his own characters in *The First Circle*) 'And the simple step of a simple courageous man is not to take part in the lie, not to support deceit. Let the lie come into the world, even dominate the world, but not through me.'

The Solzhenitsyn principle does not commit people who hold it to the view that some acts are wrong for reasons entirely independent of outcome. It is open to us to incorporate this principle in a kind of tempered consequentialism. I may think that a certain outcome is bad, and then invoke the Solzhenitsyn principle to say that *I* must not be the person who brings it about. But this is obviously a departure from the strictest consequentialism, which is concerned with total outcomes, rather than with what would ordinarily be described as the consequences of *my* act.

How can we choose between the strictest consequentialism and the Solzhenitsyn principle? If they always generated the same answer, there would be no need to choose. But clearly they do not. In the chemical warfare problem, if there are cases where side effects give overall support to taking the job, this leads to a clash with the Solzhenitsyn principle. In those cases, to obey the principle is to do so at the cost of the total outcome being worse. The strict consequentialist will say that the principle tells us to keep our hands clean, at a cost which will probably be paid by other people. It is excessively self-regarding, placing considerations either of my own feelings or purity of character far too high on the scale of factors to be considered.

Williams has considered an argument of this kind, which he calls the 'squeamishness appeal' in the context of an example of his own.

A man, arriving in a small South American town, finds that soldiers are about to shoot twenty captive Indians as a reprisal for recent anti-government protests there. The man, as a foreign visitor, is offered the privilege of shooting one Indian. If he does this, the others will be let off. There is no escape from the dilemma of accepting or refusing the offer.

Williams plausibly says that the utilitarian would think that he obviously ought to accept the offer. Williams does not himself say that the offer should be refused, but that it is not *obvious* that it should be accepted. He then refers to the criticism that a refusal might be 'self-indulgent squeamishness'. But he suggests a reply to this squeamishness appeal. He says that this appeal can only carry weight with someone already seeing the situation in terms of strict consequentialism. He says that, for anyone not seeing things from that point of view, 'he will not see his resistance to the invitation, and the unpleasant feelings he associates with accepting it, *just* as disagreeable experiences of his; they figure rather as emotional expressions of a thought that to accept would be wrong'. Williams goes on to say, 'Because our moral relation to the world is partly given by such feelings, and by a sense of what we can or cannot "live with", to come to regard those feelings from a purely utilitarian point of view, that is to say, as happenings outside one's moral self, is to lose a sense of one's moral identity; to lose, in the most literal way, one's integrity.'

This reply does have some force, but also severe limitations. In the first place, it does not show that the *utilitarian* who regards certain of his own feelings in this way has lost his integrity. He can agree that his morality is partly based on such feelings, but say that when he reflects on his feelings he finds that they cannot all be combined into anything coherent. It then seems legitimate to disregard some of them as anomalies. When I hear of some medical experiments on an animal, I may feel a revulsion against all vivisection, but this may conflict with my feelings when I reflect on the implications of this for medical research. I do not lose my integrity by deciding that my first response was exaggerated.

The second limitation of the Williams reply is that it seems to presuppose that we can readily distinguish feelings that have moral import from other feelings. But this is not clear. The atheist already mentioned is surely right to attach no moral significance to his guilt feelings when he does not go to church. But his guilt feelings may not be phenomenologically distinct from those of a man whose whole morality centres round his religion.

The final doubt about the Solzhenitsyn principle is that it appears to presuppose a conventional but questionable doctrine about the moral difference between acts and omissions. According to this doctrine, I have made a worse moral choice if something bad foreseeably comes about as the result of my deliberate act than I have if something equally bad foreseeably comes about as the result of my deliberate omission. If we eliminate a complication by removing the difference of numbers, the Solzhenitsyn principle seems to suggest that it would be worse for me to shoot an Indian than for me deliberately to refuse an invitation with the foreseen and inevitable consequence that a soldier would shoot the same Indian. To look closely at arguments normally offered for this conventional view might increase our scepticism about the principle so closely related to it.

(The criticism of a possessive attitude to one's own virtue seems to be the point of the story of the old woman and the onion in *The Brothers Karamazov*. After a wicked life, an old woman was in the lake of fire. But God heard about her only good deed: she had once given an onion from her garden to a beggar. He told her guardian angel to hold out the onion for her to catch hold of it, and to try to pull her up from the lake to paradise. She was being pulled out when other sinners in the lake caught hold of her to be pulled out. The woman kicked them, saying 'It's me who is being pulled out, not you. It's my onion, not yours.' When she said this, the onion broke and she fell back into the lake.)

12. *Judging actions and judging people*

Our inclination to make the choice I am arguing against (to prefer the Solzhenitsyn principle to strict consequentialism) is perhaps partly caused by a tendency to confuse judging actions with judging people. We ought in our thinking to keep separate the standpoints of the agent deciding between different courses of action and of the moral critic or judge, who comments on the moral quality of people's character.

The moralities of other people may lead them to perform acts that arouse our admiration, whether they are obeying absolute prohibitions or the Solzhenitsyn principle. Solzhenitsyn's own conduct while in Russia is a case in point. A more calculating, strict consequentialist morality might not have generated such a fine display of independence and bravery. (*Might* not: for the paradox here is that Solzhenitsyn's own example has done good in Russia that we cannot calculate, and has probably, in consequentialist terms, been well worth the risks taken. And even in our society, where the penalties are so much less, acts of moral independence help to create a climate where social pressures are less, and where the views of the powerful and the orthodox are treated with appropriate lack of reverence.)

Because we often admire the moral character of people following the Solzhenitsyn principle, we easily slide over into thinking their action right. But there is no equivalence here. Unless we are narrow-minded bigots, we will often admire the moral qualities of people following many different sets of beliefs: it does not follow that we are justified in following all or any of them when we have to act ourselves. The corollary of this is the platitude that we can sometimes disagree with a moral view while respecting those who act on it. Sometimes the reluctance to reject the Solzhenitsyn principle rests on neglect of this platitude.

Is there an oddity in saying that we can admire the character of those who accept the Solzhenitsyn principle just after quoting the story of the old woman and the onion?

We should distinguish here between admirable character traits on the one hand and a policy which gives exaggerated weight to preserving them on the other. Someone acting on the Solzhenitsyn principle can display such traits as honesty, loyalty, or a revulsion against killing or hurting people. These are all traits whose existence is in overall effect immensely beneficial. A consequentialist has every reason to encourage them. (This is the point sometimes exaggerated by crude consequentialists when they wrongly suggest that we admire these traits *because* of their contribution to social welfare.) We can admire these traits while thinking that they sometimes lead to the wrong decision, as happens if, in the Williams case, the man refuses to shoot an Indian. If, in explaining this, he says 'I just could not bring myself to do it', we see an admirable character trait that has too strong a grip on him. But if he says 'Before coming to South America I read an interesting article by Bernard Williams, and so I understood that I must preserve my integrity, even at the cost of nineteen lives', the onion criticism then applies.

13. *Esoteric morality*

It may be said that the consequentialist approach to these questions defended here is in some way incoherent, since if it were propagated widely, it would have disastrous consequences in its own terms. (Jonathan Harrison, in his discussion of these questions, said 'No principle is fit to be a moral principle unless it is fit that it should be universally adopted and universally applied.') The consequentialist approach leaves such decisions as whether or not to vote, or whether or not to work on chemical warfare, to be decided by sophisticated reasoning about the outcome, rather than by simple and clear rules. The suggestion is that most people do not think in a very sophisticated way, and are likely to be biased by self-interest, so that if these views were propagated, disasters would follow. Elections might collapse. If not, they might be decided by people who were either not consequentialists or else not intelligent.

One reply is that propagating the consequentialist approach would include telling people about spirals. Where sophisticated utilitarian abstention started to become common, sophisticated utilitarians would detect this. They would revise their estimates of the chances of their party winning by a narrow margin, and they would also consider the danger of helping to start a downward spiral. The tendency not to vote would be to some extent self-correcting.

Another reply is that people are not as dim as the criticism suggests. You do not really have to be a very sophisticated person to grasp say the essential point of the principle of divisibility. A recent anti-litter poster showed bits of paper falling, thick and fast, each accompanied by a speak-bubble saying 'My one bit of paper won't make any difference.' People who were not philosophers probably got the message.

But, apart from these points, there is a more central reply. A morality is not incoherent simply because, in its own terms, it would be better not propagated. I can consistently adhere to a morality which, among other things, enjoins me to practise it secretly. It is true that, if much of the morality is esoteric in this way, the bad effects on me of deceiving others will start to operate. But if the cases where deception will be justified are as few as I think they are, I can allow for them in my consequentialist calculations.

Sidgwick put the matter in an engaging sentence: 'Thus the Utilitarian conclusion, carefully stated, would seem to be this; that the opinion that secrecy may render an action right which would not otherwise be so should itself be kept comparatively secret; and similarly it seems expedient that the doctrine that esoteric morality is expedient should itself be kept esoteric.' Sidgwick appropriately buried this sentence in page 490 of *The Methods of Ethics*.

14. *Conclusions*

To summarize the position argued for:

(A) THE ARGUMENT FROM THE INSIGNIFICANT DIFFERENCE:
    (i) fails where it depends on size illusions
    (ii) fails where it depends on ignoring the principle of divisibility.

(B) THE ARGUMENT FROM NO DIFFERENCE:
    (i) is not defeated by the generalization test
    (ii) is not defeated by the appeal to justice
    (iii) often is defeated by consideration of alternatives and side effects, especially spirals.

   And

    (iv) where the side effects are inadequate to defeat the argument from no difference, this should then be accepted in preference to looking for absolute prohibitions or adopting the Solzhenitsyn principle.
    (v) In cases where the argument from no difference is accepted, this should sometimes not be publicized.

(I follow Sidgwick's example, and bury this last conclusion at the end of a paper in the Supplementary Volume of the Aristotelian Society.)

Note: In writing this paper I have been helped a lot by suggestions and criticisms by Vivette Glover, Henry West, Jim Griffin, and Derek Parfit.

REFERENCES

Gertrude Ezorsky: 'A Defense of Rule Utilitarianism Against David Lyons who insists on Tieing it to Act Utilitarianism, Plus a Brand New Way of Checking Out General Utilitarian Properties', *Journal of Philosophy*, 1968.

Jonathan Harrison: 'Utilitarianism, Universalisation, and Our Duty to be Just', *PAS*, 1952–3.

D. H. Hodgson: *Consequences of Utilitarianism* (Oxford, 1967).

David Lyons: *Forms and Limits of Utilitarianism* (Oxford, 1965), esp. p. 89 and Chap. 5 Part A.

Henry Sidgwick: *The Methods of Ethics* (Seventh edn., London, 1907).

Peter Singer: 'Is Act-Utilitarianism Self-Defeating?' *Philosophical Review*, 1972.

Jordan Howard Sobel: 'Utilitarianisms: Simple and General', *Inquiry*, 1970.

Alexander Solzhenitsyn: 'One Word of Truth . . .' (London, 1972).

Bernard Williams: 'A Critique of Utilitarianism', in J. J. C. Smart and Bernard Williams: *Utilitarianism For and Against* (Cambridge, 1973).

X

OVERPOPULATION AND THE QUALITY OF LIFE

How many people should there be? Can there be *overpopulation*: too many people living? I shall present a puzzling argument about these questions, show how this argument can be strengthened, then sketch a possible reply.*

I QUALITY AND QUANTITY

Consider the outcomes that might be produced, in some part of the world, by two rates of population growth. Suppose that, if there is faster growth, there would later be more people, who would all be worse off. These outcomes are shown in Fig. 1. The width of the

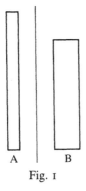

Fig. 1

* The first half of this (hitherto unpublished) essay summarizes a longer discussion in my *Reasons and Persons* (Oxford, 1984). I have been greatly helped by J. McMahan, J. R. Richards, L. Temkin, K. Kalafski, and R. Jones. For further reading on this subject, see *Obligations to Future Generations*, ed. R. I. Sikora and B. Barry (Philadelphia, 1978) and McMahan's long review of this anthology in *Ethics* 92, No. 1, 1981.

blocks shows the number of people living; the height shows how well off these people are. Compared with outcome A, outcome B would have twice as many people, who would all be worse off. To avoid irrelevant complications, I assume that in each outcome there would be no inequality: no one would be worse off than anyone else. I also assume that everyone's life would be well worth living.

There are various ways in which, because there would be twice as many people in outcome B, these people might be all worse off than the people in A. There might be worse housing, overcrowded schools, more pollution, less unspoilt countryside, fewer opportunities, and a smaller share per person of various other kinds of resources. I shall say, for short, that in B there is *a lower quality of life*.

Except for the absence of inequality, these two outcomes could be the real alternatives for some country, or mankind, given two rates of population growth over many years. Would one of these outcomes be worse than the other? I do not mean 'morally worse' in the sense that applies only to agents and to acts. But one of two outcomes can be worse in another sense that has moral relevance. It would be worse, in this sense, if more people suffer, or die young.

Would it be worse, in this sense, if the outcome was B rather than A? Part of the answer is clear. We would all agree that B would be, in one way, worse than A: it would be bad that everyone would be worse off.

On one view, this is all that matters, and it makes B worse than A. This view is expressed in

The Average Principle: If other things are equal, it is better if people's lives go, on average, better.

The *Hedonistic* version of this principle substitutes, for 'go better', 'contain more happiness'.[1]

---

[1] Of the many economists who appeal to the Average Principle, some make it true by definition. See, for example, P. A. Samuelson, *Economics* (New York, 1970), p. 551. Certain writers state this principle so that it covers only the lives that are, at any time, being lived. This makes the principle imply that it would have been better if all but the best-off people had just dropped dead. My versions of the Average Principle do not imply this absurd conclusion. If anyone with a life worth living dies earlier, this causes people's lives to go, on average, worse, and to contain a smaller average sum of happiness.

On the other main view about this question, it is good if any extra life is lived, that is worth living. On this view B might be better than A. B would be in one way worse, because everyone would be worse off. But in another way B would be better, because there would be more people living, all of whose lives would be worth living. And the fact that people would be worse off might be less important than—or *outweighed* by—the fact that there would be more people living.

Which of these views should we accept? Could a loss in the *quality* of people's lives be outweighed by a sufficient increase in the *quantity* of worthwhile life lived? If this is so, what are the relative values of quality and quantity? These are the central questions about overpopulation.[2]

The Average Principle implies that only quality matters. At the other extreme is

> *The Hedonistic Total Principle*: If other things are equal, it is better if there is a greater total sum of happiness.

This principle implies that only quantity matters. Its Non-Hedonistic version substitutes, for 'happiness', 'whatever makes life worth living'.

On the Hedonistic Total Principle, B would be better than A because each life in B would be *more than half* as happy as each life in A. Though the people in B would each be less happy than the people in A, they *together* would have more happiness—just as two bottles more than half-full hold more than a bottleful. On the non-Hedonistic version of this principle, B would be better than A because, compared with lives in A, lives in B would be *more than half* as much worth living.

These claims may seem implausibly precise. But lives in B would be more than half as much worth living if, though a move from the level in A to that in B would be a decline in the quality of life, it would take much more than another similarly large decline before

---

[2] These remarks assume that the quality of life is higher if people's lives go better, and that each life goes better if it contains a greater quantity either of happiness or of whatever else makes life worth living. 'Quality' thus means 'quantity, per life lived'. In Section 5 below I drop this assumption, thereby simplifying the contrast between quality and quantity. (If this note is puzzling, ignore it.)

people's lives ceased to be worth living. There are many actual cases in which such a claim would be true.[3]

2   THE REPUGNANT CONCLUSION

Consider Fig. 2. On the Total Principle, just as B would be better than A, C would be better than B, D better than C, and so on.

Best of all would be Z. This is an enormous population all of whom have lives that are not much above the level where they would cease to be worth living. A life could be like this either because its ecstasies make its agonies seem just worth enduring, or because it is painless but drab. Let us imagine lives in Z to be of this second kind. There is nothing bad in each of these lives; but there is little happiness, and little else that is good. The people in Z never suffer; but all they have is muzak and potatoes. Though there is little happiness in each life in Z, because there are so many of these lives Z is the outcome in which there would be the greatest total sum of happiness. Similarly, Z is the outcome in which there would be the greatest quantity of whatever makes life worth living. (The greatest mass of milk might be in a vast heap of bottles each containing only one drop.)

It is worth comparing Z with Nozick's imagined *Utility Monster.*

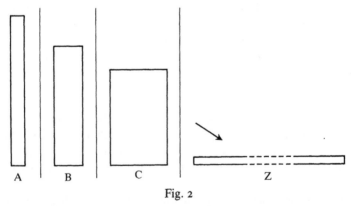

Fig. 2

[3] In what follows I assume, for convenience, that there can be precise differences between the quality of life of different groups. I believe that there could not really be such precise differences. All that my arguments require is that some people can be worse off than others, in morally significant ways, and by more or less.

This is someone who would gain more happiness than we would lose whenever he is given any of our resources. Some Utilitarians believe that the Hedonistic Total Principle should be our only moral principle. Nozick claims that, on this Utilitarian theory, it would be best if all our resources were taken away and given to his Utility Monster, since this would produce the greatest total sum of happiness. As he writes, 'unacceptably, the theory seems to require that we all be sacrificed in the monster's maw'.[4]

How could it be true that, if all mankind's resources were given to Nozick's Monster, this would produce the greatest total sum of happiness? For this to be true, this Monster's life must, compared with other people's lives, be *millions* of times as much worth living. We cannot imagine, even in the dimmest way, what such a life would be like. Nozick's appeal to his Monster is therefore not a good objection to the Total Principle. We cannot test a moral principle by applying it to a case which we cannot even imagine.

Return now to the population in outcome Z. This is another Utility Monster. The difference is that the greater sum of happiness would come from a vast increase, not in the quality of one person's life, but in the number of lives lived. And *this* Utility Monster can be imagined. We can imagine what it would for someone's life to be barely worth living—containing only muzak and potatoes. And we can imagine what it would be for there to be many people with such lives. In order to imagine Z, we merely have to imagine that there would be *very* many.

We could not in practice face a choice between A and Z. Given the limits to the world's resources, we could not in fact produce the greatest possible sum of happiness, or the greatest amount of whatever makes life worth living, by producing an enormous population whose lives were barely worth living.[5] But this would be

---

[4] R. Nozick, *Anarchy, State, and Utopia* (Oxford, 1974), p. 41.

[5] According to some versions of the widely assumed *Law of Diminishing Marginal Utility*, we could do this. The point can be made most easily in Hedonistic terms. It is assumed that, because resources produce more happiness if they are given to people who are worse off, they would produce most happiness if they are all given to people whose lives are barely worth living. There is here an obvious oversight. Many resources are needed to make each person's life even reach a level where it begins to be worth living. Such resources do not help to produce the greatest possible quantity of happiness, since they are merely being used to raise people to the level where their happiness begins to outweigh their suffering.

merely *technically* impossible. In order to suppose it possible, we merely need to add some assumptions about the nature and availability of resources. We can therefore test our moral principles by applying them to A and Z.[6]

The Total Principle implies that Z would be better than A. More generally, the principle implies

> *The Repugnant Conclusion:* Compared with the existence of very many people—say, ten billion—all of whom have a very high quality of life, there must be some much larger number of people whose existence, if other things are equal, would be *better*, even though these people would have lives that are barely worth living.[7]

As its name suggests, most of us find this conclusion hard to accept. Most of us believe that Z would be much worse than A. To keep this belief, we must reject the Total Principle. We must also reject the broader view that any loss in the quality of life could be outweighed by a sufficient increase in the total quantity of whatever makes life worth living. Unless we reject this view, we cannot avoid the Repugnant Conclusion.

When the stakes are lower, as in the comparison between A and B, most of us believe that B would be worse. We believe that, compared with the existence of ten billion people whose lives are very well worth living, it would be worse if instead there were twice

---

[6] It may help to give this illustration. Suppose that, as a *Negative Utilitarian*, I believe that all that matters morally is the relief or prevention of suffering. It is pointed out to me that, on my view, it would be best if all life on Earth was painlessly destroyed, since only this would ensure that there would be no more suffering. And suppose I agreed that this would be a very bad outcome. Could I say: 'It is true that this very bad outcome would, according to my moral view, be the best outcome. But this is no objection to my view, since we are not in fact able to bring about this outcome'? This would be no defence. On my view, I ought to *regret* our inability to bring about this outcome. Whether my view is plausible cannot depend on what is technically possible. Since this view implies that the destruction of all life on Earth would be the best outcome, if I firmly believe that this outcome would be very bad, I should reject this view.

[7] The phrase 'if other things are equal' allows for the possibility that the existence of the larger population might, in some other way, be worse. It might, for instance, involve injustice. What the Repugnant Conclusion claims is that, though the lower quality of life would make Z in one way worse than A, this bad feature could be less important than, or be outweighed by, Z's good feature: the existence of enough extra people whose lives are—even if only barely—worth living.

as many people who were all worse off. To keep this belief, we must again reject the Total Principle.

Suppose that we do reject this principle. Unfortunately, this is not enough. As I shall now argue, it is hard to defend the belief that B would be worse than A, and it is also hard to avoid the Repugnant Conclusion.

3   THE MERE ADDITION PARADOX

Consider the alternatives shown in Fig. 3. There is here a new outcome, A+. This differs from A only by the addition of an extra group of people, whose lives are well worth living, though they are worse off than the original group.

The inequality in A+ is *natural*: not the result of any kind of social injustice. Take my waves to show the Atlantic Ocean, and assume that we are considering possible outcomes in some past century, before the Atlantic had been crossed. In A+ there was one group of people living in Europe, Asia, and Africa, and another group, who were worse off, living in the Americas. A is a different possible outcome at this time, in which the Americas were uninhabited. Perhaps the Bering Straits had opened before the land was crossed.

Is A+ worse than A? Note that I am not asking whether it is *better*. If we do not believe that the existence of extra people is in itself good, we shall deny that the extra group in A+ makes A+ better than A. But is A+ *worse* than A? Would it have been better if

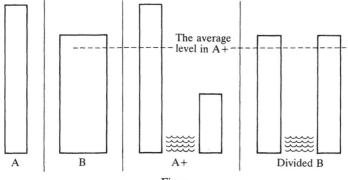

Fig. 3

the extra group had never existed? This is hard to believe. It may seem a bad feature that there is natural inequality in A+—that the extra group are, through no fault of theirs, worse off than the original group. But the inequality in A+ does not seem to justify the view that the extra group should never have existed. Why are they such a blot on the Universe?

You may think that you have no view about whether it would have been better if the extra group had never existed. It may help to consider another outcome: A + Hell. In this outcome the extra group are innocent people who all have lives which are much worse than nothing. They would all kill themselves if they could, but their torturers prevent this. We would all agree that A + Hell *is* worse than A. It would have been better if *this* extra group, as they all passionately wish, had never existed. Since we believe that A + Hell is worse than A, we must be able to compare A+ and A. Unlike the extra group in Hell, the extra people in A+ have lives that are well worth living; and their existence is not bad for anyone. Most of us could not honestly claim to believe that it would have been better if these people had never existed. Most of us would therefore believe that A+ is not worse than A.

Now suppose that, as a result of changes in the environment, A+ turned into Divided B. In both these outcomes the same number of people would exist, so we are not making one of the unfamiliar comparisons which involve different numbers of people in existence. Since the numbers are the same in A+ and Divided B, our ordinary moral principles apply.

On the principles which most of us accept, Divided B would be better than A+. On the Principle of Utility it is better if there is a greater net sum of benefits—a greater sum of benefits minus losses. Divided B would be better than A+ in utilitarian terms, since the benefits to the people who gain would be greater than the losses to the people who lose. On the Principle of Equality it is better if there is less inequality between different people. Divided B would be better than A+ in egalitarian terms, since the benefits would all go to the people who are worse off.

It might be objected that the Principle of Equality does not apply to people who cannot even communicate. But suppose that I know about two such people, one of whom is, through mere bad luck, worse off. Call these people *Poor* and *Rich*. I could either benefit Rich, or give a greater benefit to Poor. Most of us would believe that it would be better if I do the second. And we would believe that this would make the outcome better, not only because I would give Poor a greater benefit, but also because he is worse off than Rich. Most of us would believe this even though Poor and Rich cannot (except through me) communicate.

How could we deny that a change from A+ to Divided B would be a change for the better? We would have to claim that the loss to the best-off people in A+ matters more than the greater gain to the equally numerous worst-off people. This seems to commit us to the *Élitist* view that what matters most is the condition of the best-off people. This is the opposite of Rawls's famous view that what matters most is the condition of the worst-off people.[8] Most of us would reject this Élitist View. Most of us would therefore agree that Divided B would be better than A+.

Suppose finally that the Atlantic is crossed, turning Divided B into B. These two outcomes are clearly equally good. Since Divided B would be better than A+, B must be better than A+.

Let us now combine the conclusions we have reached. Most of us believe both that A+ is not worse than A, and that B is better than A+. These beliefs together imply that B is not worse than A. B cannot be worse than A if it is *better* than something—A+—which is *not worse* than A. In the same way, you cannot be taller than me if you are shorter than someone who is not taller than me. But, as I earlier claimed, most of us also believe that B *is* worse than A. We therefore have three beliefs which are inconsistent, and imply a contradiction. These beliefs imply that B both is and is not worse than A. I call this *the Mere Addition Paradox*.

This is not just a conflict between different moral principles. Suppose that we accept both the Principle of Equality and the Principle of Utility. There can be cases where these principles conflict—where greater equality would reduce the sum of benefits. But such a case does not reveal any inconsistency in our moral view. We would merely have to ask whether, given the details of the case, the gain in equality would be more important than the loss of

[8] J. Rawls, *A Theory of Justice* (Cambridge, Mass., 1971).

benefits. We would here be trying to decide what, after considering all the details, we believe would be the better outcome.

In the Mere Addition Paradox, things are different. Most of us here believe, *all things considered*, that B is worse than A, though B is better than A+, which is not worse than A. If we continue to hold these three beliefs, we must conclude that B both is and is not worse than A. But we cannot possibly accept this conclusion, any more than we could accept that you both are and are not taller than me. Since we cannot possibly accept what these three beliefs imply, at least one belief must go.

Which should go? Suppose that we keep our belief that B is better than A+, because we cannot persuade ourselves that what matters most is the condition of the best-off people. Suppose that we also keep our belief that A+ is not worse than A, because we cannot persuade ourselves that it would have been better if the extra group had never existed. We must then reject our belief that B is worse than A. We must conclude that, if these were two possible futures for some society or the world, it would *not* be worse if what comes about is B: twice the population, who are all worse off.

The Mere Addition Paradox does not force us to this conclusion. We can avoid the conclusion if we reject one of our other two beliefs. Some people reject the belief that A+ is not worse than A, because they think that the inequality in A+ is enough to make A+ worse. These people can keep their belief that B is worse than A. Note, however, that we cannot simply claim that A+ must be worse than A, since it is worse than something—B—which is worse than A. We would here be rejecting one of our three inconsistent beliefs simply on the ground that it is not consistent with the other two. This could be said against *each* belief. To avoid the paradox we must believe, without considering the rest of the argument, that A+ is worse than A. We must believe that it was bad in itself that the extra people ever lived, even though these people had lives that were well worth living, and their existence was bad for no one. To the extent that we find this hard to believe, we still face a paradox.

It may be objected: 'Your argument involves a kind of trick. When you compare A and A+, you claim that the extra group's existence was bad for no one. But by the time we have moved to B the original group have become worse off. The addition of the extra group *was* bad for the original group.'

The argument can be restated. Suppose that A+ was the actual state of the world in some past century. A is a different state of the world which was merely possible. We can ask, 'Would A have been better? Would it have been better if the worse-off group had never existed?' As I have said, most of us could not answer Yes. Suppose next that A+ did *not* in fact later change into either Divided B or B. We can ask, '*If* this change had occurred, would it have been a change for the better?' It is hard to answer No. On this version of the argument, the last objection has been met. The better-off group in A+ was not an originally existing group, to which the worse-off group was added. And the existence of the worse-off group was not bad for the better-off group.

It is worth giving another version of the argument. To ensure that there was no social injustice, we assumed that the two groups in A+ did not know of each other's existence. We could assume instead that both these groups live in the same society, and that the people in one group are worse off, not because of social injustice, but because they all have some handicap which cannot be cured. Suppose, for example, that they are deaf. If this is so, would it have been better if these people had never existed? Would this have been better even though these people's lives are worth living, their existence is not bad for anyone, and if they had never existed no one else would have existed in their place? It is hard to believe that these deaf people should never have existed. On this version of the argument, it again seems that A+ is not worse than A.

Suppose next that these deaf people could be cured, at some lesser cost to the other group. This would be like the change from A+ to B. It is again hard to deny that this change would make the outcome better. In this version of the argument, with the groups in one society, we seem again driven to conclude that, since B would be better than A+, which is not worse than A, B cannot be worse than A.

There are some other possible objections to this argument. But rather than discussing these I shall turn to another argument. This is harder to answer, and it also leads to the Repugnant Conclusion.

4   THE SECOND PARADOX

Consider the first three outcomes shown in Fig. 4. Though this argument involves many outcomes, we need to make only two comparisons.

One is between A+ and the much more populated Alpha. Suppose that Alpha will be the actual outcome at some time far in the future, after humans have colonized thousands of planets in this Galaxy. A+ is a different possible outcome at this time, in which humans have colonized only one other planet, near a distant star. As before, in neither Alpha nor A+ would the inequality between different people be the result of social injustice. Because of the difficulties of trans-Galactic travel, those who are better off could not raise the quality of life of those who are worse off.

The comparison between A+ and Alpha replaces the comparison, in the old argument, between A and A+. On one view, the natural inequality in A+ makes it worse than A. If I held this view, I would now say:

> The inequality in Alpha is in one way worse than the inequality in A+, since the gap between the better-off and worse-off people is slightly greater. But in another way the inequality is less bad. This is a matter of the relative numbers of, or the *ratio* between, those who are better-off and those who are worse-off. Half of the people in A+ are better off than the other half. This is a worse inequality than a situation in which almost everyone is equally well off, and those who are better off are only a fraction of one per cent. And this is the difference between A+ and Alpha. Because there are so many groups at level 45 (most of them not shown in the diagram), the better-off people in Alpha are only a fraction of one per cent.
>
> To put these claims together: The inequality in Alpha is in one way slightly worse than the inequality in A+, but in another way much better. There is a slightly greater gap between the better-off and worse-off groups, but a much better ratio between these groups. All things considered, the natural inequality in Alpha is not worse than the natural inequality in A+.[9]

---

[9] If you believe that the inequality is worse in Alpha than it is in A+, read (when you reach it) footnote 11.

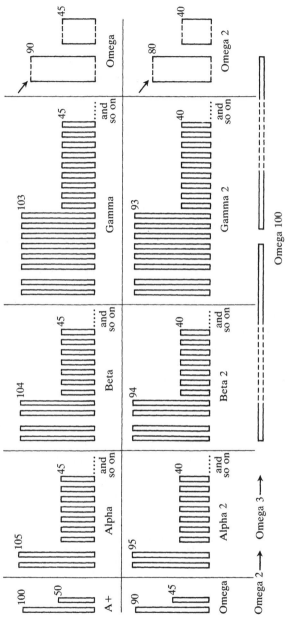

Fig. 4

It may be objected that Alpha is worse than A+ because the worst-off groups in Alpha are worse off than the worst-off group in A+. Many people accept Rawls's view that what matters most is the condition of the worst-off group. But there are two quite different ways in which any worst-off group might have been better off. This group might have existed, and been better off. This is the ordinary case, which Rawls discusses. Things would have been quite different if the worst-off group had never existed. This would have provided another sense in which the 'worst-off' group would have been better off, since some other group would then have *been* those who are worst off. Would this have made the outcome better? If we answer Yes, we must agree that it would have been even better if the second worst-off group had also never existed, and the third worst-off group, and the fourth worst-off group, and so on. It would have been best if everyone except the best-off group had never existed. Similarly, it might be best if in future only the best-off nation—such as the Norwegians—have children. Even if this would be worse for them, it might cause it to be true that, after the rest of us have died, the 'worst-off' people in the world are as well off as possible. This way of raising the level of 'the worst-off group' has no moral merit. The non-existence of all but the best-off group would not, in the morally relevant sense, make the worst-off group better off.

The inequality in Alpha is not worse than the inequality in A+; nor is Alpha worse than A+ because the worst-off groups are worse off. Nor is there any other way in which Alpha is worse than A+.[10] And, in one way, Alpha is *better* than A+. Alpha does not differ from A+ merely by involving the existence of the very many groups at level 45. All of the people in A+ are in one of two groups, and both these groups are, in Alpha, better off. (These are the groups at level 105.) I conclude that, since Alpha is in this way better than

---

[10] Alpha is worse than A+ according to the Average Principle. But this is one of the cases which show that we should reject this principle. The Average Principle could also imply that it would be best if in future all except the Norwegians have no children. For further objections to this principle, see my *Reasons and Persons*, Section 143, and J. A. McMahan, 'Problems of Population Theory', *Ethics*, Vol. 92 no. 1, Oct. 1981. It may also be claimed, 'Alpha is worse than A+ because, if we had to choose in which outcome we would prefer to exist—without knowing who we would be—it would be rational to choose A+.' For objections to this claim, see my *Reasons and Persons*, Section 133.

A+, and is in no way worse, Alpha is better than A+. We are assuming that the actual outcome at some future time is Alpha. If the outcome had been A+, this would have been worse.

Could we honestly deny this conclusion? Could we honestly claim that A+ would not have been worse than Alpha? This is the claim that it would not have been worse if the worst-off people in Alpha had never existed, even though their lives are worth living, and if they had never existed, so that the outcome had been A+, the inequality would have been no better, and *everyone who did exist would have been worse off.* That this would *not* have been worse is hard to believe.[11]

Consider next whether Beta would be better than Alpha. In a change from Alpha to Beta, the best-off group in Alpha would lose a little, but an equally large worse-off group would gain very much more. If this is all we know about this change, it would need extreme Élitism to deny that it would be a change for the better.

The rest of the argument merely involves repetition. Gamma would be better than Beta in the same way in which Beta would be better than Alpha. Delta would be better than Gamma in the same way, Epsilon better than Delta, and so on down to Omega. We then run through the argument again, on the second line of the diagram, from Omega to Omega 2. (Omega is thinner on this second line only because, to make room, all widths are reduced.) Similar steps take us to Omega 3, Omega 4, and all the way to Omega 100. Every step would be a change for the better, so Omega 100 must be the best of all these outcomes.

Since this argument implies that Omega 100 would be better than A+, it leads us to the Repugnant Conclusion. A+ might be a world with ten billion people, of whom even the worse-off half have an *extremely high* quality of life. According to this argument it would be *better* if instead there were vastly many more people, all of whose lives were *barely worth living*.

What is wrong with this argument? To avoid its conclusion, we must either deny that A+ would have been worse than Alpha, or

---

[11] Suppose you believe that the inequality in Alpha is worse than the inequality in A+. Is this enough to justify the claim that it would *not* have been worse if the actual outcome had been A+ rather than Alpha? Which would have mattered more: (1) that the inequality would have been less bad, or (2) that everyone who did exist would have been worse off? It is hard to deny that (2) would have mattered more.

deny that Beta would be better than Alpha. Unless we deny one of these claims, we cannot plausibly deny the similar claims which carry us down to Omega 100. But how can we deny that A+ would have been worse than Alpha? If the outcome had been A+, everyone who existed would have been worse off. And how can we deny that Beta would be better than Alpha? In a change to Beta some people would lose a little, but as many people who are much worse off would gain much more.

While we consider these outcomes in these simple terms, it is hard to answer this argument. There is little room for manœuvre. To find an answer we must consider other features of these outcomes.[12]

5 THE QUALITY OF SINGLE LIVES

Consider first the analogue, within one life, of the Repugnant Conclusion.[13] Suppose that I can choose between two futures. I could live for another 100 years, all of an extremely high quality. Call this *the Century of Ecstasy*. I could instead live for ever, with a life that would always be barely worth living. Though there would be nothing bad in this life, the only good things would be muzak and potatoes. Call this *the Drab Eternity*.

I believe that, of these two, the Century of Ecstasy would give me a better future. And this is the future that I would prefer. Many people would have the same belief, and preference.

On one view about what makes our lives go best, we would be making a mistake. On this view, though the Century of Ecstasy

---

[12] It may be objected that my argument is like what are called *Sorites Arguments*, which are known to lead to false conclusions. Suppose we assume that removing any single grain of sand cannot turn a heap of sand into something that is not a heap. It can then be argued that, even if we remove every single grain, we must still have a heap. Or suppose we assume that the loss of any single hair cannot cause someone who is not bald to be bald. There is a similar argument for the conclusion that, even if someone loses all his hair, this cannot make him bald. If my argument was like this, it could be referred to those who work on what is wrong with Sorites Arguments. But my argument is not like this. A Sorites Argument appeals to a series of steps, each of which is assumed to *make no difference*. My argument would be like this if it claimed that Alpha is *not worse* than A+, Beta is not worse than Alpha, Gamma is not worse than Beta, and so on. But the argument claims that Alpha is *better* than A+, Beta is better than Alpha, Gamma is better than Beta, and so on. The objections to Sorites Arguments are therefore irrelevant.

[13] This section is partly based on an unpublished paper by J. McMahan.

would have great value for me, this value would be finite, or have an upper limit. In contrast, since each day in the Drab Eternity would have the same small value for me, there would be no limit to the total value for me of this second life. This value must, in the end, be greater than the limited value of the Century of Ecstasy.

I reject this view. I claim that, though each day of the Drab Eternity would be worth living, the Century of Ecstasy would give me a better life. This is like Mill's claim about the 'difference in quality' between human and pig-like pleasures.[14] It is often said that Mill's 'higher pleasures' are merely *greater* pleasures: pleasures with more value. As Sidgwick wrote, 'all qualitative comparison of pleasures must really resolve itself in quantitative [comparison]'.[15] This would be so if the value of all pleasures lay on the same scale. But this is what I have just denied. The Century of Ecstasy would be better for me in an essentially qualitative way. Though each day of the Drab Eternity would have some value for me, *no* amount of this value could be as good for me as the Century of Ecstasy.

6 PERFECTIONISM

Return to the argument about overpopulation. Should we make a similar claim, not about the value for one person of different possible futures, but about the relative goodness of different outcomes? Cardinal Newman made such a claim about pain and sin. He believed that both of these were bad, but that no amount of pain could be as bad as the least amount of sin. He therefore wrote that, 'if all mankind suffered extremest agony, this would be less bad than if one venial sin was committed'.[16] Can we make such a claim about what is good in my outcomes A and Z?

Consider what I shall call *the best things in life*. These are the best kinds of creative activity and aesthetic experience, the best relationships between different people, and the other things which do most to make life worth living. Return next to A and B. Suppose that all of the best things in life are, in B, *better*. The people in B are all

[14] J. S. Mill, *Utilitarianism* (London, 1863), Chapter II.
[15] H. Sidgwick, *The Methods of Ethics* (London, 1907), p. 94.
[16] J. H. Newman, *Certain Difficulties Felt by Anglicans in Catholic Teaching* (London, 1885), Vol. I, p. 204.

worse off than the people in A only because they each have many fewer of these things. In B, for example, people can hear good music only a few times in their lives; in A they can often hear music that is nearly as good. If this was the difference between A and B, I would cease to believe that B would be worse.

A similar claim applies to the Repugnant Conclusion. Why is it so hard to believe that my imagined world Z—or Omega 100—would be better than a world of ten billion people, all of whom have an extremely high quality of life? This is hard to believe because in Z two things are true: people's lives are barely worth living, and most of the good things in life are lost.

Suppose that only the first of these was true. Suppose that, in Z, all of the best things in life remain. People's lives are barely worth living because these best things are so thinly spread. The people in Z do each, once in their lives, have or engage in one of the best experiences or activities. But all the rest is muzak and potatoes. If this is what Z involves, it is still hard to believe that Z would be better than a world of ten billion people, each of whose lives is very well worth living. But, if Z retains all of the best things in life, this belief is less repugnant.

Now restore the assumption that in Z, and Omega 100, most of the good things in life are lost. There is only muzak and potatoes. By appealing to the value of the best things in life, we can try to answer the argument.

The argument involves two kinds of step. One is the claim that Alpha is better than A+, Alpha 2 is better than Omega, and similar later claims. A+ contains two groups of people, all of whom are better off in Alpha. We can add the assumption that these people are better off because, in Alpha, the best things in life are even better. Appealing to the value of these best things cannot help us to reject the claim that Alpha is better than A+. And, as I argued, there seems to be no other way to reject this claim. If the actual outcome had been A+, the inequality would have been no better, and everyone who existed would have been worse off. How can we deny that this would have been worse? There seems to be little hope of answering these steps in the argument.

The other steps are all redistributive. In each step the best-off people would lose a little, but an equally large worse-off group would gain much more. Can we claim that at least one of these steps would not be a change for the better? This cannot be plausibly claimed if what we appeal to is the Élitist View. We cannot plausibly claim that it is the best-off people whose condition matters most.

What we might appeal to is not Élitism, but *Perfectionism*. In the move from Alpha to Omega 100, the best things in life must have disappeared. Suppose for instance that, in the move from Alpha to Beta, Mozart's music would be lost, in the move to Gamma, Haydn's. In the move to Delta, Venice would be destroyed, in the move to Epsilon, Verona.[17] We might claim that, even if some change brings a great net benefit to those who are affected, it is a change for the worse if it involves the loss of one of the best things in life.

When should we make this claim? It would not be plausible when we are considering outcomes that are close to Omega 100. Suppose that, in one such outcome, the best thing left is a bad performance of Ravel's Bolero; in the next outcome, it is an even worse perform-ance of Ravel's Bolero. We cannot claim that great benefits to those who are worst-off would not make the outcome better if they involved the loss of a bad performance of Ravel's Bolero. If such a claim is to have any plausibility, it must be made at the start. We must reject the change in which the music of Mozart is lost.

Has such a claim any plausibility? I believe that it has. It expresses one of our two main reasons for wanting to avoid the Repugnant Conclusion. When we are most concerned about overpopulation, our concern is only partly about the value that each life will have for the person whose life it is. We are also concerned about the disappearance from the world of the kinds of experience and activity which do most to make life worth living.

Perfectionism faces many objections. One is raised by the moral importance of relieving or preventing great suffering. We should reject the Nietzschean view that the prevention of great suffering can be ranked wholly below the preservation of creation of the best things in life. What should Perfectionists claim about great

---

[17] If, in the move from Alpha to Beta, the best-off people lose Mozart, it may seem that their quality of life cannot, as my argument assumes, fall by only a little. But I have explained how this might be so. The loss of a few performances of Mozart could for these people be nearly outweighed by many extra performances of Haydn.

suffering? But this problem is irrelevant here, since we can assume that in the various outcomes we are considering there would be no such suffering.

Another problem is raised by the fact that the good things in life do not come in quite different categories. It is because pain and sin are in such different categories that Newman believed sin to be infinitely worse. If we merely compare Mozart and muzak, these two may also seem to be in quite different categories. But there is a fairly smooth continuum between these two. Though Haydn is not as good as Mozart, he is very good. And there is other music which is not far below Haydn's, other music not far below this, and so on. Similar claims apply to the other best experiences, activities, and personal relationships, and to the other things which give most to the value of life. Most of these things are on fairly smooth continua, ranging from the best to the least good. Since this is so, it may be hard to defend the view that what is best has more value—or does more to make the outcome better—than any amount of what is nearly as good. This view conflicts with the preferences that most of us would have about our own futures. But, unless we can defend this view, any loss of quality could be outweighed by a sufficient gain in the quantity of lesser goods.

These are only two of the objections facing this view. It seems to me, at times, crazy. But at least, unlike the Élitist View, it is not morally monstrous. And without Perfectionism how can we avoid the Repugnant Conclusion?[18]

[18] I would be grateful for any comments on this essay, which could be sent to me at All Souls College, Oxford.

XI

WHAT IS WRONG WITH SLAVERY?

R. M. HARE

NEARLY everybody would agree that slavery is wrong; and I can say this perhaps with greater feeling than most, having in a manner of speaking *been* a slave. However, there are dangers in taking for granted that something is wrong; for we may then assume that it is obvious that it is wrong and indeed obvious why it is wrong; and this leads to a prevalence of very bad arguments with quite silly conclusions, all based on the so-called absolute value of human freedom. If we could see more clearly what *is* valuable about freedom, and why it is valuable, then we might be protected against the rhetoric of those who, the moment anything happens that is disadvantageous or distasteful to them, start complaining loudly about some supposed infringement of their liberty, without telling us why it is wrong that they should be prevented from doing what they would like to do. It may well *be* wrong in many such cases; but until we have some way of judging when it is and when it is not, we shall be at the mercy of every kind of demagogy.

This is but one example of the widespread abuse of the appeal to human rights. We may even be tempted to think that our politics would be more healthy if rights had never been heard of; but that would be going too far. It is the unthinking appeal to ill-defined rights, unsupported by argument, that does the harm. There is no doubt that arguments justifying some of these appeals are possible; but since the forms of such arguments are seldom understood even by philosophers, it is not surprising that many quite unjustified claims of this sort go unquestioned, and thus in the end bring any sort of appeal to human rights into disrepute. It is a tragedy that this happens, because there really are rights that ought to be defended

R. M. Hare, 'What is Wrong with Slavery', *Philosophy & Public Affairs* 8, No. 2 (Winter 1979). Copyright © 1979 by R. M. Hare. Reprinted by permission of the author and Princeton University Press.

with all the devotion we can command. Things are being done the world over which can properly be condemned as infringements of human rights; but so long as rights are used so loosely as an all-purpose political weapon, often in support of very questionable causes, our protests against such infringements will be deprived of most of their force.

Another hazard of the appeal to rights is that it is seldom that such an appeal by one side cannot be countered with an appeal to some conflicting right by the opposite side. The controversies which led finally to the abolition of slavery provide an excellent example of this, with one side appealing to rights of liberty and the other to rights of property. But we do not have to go so far back in history to find examples of this sort of thing. We have only to think of the disputes about distributive justice between the defenders of equality and of individual liberty; or of similar arguments about education. I have written about both these disputes elsewhere, in the attempt to substitute for intuitions some more solid basis for argument.[1] I have the same general motive in raising the topic of slavery, and also a more particular motive. Being a utilitarian, I need to be able to answer the following attack frequently advanced by opponents of utilitarianism. It is often said that utilitarianism must be an objectionable creed because it could in certain circumstances condone or even commend slavery, given that circumstances can be envisaged in which utility would be maximized by preserving a slave-owning society and not abolishing slavery. The objectors thus seek to smear utilitarians with the taint of all the atrocious things that were done by slave-traders and slave-owners. The objection, as I hope to show, does not stand up; but in order to see through this rhetoric we shall have to achieve a quite deep understanding of some rather difficult issues in moral philosophy; and this, too, adds to the importance and interest of the topic.

First, we have to ask what this thing, slavery, is, about whose wrongness we are arguing. As soon as we ask this question we see at

---

[1] 'Justice and Equality', in J. Arthur and W. H. Shaw, eds., *Justice and Economic Distribution* (Englewood Cliffs, 1978); 'Opportunity for What?: Some Remarks on Current Disputes about Equality in Education', *Oxford Review of Education* 3 (1977).

once, if we have any knowledge of history, that it is, in common use, an extremely ill-defined concept. Even if we leave out of account such admittedly extended uses as 'wage-slave' in the writings of Marxists, it is clear that the word 'slave' and its near-equivalents such as *servus* and *doulos* have meant slightly different things in different cultures; for slavery is, primarily, a *legal* status, defined by the disabilities or the liabilities which are imposed by the law on those called slaves; and obviously these may vary from one jurisdiction to another. Familiar logical difficulties arise about how we are to decide, of a word in a foreign language, that it means the same as the English word 'slave'. Do the relevant laws in the country where the language is spoken have to be identical with those which held in English-speaking countries before slavery was abolished? Obviously not; because it would be impossible for them to be identical with the laws of all such countries at all periods, since these did not remain the same. Probably we have a rough idea of the kind of laws which have to hold in a country before we can say that that country has an institution properly called 'slavery'; but it is pretty rough.

It would be possible to pursue at some length, with the aid of legal, historical, and anthropological books on slavery in different cultures and jurisdictions, the different shades of meaning of the word 'slave'. But since my purpose is philosophical, I shall limit myself to asking what is essential to the notion of slavery in common use. The essential features are, I think, to be divided under two heads: slavery is, first, a *status* in society, and secondly, a *relation* to a master. The slave is so called first of all because he occupies a certain place in society, lacking certain rights and privileges secured by the law to others, and subject to certain liabilities from which others are free. And secondly, he is the slave *of* another person or body (which might be the state itself). The first head is not enough to distinguish slavery from other legal disabilities; for example the lowest castes in some societies are as lacking in legal rights as slaves in some others, or more so, but are not called slaves because they are not the slaves *of* anybody.

The *status* of a slave was defined quite early by the Greeks in terms of four freedoms which the slave lacks. These are: a legally recognized position in the community, conferring a right of access to the courts; protection from illegal seizure and detention and other personal violence; the privilege of going where he wants to go; and that of working as he pleases. The first three of these features are present in a manumission document from Macedonia dated about 235 BC; the last is added in the series of manumission documents from Delphi which begins about thirty years later.[2] The state could to some extent regulate by law the treatment of slaves without making us want to stop calling them slaves, so that the last three features are a bit wobbly at the edges. But we are seeking only a rough characterization of slavery, and shall have to put up with this indefiniteness of the concept.

The *relation* of the slave to a master is also to some extent indefinite. It might seem that we could tie it up tight by saying that a slave has to be the *property* of an *owner*; but a moment's reflection will show what unsafe ground this is. So-called property-owners do not need to be reminded that legal restrictions upon the use and enjoyment of property can become so onerous as to make it almost a joke to call it property at all. I am referring not only to such recent inventions as zoning and other planning laws (though actually they are not so recent, having been anticipated even in ancient times), and to rent acts, building regulations, clean air acts and the like, but also to the ancient restrictions placed by the common law on uses of one's property which might be offensive to one's neighbours. In relation to slavery, it is also instructive to think of the cruelty-to-animals legislation which now rightly forbids one to do what one likes to one's own dog or cow which one has legally purchased. Legislation of this kind was passed in the days before abolition, and was even to some extent enforced, though not always effectively. The laws forbidding the slave trade were, of course, the outstanding example of such legislation preventing people from doing what they wanted with their own property.

However, as before, we are seeking only a general and rough characterization of slavery, and shall therefore have to put up with the open texture of the concept of property. This, like slavery itself, is defined by the particular rights and obligations which are conferred or imposed by a particular legal system, and these may vary from one such system to another. It will be enough to have a general

---

[2] See W. L. Westermann, *The Slave Systems of Greek and Roman Antiquity* (Philadelphia, 1955), p. 35.

idea of what would stop us calling a person the slave of another—
how far the law would have to go in assigning rights to slaves before
we stopped using that word of them. I have gone into these
difficulties in such detail as space has allowed only because I am now
going on to describe, for the purposes of our moral discussion,
certain conditions of life about which I shall invite the reader's
judgement, and I do not want anybody to say that what I am
describing *is* not really slavery. The case I shall sketch is admittedly
to some extent fantastic; and this, as we shall later see, is very
important when we come to assess the philosophical arguments that
have been based on similar cases. But although it is extremely
unlikely that what I describe should actually occur, I wish to
maintain that *if* it occurred, we should still call it slavery, so that *if*
imaginary cases are allowed to be brought into the arguments, this
case will have to be admitted.

It may be helpful if, before leaving the question of what slavery is,
I list a few conditions of life which have to be *distinguished* from
slavery proper. The first of these is *serfdom* (a term which, like
'slavery' itself, has a wide range of meaning). A serf is normally
tied, not directly to a master, but to a certain area of land; the rights
to his services pass with the land if it changes hands. This very
distinction, however, separates the English villein in gross, who
approximates to a slave although enjoying certain legal rights, from
the villein regardant, whose serfdom arises through his feudal
tenure of land. Those who unsuccessfully tried to persuade Lord
Mansfield in Sommersett's case that slavery could exist in England
attempted to show that the defendant was a villein in gross.[3]
Secondly, one is not a slave merely because one belongs to a *caste*
which has an inferior legal status, even if it has pretty well no rights;
as I have said, the slave has to be the slave *of* some owner. Thirdly,
slavery has to be distinguished from *indenture*, which is a form of
contract. Apprentices in former times, and football players even
now, are bound by contract, entered into by themselves or, in the
case of children, by their parents, to serve employers for a fixed
term under fixed conditions, which were in some cases extremely
harsh (so that the actual sufferings of indentured people could be as

---

[3] Summing up for defence and judgement of Lord Mansfield in Sommersett's
case, King's Bench, 12 George III, 1771–2, *Howells' State Trials* 20, pp. 1 ff.

bad as those of slaves).[4] The difference lies in the voluntariness of the contract and in its fixed term. We must note, however, that in some societies (Athens before Solon for example) one could *choose* to become a slave by selling one's person to escape debt;[5] and it might be possible to sell one's children as well, as the Greeks sometimes did, so that even the heritability of the slave status does not serve to make definite the rather fuzzy boundary between slavery and indenture.

We ought perhaps to notice two other conditions which approximate to slavery but are not called slavery. The first is compulsory *military* or *naval service* and, indeed, other forced labour. The impressed sailors of Nelson's navy no doubt endured conditions as bad as those of many slaves; Dr Johnson remarked that nobody would choose to be a sailor if he had the alternative of being put in prison.[6] But they were not called slaves, because their status as free men was only in abeyance and returned to them on discharge. By contrast, the galley slaves of the Mediterranean powers in earlier times really were slaves. Secondly, although the term 'penal servitude' was once in use, *imprisonment* for crime is not usually called slavery. This is another fuzzy boundary, because in ancient times it was possible for a person to lose his rights as a citizen and become a slave by sentence of a court for some crime;[7] though when something very like this happened recently in South Africa, it was not *called* slavery, officially.[8] Again, prisoners of war and other captives and bondsmen are not always called slaves, however grim their conditions, although in ancient times capture in war was a way of becoming a slave, if one was not fortunate enough to be ransomed.[9] I have myself, as a prisoner of war, worked on the Burma railway in conditions not *at the time* distinguishable from slavery; but because my status was temporary I can claim to have been a slave only 'in a manner of speaking'.

[4] See O. Patterson, *The Sociology of Slavery* (London: MacGibbon and Kee, 1967), p. 74; A. Sampson, *Drum* (London, 1956), chap. 3.

[5] See Westermann, *Slave Systems*, p. 4.

[6] Boswell, *Life of Johnson*, ed. G. B. Hill and L. F. Powell (Oxford, 1934), vol. 1, p. 348, 16 March 1759.

[7] See Westermann, *Slave Systems*, p. 81. In pre-revolutionary France one could be sentenced to the galleys.   [8] See Sampson, *Drum*, p. 241.

[9] See Westermann, *Slave Systems*, pp. 2, 5–7, 29.

I shall put my philosophical argument, to which we have now come, in terms of an imaginary example, to which I shall give as much verisimilitude as I can. It will be seen, however, that quite unreal assumptions have to be made in order to get the example going—and this is very important for the argument between the utilitarians and their opponents. It must also be noted that to play its role in the argument the example will have to meet certain requirements. It is intended as a fleshed-out substitute for the rather jejune example often to be found in anti-utilitarian writers. To serve its purpose it will have to be a case in which to abolish slavery really and clearly would diminish utility. This means, first, that the slavery to be abolished must really be slavery, and, secondly, that it must have a total utility clearly, but not enormously, greater than the total utility of the kind of regime which would be, in that situation, a practical alternative to slavery.

If it were not *clearly* greater, utilitarians could argue that, since all judgements of this sort are only probable, caution would require them to stick to a well-tried principle favouring liberty, the principle itself being justified on utilitarian grounds (see below); and thus the example would cease to divide them from their opponents, and would become inapposite.

If, on the other hand, the utility of slavery were *enormously* greater, anti-utilitarians might complain that their own view was being made too strong; for many anti-utilitarians are pluralists and hold that among the principles of morality a principle requiring beneficence is to be included. Therefore, if the advantages of retaining slavery are made sufficiently great, a non-utilitarian with a principle of beneficence in his repertory could agree that it ought to be retained—that is, that *in this case* the principle of beneficence has greater weight than that favouring liberty. Thus there would again be no difference, in this case, between the verdicts of the utilitarians and their opponents, and the example would be inapposite.

There is also another dimension in which the example has to be carefully placed. An anti-utilitarian might claim that the example I shall give makes the difference between the conditions of the slaves and those of the free in the supposed society too small, and the number of slaves too great. If, he might claim, I had made the number of slaves small and the difference between the miseries of the slaves and the pleasures of the slave-owners much greater, then the society might have the same total utility as mine (that is, greater than that of the free society with which I compare it), but it would be less plausible for me to maintain that if such a comparison had to be made in real life, we ought to follow the utilitarians and prefer the slave society.[10]

I cannot yet answer this objection without anticipating my argument; I shall merely indicate briefly how I would answer it. The answer is that the objection rests on an appeal to our ordinary intuitions; but that these are designed to deal with ordinary cases. They give no reliable guide to what we ought to say in highly unusual cases. But, further, the case desiderated is never likely to occur. How could it come about that the existence of a small number of slaves was necessary in order to preserve the happiness of the rest? I find it impossible to think of any technological factors (say, in agriculture or in transport by land or sea) which would make the preservation of slavery for a small class necessary to satisfy the interests of the majority. It is quite true that in the past there have been *large* slave populations supporting the higher standard of living of *small* minorites. But in that case it is hard to argue that slavery has more utility than its abolition, if the difference in happiness between slaves and slave-owners is great. Yet if, in order to produce a case in which the retention of slavery really would be optimal, we reduce the number of slaves relative to slave-owners, it becomes hard to say how the existence of this relatively small number of slaves is necessary for the happiness of the large number of free men. What on earth are the slaves doing that could not be more efficiently done by paid labour? And is not the abolition (perhaps not too abrupt) of slavery likely to promote those very technical changes which are necessary to enable the society to do without it?

The crux of the matter, as we shall see, is that in order to use an

---

[10] I am grateful to the editors of *Philosophy and Public Affairs* for pressing this objection. I deal with it only so far as it concerns slavery such as might occur in the world as we know it. Brave New World situations in which people are conditioned from birth to be obedient slaves and given disagreeable or dangerous tasks require separate treatment which is beyond the scope of this paper, though anti-utilitarian arguments based on them meet the same defence, namely the requirement to assess realistically what the consequences of such practices would actually be.

appeal to our ordinary intuitions as an argument, the opponents of utilitarianism have to produce cases which are not too far removed from the sort of cases with which our intuitions are designed to deal, namely the ordinary run of cases. If the cases they use fall outside this class, then the fact that our common intuitions give a different verdict from utilitarianism has no bearing on the argument; our intuitions could well be wrong about such cases, and be none the worse for that, because they will never have to deal with them in practice.

We may also notice, while we are sifting possible examples, that cases of *individual* slave-owners who are kind to their slaves will not do. The issue is one of whether slavery as an institution protected by law should be preserved; and if it is preserved, though there may be individuals who do not take advantage of it to maltreat their slaves, there will no doubt be many others who do.

Let us imagine, then, that the battle of Waterloo, that 'damned nice thing, the nearest run thing you ever saw in your life',[11] as Wellington called it, went differently from the way it actually did go, in two respects. The first was that the British and Prussians lost the battle; the last attack of the French Guard proved too much for them, the Guard's morale having been restored by Napoleon who in person led their advance instead of handing it over to Ney. But secondly, having exposed himself to fire as Wellington habitually did, but lacking Wellington's amazing good fortune, Napoleon was struck by a cannon ball and killed instantly. This so disorganized the French, who had no other commanders of such ability, that Wellington was able to rally his forces and conduct one of those holding operations at which he was so adept, basing himself on the Channel ports and their intricate surrounding waterways; the result was a cross between the Lines of Torres Vedras and the trench warfare of the First World War. After a year or two of this, with Napoleon out of the way and the war party discredited in England, liberal (that is, neither revolutionary nor reactionary) regimes came into power in both countries, and the Congress of Vienna

---

[11] For references, see E. Longford, *Wellington: The Years of the Sword* (London, 1969), p. 489.

reconvened in a very different spirit, with the French represented on equal terms.

We have to consider these events only as they affected two adjacent islands in the Caribbean which I am going to call Juba and Camaica. I need not relate what happened in the rest of the world, because the combined European powers could at that time command absolute supremacy at sea, and the Caribbean could therefore be effectively isolated from world politics by the agreement which they reached to take that area out of the imperial war game. All naval and other forces were withdrawn from it except for a couple of bases on small islands for the suppression of the slave trade, which, in keeping with their liberal principles, the parties agreed to prohibit (those that had not already done so). The islands were declared independent and their white inhabitants, very naturally, all departed in a hurry, leaving the government in the hands of local black leaders, some of whom were of the calibre of Toussaint l'Ouverture and others of whom were very much the reverse.

On Juba, a former Spanish colony, at the end of the colonial period there had been formed, under pressure of military need, a militia composed of slaves under white officers, with conditions of service much preferable to those of the plantation slaves, and forming a kind of élite. The senior sergeant-major of this force found himself, after the white officers fled, in a position of unassailable power, and, being a man of great political intelligence and ability, shaped the new regime in a way that made Juba the envy of its neighbours.

What he did was to retain the institution of slavery but to remedy its evils. The plantations were split up into smaller units, still under overseers, responsible to the state instead of to the former owners. The slaves were given rights to improved conditions of work; the wage they had already received as a concession in colonial times was secured to them and increased; all cruel punishments were prohibited. However, it is still right to call them slaves, because the state retained the power to direct their labour and their place of residence and to enforce these directions by sanctions no more severe than are customary in countries without slavery, such as fines and imprisonment. The Juban government, influenced by early communist ideas (though Marx had not yet come on the scene) kept the plantations in its own hands; but private persons were also allowed to own a limited number of slaves under conditions at least as protective to the slaves as on the state-owned plantations.

The island became very prosperous, and the slaves in it enjoyed a life far preferable in every way to that of the free inhabitants of the neighbouring island of Camaica. In Camaica there had been no such focus of power in the early days. The slaves threw off their bonds and each seized what land he could get hold of. Though law and order were restored after a fashion, and democracy of a sort prevailed, the economy was chaotic, and this, coupled with a population explosion, led to widespread starvation and misery. Camaica lacked what Juba had: a government with the will *and the instrument, in the shape of the institution of slavery*, to control the economy and the population, and so make its slave-citizens, as I said, the envy of their neighbours. The flood of people in fishing boats seeking to emigrate from free Camaica and insinuate themselves as slaves into the plantations of Juba became so great that the Juban government had to employ large numbers of coastguards (slaves, of course) to stop it.

That, perhaps, will do for our imaginary example. Now for the philosophical argument. It is commonly alleged that utilitarianism could condone or commend slavery. In the situation described, utility would have been lessened and not increased if the Juban government had abolished slavery and if as a result the economy of Juba had deteriorated to the level of that of Camaica. So, it might be argued, a utilitarian would have had to oppose the abolition. But everyone agrees, it might be held, that slavery is wrong; so the utilitarians are convicted of maintaining a thesis which has consequences repugnant to universally accepted moral convictions.

What could they reply to this attack? There are, basically, two lines they could take. These lines are not incompatible but complementary; indeed, the defence of utilitarianism could be put in the form of a dilemma. Either the defender of utilitarianism is allowed to question the imagined facts of the example, or he is not. First let us suppose that he is not. He might then try, as a first move, saying that in the situation *as portrayed* it would indeed be wrong to abolish slavery. If the argument descends to details, the anti-utilitarians may be permitted to insert any number of extra details (barring the actual abolition of slavery itself) in order to make sure that its retention really does maximize utility. But then the utilitarian sticks to his guns and maintains that in that case it *would* be wrong to abolish slavery, and that, further, most ordinary people, if they could be got to consider the case on its merits and not allow their judgement to be confused by association with more detestable forms of slavery, would agree with this verdict. The principle of liberty which forbids slavery is a prima-facie principle admitting of exceptions, and this imaginary case is one of the exceptions. If the utilitarians could sustain this line of defence, they would win the case; but perhaps not everyone would agree that it is sustainable.

So let us allow the utilitarian another slightly more sophisticated move, still staying, however, perched on the first horn of the dilemma. He might admit that not everyone would agree on the merits of this case, but explain this by pointing to the fantastic and unusual nature of the case, which, he might claim, would be unlikely to occur in real life. *If* he is not allowed to question the facts of the case, he has to admit that abolition would be wrong; but ordinary people, he might say, cannot see this because the principles of political and social morality which we have all of us *now* absorbed (as contrasted with our eighteenth-century ancestors), and with which we are deeply inbued, prevent us from considering the case on its merits. The principles are framed to cope with the cases of slavery which actually occur (all of which are to a greater or lesser degree harmful). Though they are the best principles for us to have when confronting the actual world, they give the wrong answer when presented with this fantastic case. But all the same, the world being as it is, we should be morally worse people if we did not have these principles; for then we might be tempted, whether through ignorance or by self-interest, to condone slavery in cases in which, though actually harmful, it could be colourably represented as being beneficial. Suppose, it might be argued, that an example of this sort had been used in anti-abolitionist writings in, say, 1830 or thereabouts. Might it not have persuaded many people that slavery *could* be an admirable thing, and thus have secured their votes against abolition; and would this not have been very harmful? For the miseries caused by the *actual* institution of slavery in the Caribbean and elsewhere were so great that it was desirable from a utilitarian point of view that people should hold and act on moral convictions which condemned slavery as such and without qualification, because this would lead them to vote for its abolition.

If utilitarians take this slightly more sophisticated line, they are left saying at one and the same time that it would have been wrong to abolish slavery in the imagined circumstances, *and* that it is a good thing that nearly everyone, if asked about it, would say that it was right. Is this paradoxical? Not, I think, to anybody who understands the realities of the human situation. What resolves the paradox is that the example *is* imaginary and that therefore people are not going to have to pronounce, as a practical issue, on what the laws of Juba are to be. In deciding what principles it is good that people have, it is not necessary or even desirable to take into account such imaginary cases. It does not really matter, from a practical point of view, what judgements people reach about imaginary cases, provided that this does not have an adverse effect upon their judgements about real cases. From a practical point of view, the principles which it is best for them to have are those which will lead them to make the highest proportion of right decisions in actual cases where their decisions make a difference to what happens—weighted, of course, for the importance of the cases, that is, the amount of difference the decisions make to the resulting good or harm.

It is therefore perfectly acceptable that we should at one and the same time feel a strong moral conviction that even the Juban slave system, however beneficial, is wrong, *and* confess, when we reflect on the features of this imagined system, that we cannot see anything specifically wrong about it, but rather a great deal to commend. This is bound to be the experience of anybody who has acquired the sort of moral convictions that one ought to acquire, and at the same time is able to reflect rationally on the features of some unusual imagined situation. I have myself constantly had this experience when confronted with the sort of anti-utilitarian examples which are the stock-in-trade of philosophers like Bernard Williams. One is led to think, on reflection, that *if* such cases were to occur, one ought to do what is for the best in the circumstances (as even Williams himself appears to contemplate in one of his cases);[12] but one is bound also to find this conclusion repugnant to one's deepest convictions; if it is not, one's convictions are not the best convictions one could have.

Against this, it might be objected that if one's deep moral convictions yield the wrong answer even in imaginary or unusual cases, they are *not* the best one could have. Could we not succeed, it might be asked, in inculcating into ourselves convictions of a more accommodating sort? Could we not, that is to say, absorb principles which had written into them either exceptions to deal with awkward cases like that in my example, or even provision for writing in exceptions *ad hoc* when the awkward cases arose? Up to a point this is a sensible suggestion; but beyond that point (a point which will vary with the temperament of the person whose principles they are to be) it becomes psychologically unsound. There are some simple souls, no doubt, who really cannot keep themselves in the straight and narrow way unless they cling fanatically and in the face of what most of us would call reason to extremely simple and narrow principles. And there are others who manage to have very complicated principles with many exceptions written into them (only 'written' is the wrong word, because the principles of such people defy formulation). Most of us come somewhere in between. It is also possible to have fairly simple principles but to attach to them a rubric which allows us to depart from them, either when one conflicts with another in a particular case, or where the case is such an unusual one that we find ourselves doubting whether the principles were designed to deal with it. In these cases we may apply utilitarian reasoning directly; but it is most unwise to do this in more normal cases, for those are precisely the cases (the great majority) which our principles *are* designed to deal with, since they were chosen to give the best results in the general run of cases. In normal cases, therefore, we are more likely to achieve the right decision (even from the utilitarian point of view) by sticking to these principles than by engaging in utilitarian reasoning about the particular case, with all its temptations to special pleading.

---

[12] See Williams, 'A Critique of Utilitarianism', in J. J. C. Smart and B. Williams, *Utilitarianism: For and Against* (Cambridge, 1973), p. 99.

I have dealt with these issues at length elsewhere.[13] Here all I need to say is that there is a psychological limit to the complexity and to the flexibility of the moral principles that we can wisely seek to build deeply, as moral convictions, into our character; and the person who tries to go beyond this limit will end up as (what he will be called) an unprincipled person, and will not in fact do the best he could with his life, even by the test of utility. This may explain why I would always vote for the abolition of slavery, even though I can admit that cases could be *imagined* in which slavery would do more good than harm, and even though I am a utilitarian.

So much, then, for the first horn of the dilemma. Before we come to the second horn, on which the utilitarian is allowed to object to his opponents' argument on the ground that their example would not in the actual world be realized, I wish to make a methodological remark which may help us to find our bearings in this rather complex dispute. Utilitarianism, like any other theory of moral reasoning that gets anywhere near adequacy, consists of two parts, one formal and one substantial. The formal part is no more than a rephrasing of the requirement that moral prescriptions be universalizable; this has the consequence that equal interests of all are to be given equal weight in our reasoning: everybody to count for one and nobody for more than one. One should not expect such a formal requirement to generate, by itself, any substantial conclusions even about the actual world, let alone about all logically possible worlds. But there is also a substantial element in the theory. This is contributed by factual beliefs about what interests people in the real world actually have (which depends on what they actually want to like or dislike, and on what they would want or like or dislike under given conditions); and also about the actual effects on these interests of different actions in the real world. Given the truth of these beliefs, we can reason morally and shall come to certain moral conclusions. But the conclusions are not generated by the formal part of the theory alone.

Utilitarianism therefore, unlike some other theories, is *exposed* to the facts. The utilitarian cannot reason *a priori* that *whatever* the

---

[13] See my 'Ethical Theory and Utilitarianism', in H. D. Lewis, ed., *Contemporary British Philosophy* 4 (London, 1976), and the references given there.

facts about the world and human nature, slavery is wrong. He has to show that it is wrong by showing, through a study of history and other factual observation, that slavery does have the effects (namely the production of misery) which make it wrong. This, though it may at first sight appear a weakness in the doctrine, is in fact its strength. A doctrine, like some kinds of intuitionism, according to which we can think up examples as fantastic as we please and the doctrine will still come up with the same old answers, is really showing that it has lost contact with the actual world with which the intuitions it relies on were designed to cope. Intuitionists think they can face the world armed with nothing but their inbred intuitions; utilitarians know that they have to look at what actually goes on in the world and see if the intuitions are really the best ones to have in that sort of world.

I come now to the second horn of the dilemma, on which the utilitarian is allowed to say, 'Your example won't do: it would never happen that way.' He may admit that Waterloo and the Congress of Vienna could have turned out differently—after all it was a damned nice thing, and high commanders were in those days often killed on the battlefield (it was really a miracle that Wellington was not), and there were liberal movements in both countries. But when we come to the Caribbean, things begin to look shakier. Is it really likely that there would have been such a contrast between the economies of Juba and Camaica? I do not believe that the influence of particular national leaders is ever so powerful, or that such perfectly wise leaders are ever forthcoming. And I do not believe that in the Caribbean or anywhere else a system of nationalized slavery could be made to run so smoothly. I should, rather, expect the system to deteriorate very rapidly. I base these expectations on general beliefs about human nature, and in particular upon the belief that people in the power of other people will be exploited, whatever the good intentions of those who founded the system.

Alternatively, if there really had been leaders of such amazing statesmanship, could they not have done better by abolishing slavery and substituting a free but disciplined society? In the example, they gave the slaves some legal rights; what was to prevent them giving others, such as the right to change residences and jobs, subject of course to to an overall system of land-use and economic planning such as exists in many free countries? Did the retention of *slavery* in particular contribute very much to the prosperity of Juba that could not have been achieved by other means? And likewise, need the government of Camaica have been so incompetent? Could it not, without reintroducing slavery, have kept the economy on the rails by such controls as are compatible with a free society? In short, did not the optimum solution lie somewhere *between* the systems adopted in Juba and Camaica, but on the free side of the boundary between slavery and liberty?

These factual speculations, however, are rather more superficial than I can be content with. The facts that it is really important to draw attention to are rather deep facts about human nature which must always, or nearly always, make slavery an intolerable condition.[14] I have mentioned already a fact about slave ownership: that ordinary, even good, human beings will nearly always exploit those over whom they have absolute power. We have only to read the actual history of slavery in all centuries and cultures to see that. There is also the effect on the characters of the exploiters themselves. I had this brought home to me recently when, staying in Jamaica, I happened to pick up a history book[15] written there at the very beginning of the nineteenth century, before abolition, whose writer had added at the end an appendix giving his views on the abolition controversy, which was then at its height. Although obviously a kindly man with liberal leanings, he argues against abolition; and one of his arguments struck me very forcibly. He argues that although slavery can be a cruel fate, things are much better in Jamaica now: there is actually a law that a slave on a plantation may not be given more than thirty-six lashes by the foreman without running him up in front of the overseer. The contrast between the niceness of the man and what he says here does perhaps more than any philosophical argument to make the point that our moral principles have to be designed for human nature as it is.

---

[14] For the effects of slavery on slaves and slave-owners, see O. Patterson, *Sociology of Slavery*; and S. M. Elkins, *Slavery* (Chicago, 1959).

[15] R. C. Dallas, *The History of the Maroons* (London, 1803; reprinted by Frank Cass, 1968). I have not been able to obtain the book again to verify this reference.

The most fundamental point is one about the human nature of the slave which makes ownership by another more intolerable for him than for, say, a horse (not that we should condone cruelty to horses). Men are different from other animals in that they can look a long way ahead, and therefore can become an object of deterrent punishment. Other animals, we may suppose, can only be the object of Skinnerian reinforcement and Pavlovian conditioning. These methods carry with them, no doubt, their own possibilities of cruelty; but they fall short of the peculiar cruelty of human slavery. One can utter to a man threats of punishment in the quite distant future which he can understand. A piece of human property, therefore, unlike a piece of inanimate property or even a brute animal in a man's possession, can be subjected to a sort of terror from which other kinds of property are immune; and, human owners being what they are, many will inevitably take advantage of this fact. That is the reason for the atrocious punishments that have usually been inflicted on slaves; there would have been no point in inflicting them on animals. A slave is the only being that is *both* able to be held responsible in this way, *and* has no escape from, or even redress against, the power that this ability to threaten confers upon his oppressor. If he were a free citizen, he would have rights which would restrain the exercise of the threat; if he were a horse or a piece of furniture, the threat would be valueless to his owner because it would not be understood. By being subjected to the threat of legal and other punishment, but at the same time deprived of legal defences against its abuse (since he has no say in what the laws are to be, nor much ability to avail himself of such laws as there are) the slave becomes, or is likely to become if his master is an ordinary human, the most miserable of all creatures.

No doubt there are other facts I could have adduced. But I will end by reiterating the general point I have been trying to illustrate. The wrongness of slavery, like the wrongness of anything else, has to be shown in the world as it actually is. We can do this by first reaching an understanding of the meaning of this and the other moral words, which brings with it certain rules of moral reasoning, as I have tried to show in other places.[16] One of the most important

---

[16] See footnote 13 above, and my *Freedom and Reason* (Oxford, 1963), especially chap. 6.

of these rules is a formal requirement reflected in the Golden Rule: the requirement that what we say we ought to do to others we have to be able to say ought to be done to ourselves were we in precisely their situation with their interests. And this leads to a way of moral reasoning (utilitarianism) which treats the equal interests of all as having equal weight. Then we have to apply this reasoning to the world as it actually is, which will mean ascertaining what will actually be the result of adopting certain principles and policies, and how this will actually impinge upon the interests of ourselves and others. Only so can we achieve a morality suited for use in real life; and nobody who goes through this reasoning in real life will adopt principles which permit slavery, because of the miseries which in real life it causes. Utilitarianism can thus show what is wrong with slavery; and so far as I can see it is the kind of moral reasoning best able to show this, as opposed to merely *protesting* that slavery is wrong.

This is a revised version of a lecture given in 1978 in the Underwood Memorial Series, Wesleyan University, Middletown, Connecticut.

XII

SEPARATE SPHERES

JANET RADCLIFFE RICHARDS

I

THE conviction which unites traditionalist opponents of feminism is that men and women should occupy *separate spheres*. There are different versions of this doctrine; opinions differ about what the nature of the sphere should be, about how much neutral space there should be belonging to neither sphere, and about the extent to which trespassing in the other sex's sphere should be tolerated. Still, through all the variations of detail the underlying theme remains constant. All traditionalists hold that men and women should at least to some extent have different functions in society, and that each sex should avoid the character and activity which is the proper preserve of the other.

Almost as constant is the argument given in defence of such a separation. The sexes should act and be treated in different ways, it is said, for the simple and obvious reason that they *are different*. In the words of one eloquent defender of the separate spheres, 'Each has what the other has not; each completes the other. They are in nothing alike, and the happiness and perfection of both depends on each asking and receiving what the other only can give.'[1] Present-day opponents of feminism may have fallen off somewhat in extremity of view as well as in style of expression, but their position

An earlier version of this chapter was delivered in the Quance Revisited Lecture Series as part of the University of Saskatchewan's 75th anniversary celebrations in Saskatoon, Canada, on 9 Oct. 1984. Parts of this hitherto unpublished essay are taken from the author's *The Sceptical Feminist* (London, 1980), but the argument has been considerably rearranged and extended. The present version has been specially written for this anthology.

[1] Ruskin, *Of Queen's Gardens*, p. 143, quoted Kate Millett, *Sexual Politics*, p. 132.

remains in essence the same. It is still widely regarded as obvious that the sexes are different, and that therefore as a matter of course any well-judging society must have different expectations of them and treat them in different ways.

Sentiments such as these are frequently expressed in such a way as to make the whole idea sound very nice and considerate: a sensitive division of labour for the good of all, with each individual being encouraged to contribute whatever is most suitable for them[2] to give. But in spite of the sugary gloss of 'equal but different' so often given to the account of the separate spheres, to the feminist it seems that the arrangement is nothing like one of equality. Scratch the egalitarian veneer even slightly, and all the differences of role between the sexes seem to depend on women's being *less* strong, *less* rational, *less* creative, and less just about everything else worth while than men, which supposed deficiencies have traditionally been the excuse for excluding women from everything men have been inclined to keep for themselves. Through all the euphemism there still comes the view of Aristotle, who attempted no such tactful suggestion of equality in difference when he said that a female was female in virtue of a certain *lack* of qualities, and Thomas Aquinas, who thought a female was a defective male.

It is not surprising, then, that when feminists protest about the lowliness of women's sphere, they nearly always start by attacking the lowly ideas about women which provide the traditional justification for keeping them confined to their place. If they are against the whole principle of separate spheres, they will deny that there are any significant differences between the sexes: differences which are admitted to have any existence at all outside the self-serving male imagination are attributed to men's own manipulation of women. If, on the other hand, they object more to the relative status of the spheres than to their existence as such, and want women's sphere to be equal or even superior to men's, they will agree that the sexes are different but maintain that tradition is wrong about the nature of the

---

[2] This is a feminist 'them', not an inadvertently ungrammatical one. I share the view that the best solution to the problem of finding a sex-neutral pronoun without doing too much violence to the language is to adopt and extend the already colloquial use of 'they' and 'them' as singular and sex-neutral. The similar extension of the plural 'you' to a singular usage, a long time ago, serves as both a precedent and a model.

differences.[3] In both cases objections to traditional views about the spheres are supported by objections to traditional beliefs about the sexes.

However, although far too many myths about the natures of women and men have been around for far too long, and although it is certainly right that they should be challenged, there are problems about doing so in this particular context. Whether by accident or design, the irritating pronouncements about female inferiority have so engrossed feminist attention that the *structure of traditionalist argument* in defence of the separate spheres has too often slipped past unnoticed, and as a result the opposition has been allowed to get away with some extraordinary sleights of hand. For the time being, therefore, it may be interesting to forget all debates about the natures of the sexes—conceding for the sake of argument even the most outrageous claims any detractor of women may care to make—and concentrate instead on the remarkable piece of reasoning by which the positions of women and men have for so long been justified.

2

The argument which derives the appropriateness of separate spheres from differences in the natures of men and women is not complete as it stands: it must be understood to have a missing premiss. To get from 'men and women are different' to 'men and women should occupy separate spheres' you obviously need some kind of statement to the effect that people should act and be treated in ways suitable to their natures. Still, since one of the main complaints traditionalists make about feminists is that they are

---

[3] Some feminists who are concerned with the nature of the spheres rather than their existence claim that women's characteristics have traditionally been *undervalued* rather than misdescribed. They typically think, for instance, that nurturing skills should have far more status than is the case at present. This means in effect that they must be seen as being more concerned with disputes about the first premiss of the argument to be discussed below than the second: they object to traditional ideas about the appropriate *treatment* of people with various kinds of quality. However, here too the disagreement is about one of the premisses of the argument, rather than its structure, and since (as will appear) the concern of this paper is with the structure, there has been no need to go into a separate discussion of this matter.

trying to distort women out of their natural femininity, they would presumably have no objection to adding such a premiss. When that is done the argument goes roughly like this:

People should act and be treated in ways suitable to their natures
Women and men are different

Therefore: women and men should act and be treated in different ways (i.e. they should occupy separate spheres).

This, of course, is only a skeleton argument, whose parts different people will want to flesh out differently. There are, in the first place, questions about what should count as suitable behaviour and treatment for different kinds of people. What is suitable treatment for the weak, for instance? Should they be given special protection, or remedial treatment to lessen their weakness, or should they perhaps be exposed at birth on grounds of being useless to the state? Should the clever be given special facilities to develop their skills, or should they be subjected to special constraints in case they become threatening? Is suitable treatment a matter of making everyone as happy as possible, or is it more to do with extracting from people every ounce of whatever they are capable of contributing to the defence of their country, or the Faith, or the Revolution? There is enormous scope for disagreement about such matters. There is also scope for considerable disagreement about the second premiss: people may hold very different opinions about the extent and nature of differences between the sexes. And, of course, differences of opinion about these two kinds of question will usually result in different conclusions about what the sexes' spheres should be like. If, for instance, you thought that the strong should help the weak and that men were strong and women weak, the argument would lead you to the conclusion that part of what was involved in the separation of the spheres was men's helping women. If, on the other hand, you thought that the weak were a drain on society and should make themselves as useful as they could without expecting much in return, you might conclude that women should be men's servants.

It is because the premisses can be filled out in different ways, to yield different conclusions about what the separate spheres should be like, that traditionalists of different colours can nevertheless produce the same general form of argument. However, since it is this general argument which is to be discussed here, we can ignore controversies about what counts as suitable treatment as well as about how different men and women actually are. Where, then, should the investigation start?

One thing which certainly needs to be done is to check the argument for ambiguities which might result in *equivocation*: the use of words in such a way that they have one meaning when first introduced, but shift to a subtly different one, essential for reaching the conclusion, during the course of the argument. We can begin, therefore, by making sure that the elements of this argument are unambiguous in all relevant ways.

Consider first the conclusion, that men and women should occupy separate spheres. This statement is a very bare one when the natures of the separate spheres are not specified, and there may seem to be no scope for problems about its interpretation. However, it does in fact contain an important ambiguity. Are we to take the separate spheres conclusion as meaning that the sexes should be *allowed to drift* into their spheres as their natures dictate—rather as children may be allowed to take a wide range of subjects in school until they find out which ones they like and are best at—or as meaning that they should be actively *pushed* towards their spheres?

There is obviously no correct answer to this question; some people may want to defend one form of the conclusion and some the other. What is important is to recognize them as distinct, and to be ready to pounce at any sign of slithering about between them. Defenders of separate spheres, whose main complaint about feminists is that they are trying to force women into activities alien to their nature, often give the impression that all they mean by women's sphere is the situation women would drift towards by nature in a society of equal opportunity where they were left to their own devices and uncorrupted by feminism. But anyone who does want to reach this version of the conclusion of the argument must recognize that they are not defending anything like the *traditional* form of the separate spheres doctrine. Tradition has never permitted such drifting. It has never simply allowed a free-for-all between the sexes, subjecting them to the same restrictions and giving them access to the same opportunities, so that men and women found themselves doing different things simply because they were differently inclined by nature. Men and women have always been subjected to *pressure* of various kinds to make them behave in different ways. Often it has been made impossible for the sexes to trespass on what has been regarded as the other's territory (as when women have been prevented from entering the professions or owning property); even more often, one sex has been discouraged from doing what is thought appropriate to the other by penalties of various sorts, ranging from severe legal punishments to varying degrees of social disapproval. The nature and extent of such sexually specific pressures has varied considerably from one society to another, but they have always existed.

Anyone who wants to defend any traditional form of separate spheres arrangement, therefore, must defend a situation in which there are pressures of various kinds—laws, institutions, conventions, and so on—to keep the sexes in their places. And, in fact, though they may not always recognize it, most apologists for separate spheres do advocate such pressures. They are likely to be in favour of such things as teaching boys and girls different subjects and training them for different kinds of work; they may be critical of women who 'take jobs from men' in times of unemployment or who are unwilling to sacrifice their own careers to their husbands'; they may be scornful of men who give up work to look after children or are bullied by their wives into sharing the housework and shopping. Anyone who has such attitudes is in favour of strongly differentiated opportunities and pressures, and since most traditionalist opponents of feminism are of this kind we shall concentrate mainly on the argument with the stronger version of the conclusion, stating that the sexes should be under pressure to keep to their spheres.

This means that the argument to be assessed now looks like this:

People should act and be treated in ways suitable to their natures
Women and men are different
———

Therefore: women and men should be *pushed* into separate spheres.

That is one important clarification, but there is also another to be made. The second premiss of the argument also provides scope for equivocation. Even though in this very general argument we are not concerned with particular ideas about what differences there might be between the sexes, nevertheless *whatever* kinds of difference there are held to be, there are two quite different ways in which this premiss might be taken. Is it supposed to be claiming that there are *universal* differences between the sexes, or merely that they are different on *average*?[4] Once again there is no correct answer; people making claims about sex differences might mean either.

Actually, once the distinction is made clear, not many people are likely to try to maintain that many—or even any—of the kinds of sexual difference usually invoked to justify the separate spheres are universal. Even the most dyed-in-grain of male supremacists, and even with women's educational disadvantages to assist his prejudices, would be hard put to it to make out that *all* women were different from *all* men in any (not purely sexual) respect; even physical strength, the most commonly invoked differentiating characteristic, does not place all men on one side of some divide and all women on the other. It is not plausible even that all women lack any significant ability usually possessed by men.[5] Claims about

---

[4] Each of these categories is intended to cover a range of variations. I am intending the average interpretation to stand in also for claims about means, medians and the like, and the universal interpretation to include not only cases in which *all* men differ from *all* women, but also ones where something is attributed to all or none of the members of *only one* sex. And in either case what is claimed for each sex might refer to a range of ability, or a specific level. These matters are not distinguished in this paper because the arguments which follow work in essentially the same way whatever the detailed interpretation of either the average or the universal form of the second premiss.

[5] The most plausible claims along these lines are that there are some levels of achievement which can be (or have been) reached by some men but no women. However, virtually none of these are of a kind achieved by *most* men but no women, and they are no use as the basis of an argument for the traditional separate spheres. Even if all the great musical geniuses have been men (and even if this is as a result of nature, not opportunity) that does not show that women should be treated differently from the massive majority of men who make no approach to genius of any kind.

average differences are usually much easier to defend. However, since we are at present concerned only with the structure of the argument and not with the acceptability of any interpretation of its premisses, we should consider both versions of the second premiss, and see how the argument fares with each in turn.

First, then, there is the universal interpretation, according to which the argument goes more or less[6] like this:

> People should act and be treated in ways suitable to their natures
> All men are different (in relevant respects) from all women
> _____
> Therefore: men and women should be pushed into separate spheres.

To assess the merits of this argument, consider a particular case. Suppose, for instance, that among your views about suitable treatment for different kinds of people is the idea that only the very clever should go to university. Suppose also that you think no women are in fact clever enough. Does that support the conclusion that there should be a rule specifically preventing women from going to university?

According to the way the argument works, the unsuitability of women is supposed to derive from a general principle, expressed by the first premiss, about the unsuitability of people who are not clever. If, therefore, you are to reach the conclusion that there should actually be *policies* to exclude these unsuitable women, you must interpret the first premiss as specifying that there should be policies to exclude *everyone* who is unsuitable; the argument presents no reason for having rules about one unsuitable group but

---

[6] It will be noticed that although this schematic statement of the argument refers to ways in which *all* men differ from *all* women, the illustration which follows takes a case in which it is claimed only that *no woman* can do something, without any corresponding suggestion that all men can. This is in fact a far commoner type of case than the other; most of the arguments about separate treatment for the sexes appeal to women's supposed unsuitability for various activities, leaving undiscussed the question of how many men are suitable. It should be noted that arguments like these lead to a less thoroughgoing theory of the spheres, specifying what one sex *should not* be doing but not what the other *should* be doing. This is another much-exploited fuzziness in debates about the separate spheres argument. However, I have ignored the distinction in this paper because, as I have already claimed, the arguments presented here work equally well in both cases.

not about others.[7] But then, if there should be rules to exclude all unsuitable people, *women's being unsuitable* (the only reason given by the argument) obviously cannot provide any justification for an *additional* rule to exclude them, since a general rule would already exclude everyone unsuitable. As Mill said, 'What women by nature cannot do, it is quite superfluous to forbid them from doing.'[8] You might just as well argue that because literacy was a minimum requirement for university entrance, and all gorillas were well known to be illiterate, university admission regulations should include a specific clause excluding gorillas.

It now becomes clear, incidentally, why it was important to distinguish between the weak and strong interpretations of the conclusion of the original argument. If the sexes really were entirely different from each other in socially relevant ways, *general* social rules specifying how people should be treated and what opportunities everyone should be given would result in the sexes making different choices and being selected for different kinds of work. In other words, they would in such circumstances *drift* into at least partially separate spheres. But our question now is not of whether the premisses can support the conclusion that a *drift* into separate spheres will *happen*; it is of whether they support the conclusion that *pressures* to bring the spheres about can be *justified*, and, at least as so far interpreted, they do not. The argument as it stands provides no reason for adding to general social rules and conventions ones which apply specifically to women or men. With the universal interpretation of the second premiss, the traditional argument for the separate spheres is a failure.

Since this is so, let us see whether the average interpretation makes things any better. The argument now becomes:

People should act and be treated in ways suitable to their natures
The average woman is different from the average man

---

[7] It is important that throughout this section the discussion is of the argument *as it stands*, and not as it might be made by the addition of new premisses explaining why women need special treatment. Such possible amendments are discussed in the next section. In this argument the only reason given for special policies to exclude women is women's unsuitability.

[8] John Stuart Mill, *The Subjection of Women*, London, 1983, p. 48.

Therefore: men and women should be pushed into separate spheres.

Once again, we can best assess the merits of the argument by considering a particular illustration. Suppose we start with the idea that the strong should be under pressure to help the weak (as before, the suitability premiss needs to include the idea of pressure), and also that men are stronger than women. If we take the average interpretation of the second premiss, does the argument support the conclusion that there should be social rules and conventions about men's helping women?

We have seen that the argument fails when it uses a universal interpretation of the second premiss, because no reason is given for thinking that a specific rule about women and men will achieve anything not already achieved by the general rule referred to in the first premiss. With the average interpretation this is not the case; the rule about men and women does achieve something new. Unfortunately for the argument, however, that only makes things worse.

If there are general conventions about the strong helping the weak, they will have the effect of putting all strong men under pressure to help all weak women, without the need for any additional convention specifically applying to men and women. It follows, therefore, that the only people to whom a specific rule about men and women can make any difference are *men who are weak* and *women who are strong*. If you add to general rules about the strong helping the weak a rule about men helping women, the effect of that additional rule is to *override* the general rules, and bring it about that the non-average puny little man has to lug around heavy loads for hefty amazonian women. And whether or not that can be justified (perhaps it can be), what is quite certain is that it cannot be justified by principles about the suitability of the strong helping the weak. On this interpretation of the argument the conclusion does not merely fail to follow from the premisses; it actually contradicts them.

The situation then is this. We started with the familiar argument that men and women should act and be treated differently because they were different. This argument was spelt out, and then checked for ambiguity. As a result its conclusion was clarified: any defender of tradition needed a conclusion about putting *pressure* on the sexes to keep them in their spheres. The second premiss was also found to be ambiguous, so the argument was tried using both possible versions. In both cases the argument failed. On one interpretation the conclusion did not follow from the premisses; on the other, it was inconsistent with them. And in fact the superficial plausibility of the argument depends entirely on equivocation. The plausible idea that there are differences on average between the sexes is conflated with the idea that these are universal, the idea of enforced separate spheres is conflated with the idea of naturally occurring ones, and because a universal difference would explain a natural separation, an average difference is mistakenly taken to justify an imposed one. Confusion could hardly be worse confounded.

If this argument, so widely taken to justify the separation of the sexes into their traditional spheres, is an example of the logic which men have counted as their special preserve, perhaps it is not surprising that some feminists have decided that men are welcome to it.

3

I am not claiming that the forces of darkness—or even those among their number capable of recognizing such a thing as rout by argument—should by now have scattered in disarray. Much more can be said before the defence of separate spheres need be abandoned, and sometimes traditionalists scarcely seem to notice this breach of their front line, so immediately do they regroup and try again.

The next moves are as predictable as the original argument. Nearly all appeal to some general good to be brought about through selection efficiency and the saving of time, or, perhaps slightly less often, to ideas that women are incompetent to understand their own best interests. So, for instance, it may be said that in fact there often is a need for rules specifically excluding women from certain activities, even though none of them would get in on the basis of existing criteria, because for their own good women should not be allowed to waste their energies in pursuit of goals which will always elude them. Or it may be said that considerations of efficiency often demand that all women should be excluded from something even when only most women are unsuitable, because if we allowed selection systems to be clogged with swarms of incompetent applicants just for the sake of one or two exceptional ones who did happen to be competent, everyone would suffer in the long run.

There is no space to go into these by ways here (which is a pity, because they are most entertaining) but there are important things to say about such arguments in general.

First, although they are often presented as such, they do not work as refutations of the kinds of argument I have been putting forward so far. My arguments have themselves been rebuttals of another argument, and all I claim to have done is show that *that particular argument* in support of the separate spheres does not work. This is, of course, quite compatible with the spheres' being effectively defended in other ways, and the possible arguments about efficiency and the like are not objections to my dismissal of the original argument, but *new arguments to the original conclusion*. They invariably bring in additional premisses. It has already been shown that premisses about women's unsuitability for particular kinds of work (for instance) are not enough on their own to justify special woman-excluding rules, and in order to escape this difficulty it is necessary for them to be supplemented with claims about such matters as the damage women will do to themselves or others if they are allowed to compete. These new arguments do not rescue the original argument, therefore, and they seem to be tried only when that has failed (at least, I have never seen them given as the original argument in favour of separate spheres).

In one way, of course, that does not matter, since if someone produces a good argument for the separate spheres at the fifteenth attempt it is none the less a good argument. Still, it is a matter of some political and psychological interest that so many people's conviction that there should be separate spheres seems to remain constant while their justifications tag along behind. People who produce the original argument usually present it as their *reason* for wanting the separate spheres; if on its failure they anxiously seek around for other justifications it is not unreasonable to suspect that their real reasons for wanting the separation have little to do with the arguments they are putting forward, and that those real reasons, whatever they are (and whether or not they are consciously held), may be unsuitable for public exposure.

Second, all such rescue attempts are direct responses to the challenge addressed to the *logic* of the traditional argument, and concentrate on avoiding that particular pitfall. To that extent they usually succeed. However, what their producers seem sometimes to forget is that even though an argument must be unsound if its logic is bad, it is not necessarily sound if its logic is good. Premisses have to be plausible or otherwise acceptable as well. So far in this paper traditionalist premisses have been left unchallenged for the sake of demonstrating the mistakes in traditionalist logic, but that is not a thing to be allowed indefinitely; a good argument must be good in all respects, and anyone arguing in defence of a conclusion must be able to provide a positive justification of the premisses used (it is not enough to produce premisses which the opposition cannot *prove wrong*). There is, however, a strong tendency for the arguments in the second line of defence of the separate spheres to achieve logical success only at the cost of falling headlong into empirical or moral absurdity.[9] For instance, in order to carry through a paternalistic argument that there should be rules specifically excluding women from certain activities for their own good, it would be necessary to find *good grounds*—not just prejudice and wishful thinking—for believing both that these activities were particularly bad for women *and* that women were so generally incompetent to judge their own interests that they would be seriously damaged by being allowed to try. Most of the second-line arguments turn out to have problems of these kinds. This is not to say that it is impossible to find a good argument to the desired conclusion, but the task may not be as straightforward as some people appear to think.

Finally, anyone who is inclined to join in the attempts to save the traditionalist position should be aware of yet another requirement which must be met by any successful argument. If the idea is to defend anything like the traditional separate spheres, the argument produced must justify not just *any* kind of separation, but one of the right sort. Another mistake made by many would-be defenders of

---

[9] I discuss this matter in slightly more detail in 'Discrimination', Proceedings of the Aristotelian Society Supp. Vol. LIX, 1985.

tradition is that of producing arguments which, even if they worked in other respects, would succeed only in justifying a separate-spheres arrangement quite unlike the traditional one. Before people get too far in their attempts to find new justifications for the separate spheres, therefore, they should make sure they know what it is they need to justify.

4

It is at this point that questions about the relative status of the traditional spheres start to arise. Defenders of tradition, as was said earlier, often make out that what they want is nothing more than a useful division of labour for the convenience of all, with no question of any inequality. Even though they may have some difficulty in finding a justification of the division in the first place, therefore, they may still fall back on claims about the spheres' essential equality. It is frequently claimed that the pressures which separate the sexes provide no ground for *feminist* fuss in particular, since men are quite as badly off in their own sphere as women are in theirs; indeed, let pursuers of this line warm to their task for a little, and it is usually not long before they start to claim that things are actually much worse for men than women.

This would be very surprising, if true. Notwithstanding some obvious potential disadvantages of the male role (conscription, some conventions of chivalry and so on) women bent on escape from the female sphere do not usually run into hordes of oppressed men swarming in the opposite direction, trying to change places with their wives and secretaries. Anyone committed to the project of believing six impossible things before breakfast might try interpreting this striking lack of enthusiasm as a sign of generosity to women, but it is much easier to suspect that it shows where the real advantage lies. However, to confirm this suspicion we must con-sider directly the natures of the traditional spheres.

These have varied a good deal over space and time, and it is impossible to attempt any historical or geographical survey here; the discussion will unfortunately have to be limited to recent Western culture and stay at a very general level. However, it is probably true that the essentials of the arrangements have always been much the same, so that a discussion even of such a restricted period and area is likely to have at least limited application elsewhere.[10] This is particularly likely to be true if we start by going back in time a little, since present conventions and attitudes can often be better understood through the more clearly defined social arrangements out of which they developed. What, then, were the arrangements for the position of each sex a century or two ago, before recent reforms modified them?

The essence of the situation is unmistakable. There was far more to the separate spheres than any convenient division of labour. In fact most of the social arrangements, institutions, and customs which defined the relative position of the sexes had the effect of *placing women in the power and service of some man.*[11]

There is no exaggeration here. It must be remembered that what is at issue has nothing to do with anyone's feelings, nor even with the treatment of individual women by individual men. We are concerned with the formal and informal social institutions of various kinds which have brought the sphere separation about, and so many of these have been completely explicit that the facts about them are incontrovertible. There were laws about the control of husbands over wives and fathers over daughters, and obstacles in the way of women's controlling property. There were rules keeping women from nearly every kind of activity which might have given them status or independence (reinforced by their being kept out of any education which might have suited them to such activities), and as a result forcing them to depend for support on men. The kind of work regarded as the proper province of women was 'private', and

[10] If there are any societies where the treatment of women is radically different from what is to be outlined here, the remaining arguments of this paper will not apply to them. It is not essential to feminism to claim that the oppression of women *must* be essentially the same the world over—even though, as a matter of fact, it probably is much the same in kind, and different mainly in degree.

[11] The arrangement of the separate spheres is actually rather more complicated than this account suggests: there is *also* a straightforward element of simply designating some kinds of work as women's and some as men's, and the two elements interact in complicated ways. However, a full account of the situation would take far more space than is available here, and would not much affect my arguments. The element I discuss is the most important one. Furthermore, anyone trying to defend the separate spheres in their full traditional complexity would have to defend the element I discuss *and* others as well, so the simplification of the account works to my opponents' advantage, not to mine.

could take place only within a home headed by a breadwinning man, so that women who were forced to make their own living found that the only work available to them was of low status and appallingly paid. There were severe penalties for 'fallen women', which kept women bound to a particular man. There were laws which made it pretty well impossible for women to escape from the power of tyrannical husbands, since they would have had to sacrifice nearly everything, including their children, in the process. And to ratify it all, women were formally excluded from the making of law, so that until some men were willing to champion their cause there was little hope of their being able to change much of it.

To see the position of women in this way is to see clearly what the feminine sphere traditionally was: it was one in which all endeavour and activity was confined to achieving a particular end. The ideal woman has never been one who was weak and incompetent; hardly any man can ever have wanted a total loss of a woman. Female perfection was a matter of devoting all abilities to being useful to a particular man and his offspring, using a great deal of skill (the more the better) but always carefully directing it so that it presented no threat to men's position. Unfemininity lay in showing signs of trying to escape this situation. It was unfeminine of women to want to study at universities or have the vote or urge their own opinions against their husbands because in doing so they were displaying ideas about stepping beyond their allotted sphere. Higher education, political power and independent opinions were not among the requirements for being a wife and mother, and to seek them was to try to compete with men and become independent of them, rather than remaining in service.

So the separation of spheres never produced anything like an *equal* division of function between men and women; there is nothing in the least comparable about the male sphere. The demands of the male sphere have never involved dependence on women, or even much adaptation to them, except for certain responsibilities to families and certain conventions of chivalry and courtship. In fact the male sphere has contained virtually everything generally valued in society, and the main way in which reference to women comes into the account of masculinity is in the demand that a man should be of higher status than his womenfolk and exert proper authority over them (the least masculine man is the one who is henpecked). This is why 'femininity had to be achieved, cultivated and preserved, while masculinity could be left to look after itself'.[12]

Of course, things are now nothing like as bad as they used to be: rules and conventions directing women towards the service of men have lessened considerably both in extent and in firmness of enforcement. Nevertheless, *to the extent* that there do still remain different conventions for proper male and female activity and demeanour, nearly all are of the traditional kind. Although they no longer force all women into the power of men, they still create an asymmetry of status and dependence.

For instance, to the extent that boys and girls are given different educations, what distinguishes the girls' is that it is home-directed, with needlework, cooking, 'home economics', and so on. The 'commercial' courses which are the exception still prepare them for what is nearly always service to a man outside the home. Consider also the significance of girls' having been encouraged to take arts rather than science subjects, or biology rather than the hard sciences.[13] Then, away from school, it is a rare home in which the man will not presume as a matter of course that whatever a woman's professional or other commitments, she will take responsibility for domestic matters (even if he occasionally 'does the washing up for Mary', so making it clear that the act is supererogatory because it is really Mary's job). Again, to the extent that different behaviour is approved for men and women, it usually involves women's not putting themselves forward, not nagging, being loyal, dropping tactful hints instead of making open criticisms, going along with what the man suggests and so on. Women's magazines still dispense advice about how to be a highly competent assistant or partner to a man without making him feel threatened: how to cover up for your boss when he makes mistakes; how to get what you want for the family by letting your husband think he thought of it. At a more sophisticated level, manuals of sexual success instruct experienced women in the art of leading men sexually while giving the

---

[12] Pauline Marks, 'Femininity in the classroom', in *The Rights and Wrongs of Women*, eds. Mitchell and Oakley, p. 183.

[13] See, e.g. Alison Kelly (ed.), *The Missing Half: Girls and Science Education*, 1981, *passim*.

impression that it is the men who are taking the initiative. And, even now, few people outside the feminist movement give a thought to the highly significant universal presumption that a woman and her children should take her husband's surname. The special demands made of women have lessened in their scope and rigidity, but their nature is the same as it ever was. A woman who tries to cross the border into the territory of men is still presumptuous; a man who slips into women's is still degraded.

This means that although present-day defenders of separate spheres may not want to return to the extreme asymmetry of the past, even those who want to maintain the present state of things are in favour of a conventional inequality of power and dependence. Others, who think that the feminist rot has already gone too far and want to recover at least part of the past, want in effect an increase of present inequality. Anyone who is in favour of the separate spheres in anything like their traditional form, therefore, needs to find a justification for this kind of inequality. It is not enough (as some people seem to think) to point out that the worst aspects of the past have now gone, as if that in itself constituted a justification of all that remained.

5

How, then, can traditionalists set about justifying this asymmetrical arrangement? Their arguments vary in detail, but as usual they tend to depend on claims about the natures of men and women of a kind which provoke (usually legitimate) feminist wrath, nearly all having to do with male strength and dominance, female helplessness and need of protection, and consequent female need of the male. However, it is once again worth resisting the temptation to be distracted into squabbles about these questions of fact, and concentrating instead on the logic of the arguments.

The simplest of the familiar arguments are to the effect that social arrangements reflect the natural state of things: men dominate women just because they are dominant; women are attached to men and dependent on them because they are naturally inclined to attachment and dependence. But if men and women just are like that, what is the purpose of the rules and pressures supposed to be?

You can hardly justify the existence of pressures by claims that what they are supposed to achieve would happen anyway, without them. You cannot sneer at a henpecked man on the grounds that a man ought to be head of his household *and* claim that men should be heads of households because they are naturally dominant; if they all were, there would be nothing to sneer at, and if there is something to sneer at, some men at least are by the criterion of dominance unsuited to the position of headship. All such simple arguments, at least in their familiar forms, are non-starters.

The more complex arguments are about women's need of men. The weak need the protection of the strong, it is said, or childbearing women need men to look after them and get the food. Here, however, things get even worse. These arguments not only run into the already discussed difficulties of trying to deduce conclusions about men and women from premisses about such qualities as strength and weakness; they also manage to get into new and impressive tangles of their own.

To take the argument about strength and weakness first, consider what you would do if you were really setting out in an unprejudiced way to arrange for the protection of the weak. You would probably start by trying to make the weak stronger, or by giving them extra powers to defend themselves. You might also try to lessen the power of the strong, or at least make rules to prevent their getting out of hand. The very last thing you would do is systematically deprive the weak of all other options in order to force them to depend on the strong, and then provide social and legal powers to make the strong stronger still, as has been the case with women and men. The idea that the weak can be protected by being abandoned to the power of the strong involves as remarkable a piece of twisted reasoning as can ever have been devised.[14]

Much the same goes for arguments about the needs of childbearing women. If you were really concerned about the well-

---

[14] It is, of course, irrelevant to point out that men often *do* protect their women. This is one of many matters made clear by Mill. 'Whether the institution to be defended is slavery, political absolutism, or the absolutism of the head of a family, we are always expected to judge of it from its best instances. . . . Who doubts that there may be great goodness, and great happiness, and great affection, under the absolute government of a good man? Meanwhile, laws and institutions require to be adapted, not to good men, but to bad.' (Ibid., p. 62.)

being of women and children, and also thought that women needed men[15] to help them, you would be most unlikely to think of rules tying *women* to *men* since women would presumably be anxious to hold on to men anyway. What you would need would be rules to keep *men* in order. You might reasonably insist that *men* should be chaperoned to make sure they did not go around idly begetting children without committing themselves to their support, and that *men* should be subject to social ostracism if they were found to have eluded this vigilance and 'fallen'. And given that your concern was for the protection of women and children, you would also want to make sure that they were left as well off as possible whenever men did manage to evade their responsibilities. Nothing could be further from this than the traditional arrangements, which not only allowed men to father illegitimate children without suffering much in the way of social consequences, but also systematically deprived women of any means of supporting themselves independently of men, and made matters even worse by heaping ferocious social penalties on unsupported women and unauthorized children.

In other words, the usual justifications of the nature of the sexes' spheres are as full of structural holes as are the usual justifications for the existence of any such spheres in the first place. It will be found, furthermore, that such arguments are just as inadequate to defend the recent, modified, forms of the separate spheres as they are for the full-blooded traditional versions. Once again, feminists need hardly bother to dispute traditionalist premisses as long as traditionalist logic is in such a ramshackle state.

6

Given the high casualty rate among arguments in defence of the separate spheres doctrine, the question naturally arises of why anyone should want to enforce or encourage it at all. Since this enquiry is philosophical rather than anthropological or psychological it cannot go into that question directly, but it can raise the related one of what a logically sound and empirically plausible justification of the separate spheres would look like. And in view of

---

[15] Most of these arguments do not even attempt to explain why the supposedly necessary support could not be given by other *women*.

the extreme perversity of traditional arguments, radical measures suggest themselves. Rather like the Fairy Queen in *Iolanthe*, who sorted out an intractable tangle of problems by the simple expedient of inserting the word 'not' into an inconvenient item of fairy law, we might see whether we could improve on traditional arguments just by denying what was usually asserted.

We can start with another observation of Mill's:

> The general opinion of men is supposed to be that the natural vocation of a woman is that of a wife and mother. I say, is supposed to be, because judging from acts—from the whole of the present constitution of society— one might infer that their opinion was the direct contrary. They might be supposed to think that the alleged natural vocation of women was of all things the most repugnant to their nature, insomuch that if they are free to do anything else . . . there will not be enough of them who will be willing to accept the condition said to be natural to them.[16]

As we have seen, for a rule to have a point it must bring about something which would not have happened otherwise. If women really wanted to attach themselves to men in the traditional way, there would be no need for all the rules designed to bring such attachment about. However, the rules and pressures binding women to men *would* have a point if women did *not* naturally want this kind of arrangement, so we can start by considering that possibility. We may also suggest that since the attachment of women to men is asymmetrical—rules and conventions have not forced men into dependence on women—men do *not* have to be coerced. The rules have a very clear purpose if we start from the proposition that men want women—at least in the way suggested by the rules—considerably more than women want men.

That avoids one striking problem of the traditional account. However, if we are to come up with an acceptable argument we need to think of a reason which would account adequately both for men's wanting women more than women want men, and for the nature of traditional arrangements. Tradition explained women's wanting men by making men out to be strong, brave, adventurous, creative, inclined to genius, and all the rest, while women were passive, timorous, incapable of coping on their own, and generally

[16] Mill, op. cit., p. 49.

nondescript. Should we try to explain men's wanting women by reversing tradition here too, and say that it is really men who have all the negative qualities and women all the good and desirable ones?

That may be tempting for various reasons, but it will not do. Quite apart from any questions about empirical plausibility (and feminists must not copy their opponents' habit of inventing convenient facts) this would involve falling into another of the logical confusions of traditionalist argument. Once again, conclusions about rules organizing the relationship of men and women cannot be reached in any obvious way (if at all) on the basis of arguments about non-sexual characteristics such as strength and weakness, activity and passivity, sensitivity and aggressiveness or anything else of the kind. If we are to think of reasons for *men*'s wanting *women* we need to get away from all the incidental and derivative characteristics which may tend to be associated with one sex more than the other, and turn our attention to what *really* differentiates the sexes: to what each really has which the other has not, and makes men as such different from women as such.

This is not too difficult. Leaving aside such modern discoveries as hormones and chromosomes, since they are not directly relevant to the making of social arrangements, there seem to be only three differences of any importance.

One of these is difference of function in conception; sperm and ovum are different. In this difference, however, it is hard to see any grounds for one sex wanting to bind the other to it more strongly than the other was willing to be bound, since the difference is completely reciprocal. Each sex is so far necessary to the other, and there is to this extent (for once) genuine equality in their difference.

Another difference comes in sexual relationships as ends in themselves. Once again, the sexes' functions are reciprocal, but here it might be claimed that inequality did begin to set in. There are various kinds of evidence (though not undisputed) to suggest that the male desire for sex is a good deal stronger than that of the female, which would mean that women might often have to be constrained to co-operate if men were to be satisfied. However, although that certainly would provide a reason for men's wanting women more than women wanted men, it is still no use as part of a justification of the forms which sexual laws and conventions have traditionally taken. If social constraints were needed at all to bring about female co-operation they could not possibly take the form of demands for monogamy and chastity, since those *limit* women's sexual activity. On the contrary, social pressures should be needed to make women co-operate whenever required whether they liked it or not.

That leaves what is undoubtedly the most significant universal difference between the sexes. *Only the female has the ability to carry, give birth to, and nurse the offspring*; an ability corresponding to which the male has nothing at all.

It is worth commenting at this point on the remarkable fact that nearly everyone, when asked about differences between the sexes, will embark on a list of (supposed) differences which characterize women almost entirely in terms of inferiority to men. Most of these claims are anyway highly disputable, but even if they were not, they all still concern characteristics which differentiate the sexes only on *average*, or, occasionally, which are possessed by some men but no women. It is one of the most pernicious consequences of shoddy traditionalist argument that people have begun to think that differences of average ability between the sexes are what *actually differentiate* them. As a matter of logic, questions about the average differences between two groups cannot even be raised until they have been distinguished as groups, and the essential differences between men and women must actually be *sexual differences*. When the question is not about the derivative, average differences between the sexes, but about what makes them male and female— what puts all men on one side of the divide and all women on the other—the difference obviously has to do with reproductive capacity. And in this the sexes have generally reciprocal abilities, with the striking exception that *women* can do something which *men* cannot. The principal difference between the sexes, in other words, is *women's having an ability which men have not*, and (to reverse along with other aspects of tradition the Aristotelian contribution to sexism) it would be closer to the truth to say that *men* were *men* in virtue of a lack of qualities, rather than that women were women on that account.

This certainly looks promising as the beginning of an account of why men should want women attached to them; if one group has some ability another lacks, there is a *prima-facie* reason for its being wanted by that other group. And in this case the way in which women have been attached to men suggests exactly what men might have wanted from the arrangement. Women are by nature able to *identify* and therefore devote special attention to their own offspring; men are not, as long as women are on the loose.

Here, then, is a possible reason for men's wanting women in ways different from those in which women want men, and also for their wanting to make it difficult for women to support themselves and their children alone, and imposing on them conventions of monogamy and chastity. So far the simple reversal of traditional ideas puts us well on the way to a sound argument leading to the conclusion that there should be separate spheres of the traditional forms.

To complete the argument we need some kind of general principle about what *ought* to be the case, from which the conclusion can be deduced that women should be subservient to men. Tradition is apt to invoke benefits for women here, or, failing that, some general social good. The first is pretty implausible, since women apparently have to be coerced into their attachment to men, and although the second looks more like a possibility, an argument appealing to the good of society would need a very complicated set of premises indeed (full of counterfactuals about the kinds of thing which would happen if women were not tied to men, and so on), all of which would need good supporting evidence (not just an absence of contrary evidence). On the other hand, if we reverse these traditionalist claims to altruism, and put in their place a simple premiss to the effect that *men* should get what they want, the argument is straightforward. It goes something like this:

Society should be organized so that men get what they want
Men want to control women in order to identify their children, which women, unconstrained, cannot be relied on to allow them to do

Therefore: women must be kept attached and subordinate to men.

So there, mainly by means of reversing various parts of the traditional defence of separate spheres, we find a logically and empirically sound argument to the conclusion that the sexes should keep their traditional positions. Its only problem is that it is morally and politically doubtful, and certainly not well adapted to the purpose of persuading a subject group of the natural inevitability of its position. Perhaps that is why this kind of justification does not often appear in public.[17]

This argument does, of course, also provide a plausible candidate answer to the factual question of why the spheres ever came about in the first place (if not of why people should want to keep them now). However, that interesting matter need not be gone into here, since here the argument is being presented not as an explanation, but only as a possible justification: an *argument* leading to the conclusion that men and women *should* occupy their traditional positions.[18] It is not even offered as the only possible justification. Still, it does present a challenge to anyone who would have us believe that the separate spheres are an arrangement for the good of all. The situation *can* be defended by an argument based on the advantage of men, so until someone produces an alternative defence we are entitled to say that we can see no other justification for the spheres than their benefiting men, and act accordingly.[19]

Perhaps sufficiently ingenious searching could produce more acceptable justifications, but it seems rather unlikely. Here we are, after all, expected to swallow arguments in defence of tradition which depend on our accepting that rules are necessary to bring about what would have happened anyway, that rules whose only effect is to prevent people's acting in ways suitable to their natures can be justified by principles about suitability, that the weak can be protected by being abandoned to the control of the strong, and that childbearing women can be protected by rules and conventions

---

[17] Hume does give essentially this argument for 'the modesty and chastity which belong to the fair sex' (*Treatise of Human Nature*, III, xii).

[18] Even this does not work as a justification of recent modified versions of traditional arrangements. Although these are less bad in themselves they are even harder to justify in *any* coherent way, acceptable or unacceptable.

[19] In general, if some social arrangement gives benefits to one group of people, the onus of proof is on anyone who wants to argue that the arrangements also produce some *general* good. I discuss this matter more fully in 'Discrimination', ibid.

which make them helpless without the protection of a man. We are also expected to overlook women's rather striking extra ability, and see the whole essence of femaleness as a series of inadequacies and absences, while at the same time transforming men's inability to bear children into a special aptitude for everything else. If such contortions form the basis of the best set of arguments in defence of the traditional spheres which can be produced for public consumption, it may reasonably be presumed that ones which are morally, logically, and empirically acceptable cannot lie immediately to hand.

7

If the arguments of this essay are right, they suggest an interesting division in the ranks of feminism's opponents. On the one hand, there are the real opponents: the still-determined defenders of tradition, who should now either admit that they are straightforwardly out to defend the privileges of men, or subside until they manage to find a better defence of the separate spheres. On the other hand, there is a large and surprising group who count themselves among the opposition, but who now turn out, according to their own principles, to have been against the separate spheres all along. All those traditionalists who complain that feminists are putting pressure on women to make them act against their natures can now see that they must in consistency (unless they want to allow feminists to monopolize logic) join feminists in their opposition to any kind of imposed sphere separation, since such arrangements distort women and men alike. The same is true of anyone who wants to defend the weak conclusion of the original separate spheres argument (to return to that at last), and thinks that there should be separate spheres because the sexes would drift into them by nature if left to their own devices. Such people should be delighted to have the opportunity to prove their point about natural sex differences by joining in the struggle to get rid of the artificially imposed ones.

However, feminists would perhaps be unwise to depend on a rush of support from these improbable allies. For one thing, it is not unheard of for people to persist in incoherent opinions. For another, even people who do recognize that their arguments commit them to opposing the traditional separate spheres may just change their tack. They may start claiming instead that arguments about justifiability are now entirely beside the point, since the spheres disappeared altogether some time ago.

This is a very common line of argument, and it means that feminists need to be able to show not only that pressures to bring about the separate spheres are unjustified, but also that they do still exist. This is, of course, largely an empirical task, but there is still philosophical work to be done in clarifying the various forms social pressures may take. It is important to be able to block the familiar move from 'women can do anything now' (which is in some sense true) to the false conclusion that if women still find themselves in a situation of inferiority to men that must be because they just are inferior.

It is true that feminists are not entitled to make any inference from the relative situations of men and women to the conclusion that there are still restraints on women: the possibility has to be allowed for that there are real differences of capability between the sexes which would remain even in a situation of equal opportunity. On the other hand, neither are the opponents of feminism entitled to claim that because (at least in the liberal West) women can now choose to own property, enter the professions and even bring up children alone, all traces of the separating pressures have disappeared. The spheres may be much more nebulous than formerly, but as long as social forces of any kind make anything *more difficult* for the members of one sex as such than for the other, men and women are still pushed in different directions, and the spheres still exert their influence.[20] And in fact, once the various ways in which they manifest themselves are recognized, differentiating pressures can still be seen to pervade even the most liberal of societies.

---

[20] It is important to remember that *general* social rules or pressures might still affect one sex more than the other, because of natural differences (average or universal) between them. (It can be argued, though the matter is complicated, that even rules which *can* only apply to one sex, such as abortion laws, may be general in the relevant sense). If women and men found themselves in different situations as a result of tendencies to difference in nature when all rules were general they would have *drifted* into separate spheres, rather than being *pushed* into them, so these spheres would not be open to the objections raised by this paper.

First, even the formal rules and institutions which differentiate the sexes have still not vanished completely. In the world as a whole there are enormous numbers of them, but even in liberal countries they still exist: there are still asymmetrical tax, social security, and pension laws, for instance. So even among formal institutions there is work to be done.

Far more pervasive, however, are informal conventions, which are also powerful exerters of pressure. The nature and extent of these differ widely among social groups, but in general people do still to a large extent approve or disapprove of actions not just in themselves, but according to the sex of their agent. Expressions of disapproval vary in strength, and may be very subtle, but where disapproval is felt there can be little doubt that it is usually shown, and approval and disapproval are often sex-connected. How many people, even among the most enlightened, would be perfectly unaffected by the sexes of the people involved when reacting to someone's playing with dolls, dressing with ostentatious care, answering the front door in an apron, making open sexual advances, wolf-whistling, riding pillion on a motor bike driven by someone of the other sex, or giving up a career to follow a spouse or care for children? As long as social approval and disapproval are connected with sex, some activities are made easier for one group than the other (because its members do not have to sacrifice social acceptability to do them), and there is pressure towards separate spheres for the sexes.

And there are other pressures less obtrusive still. There are compelling grounds for believing that the separate spheres perpetuate themselves even in the different expectations people have of men and women.

In the first place, experiments have shown that beliefs about the differences between the sexes have further-reaching effects than most people have any idea of. They influence not only predictions about the way men and women will perform, but even the way their actual performance is perceived and described. For instance, in one experiment groups of young mothers were watched on different occasions as they played with toddlers: first with one in blue dungarees called Adam, and then with one in a pink frilly dress, called Beth. Adam and Beth were treated and described differently; they were the same child.[21] In another experiment groups of women undergraduates were given articles to read, three by women and three by men, dealing with fields generally thought of as masculine, feminine, and neutral. For half of these groups, the articles written by men were attributed to women, and vice versa. 'A general bias against women was found regardless of the field, and even in traditional feminine fields an article was considered more valuable and its author more competent when that author was a man. The bias was strongest in the case of "masculine" fields with a female author.'[22] In both these cases the subjects of the experiment would doubtless have claimed to be responding only to what was immediately before them; in both the structure of the experiment shows that they would have been mistaken. There have been a great many such experiments, consistently showing a strong bias against women.

Then, in addition to this, there is a mass of psychological evidence which shows that expectation affects performance; that if, for instance, a teacher is told that some randomly selected children are high-flyers, that group will do far better than it otherwise would have done. (I gather that the same is true even when experimenters are told they are dealing with high-flying rats.) If it is generally believed that women are inferior to men in most respects, that is enough in itself to account for their turning out to be so.

And finally (to reverse yet another part of traditional mythology) present beliefs about the differences between the sexes are to a considerable extent the effect, rather than the cause, of the separate spheres. There may well be (as a good deal of evolutionary and genetic evidence suggests) deeply rooted tendencies towards difference of character and ability in women and men, and if the sexes ever come to have genuine equality of opportunity perhaps women may indeed turn out to have generally fewer abilities than men—or, let it not be forgotten, the other way round. As yet, however, there is no adequate evidence for any such conclusion. We know to start with that the imposition of the spheres has

[21] A. Lake (1975), 'Are we born into our sex roles or programmed into them?' *Woman's Day*, January, pp. 24–5, quoted Ann Oakley, *Subject Women* (1981), p. 96.

[22] P. Goldberg (1968), 'Are women prejudiced against women?' *Transaction*, 5, no. 5, pp. 28–30, quoted Oakley, op. cit., p. 126.

systematically deprived women of equal opportunity with men to demonstrate what abilities they have, so that little if anything about their nature can be inferred from their actual performance. We have also seen how important it has been to traditional ideology to foster appropriate beliefs about the nature of women: any competent oppressor will, of course, try to disguise what is going on by persuading everyone that social arrangements are the result of nature rather than contrivance. The idea that women are naturally suited to their subordinate sphere has become one of the most entrenched parts of tradition, and remarkably resistant to change (as other research shows) even in the face of overwhelming evidence. We know, therefore, that strongly held convictions about the natural inferiority of women are not adequately justified by present evidence. These convictions must themselves be regarded as a legacy of the differential treatment of women and men. It follows that beliefs and expectations provide yet another method of entrenching the separate spheres, probably at least as effective as any rules, and far more sinister because almost invisible.

The separate spheres have shrunk and become blurred round the edges in many societies, but they have by no means vanished completely. Differentiating pressures still systematically place women at a disadvantage to men. Furthermore, although that disadvantage is considerably less than it once was, other difficulties have arisen in its place: the subtlety of the pressures which remain makes them far more difficult to identify, to demonstrate to the sceptical, and to deal with than was ever the case with formal laws and institutions. Problems for *women* may have lessened with the shrinking of the spheres, but the problems faced by *feminists* remain as formidable as ever.

XIII

ALL ANIMALS ARE EQUAL

PETER SINGER

IN recent years a number of oppressed groups have campaigned vigorously for equality. The classic instance is the Black Liberation movement, which demands an end to the prejudice and discrimination that has made blacks second-class citizens. The immediate appeal of the Black Liberation movement and its initial, if limited, success made it a model for other oppressed groups to follow. We became familiar with liberation movements for Spanish-Americans, gay people, and a variety of other minorities. When a majority group—women—began their campaign, some thought we had come to the end of the road. Discrimination on the basis of sex, it has been said, is the last universally accepted form of discrimination, practised without secrecy or pretence even in those liberal circles that have long prided themselves on their freedom from prejudice against racial minorities.

One should always be wary of talking of 'the last remaining form of discrimination'. If we have learnt anything from the liberation movements, we should have learnt how difficult it is to be aware of latent prejudice in our attitudes to particular groups until this prejudice is forcefully pointed out.

A liberation movement demands an expansion of our moral horizons and an extension or reinterpretation of the basic moral principle of equality. Practices that were previously regarded as natural and inevitable come to be seen as the result of an unjustifiable prejudice. Who can say with confidence that all his or her attitudes and practices are beyond criticism? If we wish to avoid being numbered amongst the oppressors, we must be prepared to re-think even our most fundamental attitudes. We need to consider them from the point of view of those most disadvantaged by our

Part of this essay appeared in the *New York Review of Books* (5 Apr. 1973), and is reprinted by permission of the Editor. This version is an abridged form of an essay which was first published in *Philosophic Exchange* vol. 1, no. 5 (Summer 1974).

attitudes, and the practices that follow from these attitudes. If we can make this unaccustomed mental switch we may discover a pattern in our attitudes and practices that consistently operates so as to benefit one group—usually the one to which we ourselves belong—at the expense of another. In this way we may come to see that there is a case for a new liberation movement. My aim is to advocate that we make this mental switch in respect of our attitudes and practices towards a very large group of beings: members of species other than our own—or, as we popularly though misleadingly call them, animals. In other words, I am urging that we extend to other species the basic principle of equality that most of us recognize should be extended to all members of our own species.

All this may sound a little far-fetched, more like a parody of other liberation movements than a serious objective. In fact, in the past the idea of 'The Rights of Animals' really has been used to parody the case for women's rights. When Mary Wollstonecraft, a forerunner of later feminists, published her *Vindication of the Rights of Women* in 1792, her ideas were widely regarded as absurd, and they were satirized in an anonymous publication entitled *A Vindication of the Rights of Brutes*. The author of this satire (actually Thomas Taylor, a distinguished Cambridge philosopher) tried to refute Wollstonecroft's reasonings by showing that they could be carried one stage further. If sound when applied to women, why should the arguments not be applied to dogs, cats, and horses? They seemed to hold equally well for these 'brutes'; yet to hold that brutes had rights was manifestly absurd; therefore the reasoning by which this conclusion had been reached must be unsound, and if unsound when applied to brutes, it must also be unsound when applied to women, since the very same arguments had been used in each case.

One way in which we might reply to this argument is by saying that the case for equality between men and women cannot validly be extended to non-human animals. Women have a right to vote, for instance, because they are just as capable of making rational decisions as men are; dogs, on the other hand, are incapable of understanding the significance of voting, so they cannot have the right to vote. There are many other obvious ways in which men and women resemble each other closely, while humans and other animals differ greatly. So, it might be said, men and women are similiar beings, and should have equal rights, while humans and non-humans are different and should not have equal rights.

The thought behind this reply to Taylor's analogy is correct up to a point, but it does not go far enough. There *are* important differences between humans and other animals, and these differences must give rise to *some* differences, in the rights that each have. Recognizing this obvious fact, however, is no barrier to the case for extending the basic principle of equality to non-human animals. The differences that exist between men and women are equally undeniable, and the supporters of Women's Liberation are aware that these differences may give rise to different rights. Many feminists hold that women have the right to an abortion on request. It does not follow that since these same people are campaigning for equality between men and women they must support the right of men to have abortions too. Since a man cannot have an abortion, it is meaningless to talk of his right to have one. Since a pig can't vote, it is meaningless to talk of its right to vote. There is no reason why either Women's Liberation or Animal Liberation should get involved in such nonsense. The extension of the basic principle of equality from one group to another does not imply that we must treat both groups in exactly the same way, or grant exactly the same rights to both groups. Whether we should do so will depend on the nature of the members of the two groups. The basic principle of equality, I shall argue, is equality of consideration; and equal consideration for different beings may lead to different treatment and different rights.

So there is a different way of replying to Taylor's attempt to parody Wollstonecraft's arguments, a way which does not deny the differences between humans and non-humans, but goes more deeply into the question of equality, and concludes by finding nothing absurd in the idea that the basic principle of equality applies to so-called 'brutes'. I believe that we reach this conclusion if we examine the basis on which our opposition to discrimination on grounds of race or sex ultimately rests. We will then see that we would be on shaky ground if we were to demand equality for blacks, women, and other groups of oppressed humans while denying equal consideration to non-humans.

When we say that all human beings, whatever their race, creed, or sex, are equal, what is it that we are asserting? Those who wish to defend a hierarchical, inegalitarian society have often pointed out that by whatever test we choose, it simply is not true that all humans are equal. Like it or not, we must face the fact that humans come in different shapes and sizes; they come with differing moral capacities, differing intellectual abilities, differing amounts of benevolent feeling and sensitivity to the needs of others, differing abilities to communicate effectively, and differing capacities to experience pleasure and pain. In short, if the demand for equality were based on the actual equality of all human beings, we would have to stop demanding equality. It would be an unjustifiable demand.

Still, one might cling to the view that the demand for equality among human beings is based on the actual equality of the different races and sexes. Although humans differ as individuals in various ways, there are no differences between the races and sexes *as such*. From the mere fact that a person is black, or a woman, we cannot infer anything else about that person. This, it may be said, is what is wrong with racism and sexism. The white racist claims that whites are superior to blacks, but this is false—although there are differences between individuals, some blacks are superior to some whites in all of the capacities and abilities that could conceivably be relevant. The opponent of sexism would say the same: a person's sex is no guide to his or her abilities, and this is why it is unjustifiable to discriminate on the basis of sex.

This is a possible line of objection to racial and sexual discrimination. It is not, however, the way someone really concerned about equality would choose, because taking this line could, in some circumstances, force one to accept a most inegalitarian society. The fact that humans differ as individuals, rather than as races or sexes, is a valid reply to someone who defends a hierarchical society like, say, South Africa, in which all whites are superior in status to all blacks. The existence of individual variations that cut across the lines of race or sex, however, provides us with no defence at all against a more sophisticated opponent of equality, one who proposes that, say, the interests of those with IQ ratings above 100 be preferred to the interests of those with IQs below 100. Would a hierarchical society of this sort really be so much better than one based on race or sex? I think not. But if we tie the moral principle of equality to the factual equality of the different races or sexes, taken as a whole, our opposition to racism and sexism does not provide us with any basis for objecting to this kind of inegalitarianism.

There is a second important reason why we ought not to base our opposition to racism and sexism on any kind of factual equality, even the limited kind which asserts that variations in capacities and abilities are spread evenly between the different races and sexes: we can have no absolute guarantee that these abilities and capacities really are distributed evenly, without regard to race or sex, among human beings. So far as actual abilities are concerned, there do seem to be certain measurable differences between both races and sexes. These differences do not, of course, appear in each case, but only when averages are taken. More important still, we do not yet know how much of these differences is really due to the different genetic endowments of the various races and sexes, and how much is due to environmental differences that are the result of past and continuing discrimination. Perhaps all of the important differences will eventually prove to be environmental rather than genetic. Anyone opposed to racism and sexism will certainly hope that this will be so, for it will make the task of ending discrimination a lot easier; nevertheless it would be dangerous to rest the case against racism and sexism on the belief that all significant differences are environmental in origin. The opponent of, say, racism who takes this line will be unable to avoid conceding that if differences in ability did after all prove to have some genetic connection with race, racism would in some way be defensible.

It would be folly for the opponent of racism to stake his whole case on a dogmatic commitment to one particular outcome of a difficult scientific issue which is still a long way from being settled. While attempts to prove that differences in certain selected abilities between races and sexes are primarily genetic in origin have certainly not been conclusive, the same must be said of attempts to prove that these differences are largely the result of environment. At this stage of the investigation we cannot be certain which view is correct, however much we may hope it is the latter.

Fortunately, there is no need to pin the case for equality to one particular outcome of this scientific investigation. The appropriate response to those who claim to have found evidence of genetically-based differences in ability between the races or sexes is not to stick to the belief that the genetic explanation must be wrong, whatever evidence to the contrary may turn up: instead we should make it quite clear that the claim to equality does not depend on intelligence, moral capacity, physical strength, or similar matters of fact. Equality is a moral ideal, not a simple assertion of fact. There is no logically compelling reason for assuming that a factual difference in ability between two people justifies any difference in the amount of consideration we give to satisfying their needs and interests. The principle of the equality of human beings is not a description of an alleged actual equality among humans: it is a prescription of how we should treat humans.

Jeremy Bentham incorporated the essential basis of moral equality into his utilitarian system of ethics in the formula: 'Each to count for one and none for more than one.' In other words, the interests of every being affected by an action are to be taken into account and given the same weight as the like interests of any other being. A later utilitarian, Henry Sidgwick, put the point in this way: 'The good of any one individual is of no more importance, from the point of view (if I may say so) of the Universe, than the good of any other.'[1] More recently, the leading figures in modern moral philosophy have shown a great deal of agreement in specifying as a fundamental presupposition of their moral theories some similar requirement which operates so as to give everyone's interests equal consideration—although they cannot agree on how this requirement is best formulated.[2]

It is an implication of this principle of equality that our concern for others ought not to depend on what they are like, or what abilities they possess—although precisely what this concern requires us to do may vary according to the characteristics of those affected by what we do. It is on this basis that the case against racism and the case against sexism must both ultimately rest; and it is in accordance with this principle that speciesism is also to be condemned. If possessing a higher degree of intelligence does not

[1] *The Methods of Ethics* (7th edn.), p. 382.
[2] For example, R. M. Hare, *Freedom and Reason* (Oxford, 1963) and J. Rawls, *A Theory of Justice* (Harvard, 1972); for a brief account of the essential agreement on this issue between these and other positions, see R. M. Hare, 'Rules of War and Moral Reasoning', *Philosophy and Public Affairs*, vol. I, no. 2 (1972).

entitle one human to use another for his own ends, how can it entitle humans to exploit non-humans?

Many philosophers have proposed the principle of equal consideration of interests, in some form or other, as a basic moral principle; but, as we shall see in more detail shortly, not many of them have recognized that this principle applies to members of other species as well as to our own. Bentham was one of the few who did realize this. In a forward-looking passage, written at a time when black slaves in the British dominions were still being treated much as we now treat non-human animals, Bentham wrote:

The day *may* come when the rest of the animal creation may acquire those rights which never could have been witholden from them but by the hand of tyranny. The French have already discovered that the blackness of the skin is no reason why a human being should be abandoned without redress to the caprice of a tormentor. It may one day come to be recognized that the number of the legs, the villosity of the skin, or the termination of the *os sacrum*, are reasons equally insufficient for abandoning a sensitive being to the same fate. What else is it that should trace the insuperable line? Is it the faculty of reason, or perhaps the faculty of discourse? But a full-grown horse or dog is beyond comparison a more rational, as well as a more conversable animal, than an infant of a day, or a week, or even a month, old. But suppose they were otherwise, what would it avail? The question is not, Can they reason? nor Can they *talk*? but, *Can they suffer?*[3]

In this passage Bentham points to the capacity for suffering as the vital characteristic that gives a being the right to equal consideration. The capacity for suffering—or more strictly, for suffering and/or enjoyment or happiness—is not just another characteristic like the capacity for language, or for higher mathematics. Bentham is not saying that those who try to mark 'the insuperable line' that determines whether the interests of a being should be considered happen to have selected the wrong characteristic. The capacity for suffering and enjoying things is a pre-requisite for having interests at all, a condition that must be satisfied before we can speak of interests in any meaningful way. It would be nonsense to say that it was not in the interests of a stone to be kicked along the road by a schoolboy. A stone does not have interests because it cannot suffer. Nothing that we can do to it could possibly make any difference to

[3] *Introduction to the Principles of Morals and Legislation*, ch. XVII.

its welfare. A mouse, on the other hand, does have an interest in not being tormented, because it will suffer if it is.

If a being suffers, there can be no moral justification for refusing to take that suffering into consideration. No matter what the nature of the being, the principle of equality requires that its suffering be counted equally with the like suffering—in so far as rough comparisons can be made—of any other being. If a being is not capable of suffering, or of experiencing enjoyment or happiness, there is nothing to be taken into account. This is why the limit of sentience (using the term as a convenient, if not strictly accurate, shorthand for the capacity to suffer or experience enjoyment or happiness) is the only defensible boundary of concern for the interests of others. To mark this boundary by some characteristic like intelligence or rationality would be to mark it in an arbitrary way. Why not choose some other characteristic, like skin colour?

The racist violates the principle of equality by giving greater weight to the interests of members of his own race, when there is a clash between their interests and the interests of those of another race. Similarly the speciesist allows the interests of his own species to override the greater interests of members of other species.[4] The pattern is the same in each case. Most human beings are speciesists. I shall now very briefly describe some of the practices that show this.

For the great majority of human beings, especially in urban, industrialized societies, the most direct form of contact with members of other species is at meal-times: we eat them. In doing so we treat them purely as means to our ends. We regard their life and well-being as subordinate to our taste for a particular kind of dish. I say 'taste' deliberately—this is purely a matter of pleasing our palate. There can be no defence of eating flesh in terms of satisfying nutritional needs, since it has been established beyond doubt that we could satisfy our need for protein and other essential nutrients far more efficiently with a diet that replaced animal flesh by soy beans, or products derived from soy beans, and other high-protein vegetable products.[5]

---

[4] I owe the term 'speciesism' to Richard Ryder.

[5] In order to produce 1 lb. of protein in the form of beef or veal, we must feed 21 lb. of protein to the animal. Other forms of livestock are slightly less inefficient, but the average ratio in the US is still 1:8. It has been estimated that the amount of

It is not merely the act of killing that indicates what we are ready to do to other species in order to gratify our tastes. The suffering we inflict on the animals while they are alive is perhaps an even clearer indication of our speciesism than the fact that we are prepared to kill them.[6] In order to have meat on the table at a price that people can afford, our society tolerates methods of meat production that confine sentient animals in cramped, unsuitable conditions for the entire durations of their lives. Animals are treated like machines that convert fodder into flesh, and any innovation that results in a higher 'conversion ratio' is liable to be adopted. As one authority on the subject has said, 'cruelty is acknowledged only when profitability ceases'.[7]

Since, as I have said, none of these practices cater for anything more than our pleasures of taste, our practice of rearing and killing other animals in order to eat them is a clear instance of the sacrifice of the most important interests of other beings in order to satisfy trivial interests of our own. To avoid speciesism we must stop this practice, and each of us has a moral obligation to cease supporting the practice. Our custom is all the support that the meat industry needs. The decision to cease giving it that support may be difficult, but it is no more difficult than it would have been for a white Southerner to go against the traditions of his society and free his slaves: if we do not change our dietary habits, how can we censure those slave-holders who would not change their own way of living?

The same form of discrimination may be observed in the widespread practice of experimenting on other species in order to

protein lost to humans in this way is equivalent to 90 per cent of the annual world protein deficit. For a brief account, see Frances Moore Lappé, *Diet for a Small Planet* (Friends of The Earth/Ballantine, New York, 1971), pp. 4–11.

[6] Although one might think that killing a being is obviously the ultimate wrong one can do to it, I think that the infliction of suffering is a clearer indication of speciesism because it might be argued that at least part of what is wrong with killing a human is that most humans are conscious of their existence over time, and have desires and purposes that extend into the future—see, for instance, M. Tooley, 'Abortion and Infanticide', *Philosophy and Public Affairs*, vol. 2, no. 1 (1972). Of course, if one took this view one would have to hold—as Tooley does—that killing a human infant or mental defective is not in itself wrong, and is less serious than killing certain higher mammals that probably do have a sense of their own existence over time.

[7] Ruth Harrison, *Animal Machines* (London, 1964). For an account of farming conditions, see my *Animal Liberation* (New York, 1975).

see if certain substances are safe for human beings, or to test some psychological theory about the effect of severe punishment on learning, or to try out various new compounds just in case something turns up . . .

In the past, argument about vivisection has often missed this point, because it has been put in absolutist terms: Would the abolitionist be prepared to let thousands die if they could be saved by experimenting on a single animal? The way to reply to this purely hypothetical question is to pose another: Would the experimenter be prepared to perform his experiment on an orphaned human infant, if that were the only way to save many lives? (I say 'orphan' to avoid the complication of parental feelings, although in doing so I am being over-fair to the experimenter, since the non-human subjects of experiments are not orphans.) If the experimenter is not prepared to use an orphaned human infant, then his readiness to use non-humans is simple discrimination, since adult apes, cats, mice, and other mammals are more aware of what is happening to them, more self-directing and, so far as we can tell, at least as sensitive to pain, as any human infant. There seems to be no relevant characteristic that human infants possess that adult mammals do not have to the same or a higher degree. (Someone might try to argue that what makes it wrong to experiment on a human infant is that the infant will, in time and if left alone, develop into more than the non-human, but one would then, to be consistent, have to oppose abortion, since the foetus has the same potential as the infant—indeed, even contraception and abstinence might be wrong on this ground, since the egg and sperm, considered jointly, also have the same potential. In any case, this argument still gives us no reason for selecting a non-human, rather than a human with severe and irreversible brain damage, as the subject for our experiments.)

The experimenter, then, shows a bias in favour of his own species whenever he carries out an experiment on a non-human for a purpose that he would not think justified him in using a human being at an equal or lower level of sentience, awareness, ability to be self-directing, etc. No one familiar with the kind of results yielded by most experiments on animals can have the slightest doubt that if this bias were eliminated the number of experiments performed would be a minute fraction of the number performed today.

Experimenting on animals, and eating their flesh, are perhaps the two major forms of speciesism in our society. By comparison, the third and last form of speciesism is so minor as to be insignificant, but it is perhaps of some special interest to those for whom this article was written. I am referring to speciesism in modern philosophy.

Philosophy ought to question the basic assumptions of the age. Thinking through, critically and carefully, what most people take for granted is, I believe, the chief task of philosophy, and it is this task that makes philosophy a worthwhile activity. Regrettably, philosophy does not always live up to its historic role. Philosophers are human beings and they are subject to all the preconceptions of the society to which they belong. Sometimes they succeed in breaking free of the prevailing ideology: more often they become its most sophisticated defenders. So, in this case, philosophy as practised in the universities today does not challenge anyone's preconceptions about our relations with other species. By their writings, those philosophers who tackle problems that touch upon the issue reveal that they make the same unquestioned assumptions as most other humans, and what they say tends to confirm the reader in his or her comfortable speciesist habits.

I could illustrate this claim by referring to the writings of philosophers in various fields—for instance, the attempts that have been made by those interested in rights to draw the boundary of the sphere of rights so that it runs parallel to the biological boundaries of the species *Homo sapiens*, including infants and even mental defectives, but excluding those other beings of equal or greater capacity who are so useful to us at meal-times and in our laboratories. I think it would be a more appropriate conclusion to this chapter, however, if I concentrated on the problem with which we have been centrally concerned, the problem of equality.

It is significant that the problem of equality, in moral and political philosophy, is invariably formulated in terms of human equality. The effect of this is that the question of the equality of other animals does not confront the philosopher, or student, as an issue itself— and this is already an indication of the failure of philosophy to

challenge accepted beliefs. Still, philosophers have found it difficult
to discuss the issue of human equality without raising, in a
paragraph or two, the question of the status of other animals. The
reason for this, which should be apparent from what I have said
already, is that if humans are to be regarded as equal to one
another, we need some sense of 'equal' that does not require any
actual, descriptive equality of capacities, talents, or other qualities.
If equality is to be related to any actual characteristics of humans,
these characteristics must be some lowest common denominator,
pitched so low that no human lacks them—but then the philosopher
comes up against the catch that any such set of characteristics which
covers *all* humans will not be possessed *only by humans*. In other
words, it turns out that in the only sense in which we can truly say, as
an assertion of fact, that all humans are equal, at least some
members of other species are also equal—equal, that is, to each
other and to humans. If, on the other hand, we regard the statement
'All humans are equal' in some non-factual way, perhaps as a
prescription, then, as I have already argued, it is even more difficult
to exclude non-humans from the sphere of equality.

   This result is not what the egalitarian philosopher originally
intended to assert. Instead of accepting the radical outcome to
which their own reasonings naturally point, however, most philosophers try to reconcile their beliefs in human equality and animal
inequality by arguments that can only be described as devious.

   As an example, I take William Frankena's well-known article,
'The Concept of Social Justice'. Frankena opposes the idea of
basing justice on merit, because he sees that this could lead to highly
inegalitarian results. Instead he proposes the principle that '. . . all
men are to be treated as equals, not because they are equal, in any
respect, but simply because they are human. They are human
because they have emotions and desires, and are able to think, and
hence are capable of enjoying a good life in a sense in which other
animals are not.'[8]

   But what is this capacity to enjoy the good life which all humans
have, but no other animals? Other animals have emotions and
desires, and appear to be capable of enjoying a good life. We may
doubt that they can think—although the behaviour of some apes,

----

   [8] In R. Brandt (ed.), *Social Justice* (Englewood Cliffs, 1962), p. 19.

dolphins, and even dogs suggests that some of them can—but what is the relevance of thinking? Frankena goes on to admit that by 'the good life' he means 'not so much the morally good life as the happy or satisfactory life', so thought would appear to be unnecessary for enjoying the good life; in fact to emphasize the need for thought would make difficulties for the egalitarian since only some people are capable of leading intellectually satisfying lives, or morally good lives. This makes it difficult to see what Frankena's principle of equality has to do with simply being *human*. Surely every sentient being is capable of leading a life that is happier or less miserable than some alternative life, and hence has a claim to be taken into account. In this respect the distinction between humans and non-humans is not a sharp division, but rather a continuum along which we move gradually, and with overlaps between the species, from simple capacities for enjoyment and satisfaction, or pain and suffering, to more complex ones.

Faced with a situation in which they see a need for some basis for the moral gulf that is commonly thought to separate humans and animals, but can find no concrete difference that will do the job without undermining the equality of humans, philosophers tend to waffle. They resort to high-sounding phrases like 'the intrinsic dignity of the human individual'.[9] They talk of the 'intrinsic worth of all men' as if men (humans?) had some worth that other beings did not,[10] or they say that humans, and only humans, are 'ends in themselves', while 'everything other than a person can only have value for a person'.[11]

This idea of a distinctive human dignity and worth has a long history; it can be traced back directly to the Renaissance humanists, for instance to Pico della Mirandola's *Oration on the Dignity of Man*. Pico and other humanists based their estimate of human dignity on the idea that man possessed the central, pivotal position in the 'Great Chain of Being' that led from the lowliest forms of matter to God himself; this view of the universe, in turn, goes back to both classical and Judaeo-Christian doctrines. Modern philos-

[9] Frankena, op. cit., p. 23.
[10] H. A. Bedau, 'Egalitarianism and the Idea of Equality' in *Nomos IX: Equality*, ed. J. R. Pennock and J. W. Chapman, New York, 1967.
[11] G. Vlastos, 'Justice and Equality' in Brandt, *Social Justice*, p. 48.

ophers have cast off these metaphysical and religious shackles and freely invoke the dignity of mankind without needing to justify the idea at all. Why should we not attribute 'intrinsic dignity' or 'intrinsic worth' to ourselves? Fellow humans are unlikely to reject the accolades we so generously bestow on them, and those to whom we deny the honour are unable to object. Indeed, when one thinks only of humans, it can be very liberal, very progressive, to talk of the dignity of all human beings. In so doing, we implicitly condemn slavery, racism, and other violations of human rights. We admit that we ourselves are in some fundamental sense on a par with the poorest, most ignorant members of our own species. It is only when we think of humans as no more than a small sub-group of all the beings that inhabit our planet that we may realize that in elevating our own species we are at the same time lowering the relative status of all other species.

The truth is that the appeal to the intrinsic dignity of human beings appears to solve the egalitarian's problems only as long as it goes unchallenged. Once we ask *why* it should be that all humans—including infants, mental defectives, psychopaths, Hitler, Stalin, and the rest—have some kind of dignity or worth that no elephant, pig, or chimpanzee can ever achieve, we see that this question is as difficult to answer as our original request for some relevant fact that justifies the inequality of humans and other animals. In fact, these two questions are really one: talk of intrinsic dignity or moral worth only takes the problem back one step, because any satisfactory defence of the claim that all and only humans have intrinsic dignity would need to refer to some relevant capacities or characteristics that all and only humans possess. Philosophers frequently introduce ideas of dignity, respect, and worth at the point at which other reasons appear to be lacking, but this is hardly good enough. Fine phrases are the last resource of those who have run out of arguments.

XIV

GAMES THEORY AND THE NUCLEAR ARMS RACE

NICHOLAS MEASOR

I

GAMES theory is a mathematical theory invented by J. von Neumann and first described at length by him and O. Morgenstern in their classic text 'Theory of Games and Economic Behaviour'.[1] It is designed to enable one rationally to choose the optimum strategy in a game.

Although games theory is a theory about *games*, it is often claimed on its behalf that its implications are considerably more wide-ranging, and that it can be put to work in the context of divers political, economic, and international situations which are supposed to be in some respect analogous to games. The subject of this chapter is the question of whether this claim can be made good in the case of nuclear deterrence.

It is frequently thought that if games-theoretic reasoning is applicable in this area it would lead to the conclusion that our nuclear arsenal should be retained. One type of strategy, therefore, which unilateralists adopt against a games-theoretic pro-armament stance is to deny that games theory is applicable to complicated strategic situations. I argue here, on the other hand, that even if one does adopt a games-theoretic approach it will lead to a type of unilateralist conclusion. Those who are agnostic (or even sceptical) about games theory can read what I say as simply an *ad hominem* argument against a certain type of pro-advocate of nuclear arma-

Nicholas Measor, 'Games Theory and the Nuclear Arms Race' from *Danger of Deterrence*, eds. Nigel Blake & Kay Pole (1983), pp. 132–56. Reprinted by permission of Routledge & Kegan Paul PLC.

[1] J. von Neumann and O. Morgenstern, *Theory of Games and Economic Behaviour* (Princeton, 1947).

ment, but I think myself that enough of the games theory approach is worth while to give any unilateralist argument some strength in its own right.

A preliminary distinction which circumscribes my subject matter is between two-person games and n-person games where n > 2. I shall only discuss two-person games, even though the 'game' of international relations involves rather more players than that. Let us think of the arms race as a contest between just two parties—which is not, in any case, a gross misrepresentation. When I talk henceforward of 'unilateral disarmament' I mean one of the two superpowers resigning from the struggle. I shall not take account of the added complexity created by the fact that the United Kingdom participates as a junior partner of one of the main contestants.

The outcomes of the various possible combinations of moves by the players in a two-person game can be represented in a two-dimensional matrix. Consider an adaptation of a well-known children's game. Each player starts with an equal number of sweets (the players are A and B). Immediately after the command 'go' (given by the referee) each player must raise his hand either in a shape so as to represent scissors or in a shape to represent paper (Figure 1).

		Player B	
		Scissors	Paper
Player A	Scissors	0, 0	+15, −15
	Paper	−15, +15	0, 0

Figure 1

Here the top right-hand compartment, for example, represents the pay-offs to the players if A does scissors and B does paper. The first number represents the number of sweets lost or won by A, the second the number lost or won by B.

Clearly the only rational move for either player is scissors. If he makes this move the worst that can happen to him is a draw, and he may in theory win fifteen sweets if the other player is sufficiently ill-advised as to try paper. In practice if both players are rational the ıpshot will be a monotonous game: an endless series of draws with both players repeating scissors.

This is an example of what is known technically as a 'zero-sum' game. It is sufficient for our present purposes if I define a zero-sum game as one in which in each box the pay-offs for the two players in that box sum to zero. In practice this means that such a game is strictly competitive. Since no money or other asset is coming into the reckoning during the game but the players are merely redividing between themselves the assets which they already have, no advantage is to be gained by them forming any agreement between themselves. There is no scope for fruitful 'preplay jockeying'.

Contrast with this the most famous example of a *non* zero-sum game, the so-called 'Prisoners' Dilemma' (attributed to A. W. Tucker) (Figure 2).

B

		Confession	No Confession
	Confession	$-2, -2$	$+15, -15$
A	No Confession	$-15, +15$	$0, 0$

Figure 2

This matrix has associated with it a somewhat bizarre anecdote. Two prisoners (here, A and B) have been incarcerated in separate cells, unable to communicate with one another. Both are suspected of a serious crime for which the penalty is fifteen years in prison. In order to obtain a confession the authorities resort to guile. Each prisoner is addressed by his interrogator as follows:

If you confess and the other prisoner confesses then you will both be given a nominal sentence for a minor offence which we would be able to get you convicted of—two years in prison would be the total you would serve. If neither of you confesses then you will both be released without charge. *But* (and this is a big but) if one of you confesses and the other does not then the confessor will be awarded a free holiday in the Bahamas but the other prisoner will be sent to prison for the full term of fifteen years.

In the matrix +15 represents the value of a holiday in the Bahamas, −15 that of fifteen years in jail, 0 release scot-free, and −2 the nominal sentence.

By what process of reasoning should the prisoner decide on his course of action? In fact, if he is reasonably sensible he will argue like this:

> Either the other prisoner will confess, or he will not. Let's first suppose that he does. Then if I confess I shall receive a nominal sentence but if I do not then I shall find myself in prison for fifteen years. So I'll be better off confessing. Suppose on the other hand that he keeps quiet. Then if I confess I'll earn myself a fabulous holiday, but if I clam up I'll simply be allowed to return home. So whatever he does I'd be better advised to confess.

The practical import of the reasoning should be clear enough. Both prisoners will reason in this fashion, so both will confess, and they will always finish up in the top left-hand box. But there is often thought to be something paradoxical or absurd about this. For if both had instead not confessed they would have found themselves in the bottom right-hand box, and both would have been better off. From the individual's point of view the reasoning seems to be impeccable, but the result of collective irrationality which damages the personal interests of both.

A simple solution to the problem seems attractive at first sight. In the example given the prisoners cannot communicate with each other. Change the story, then, so that they can. *Now*, one first wants to say, the sensible thing will be for them to get together and *agree* that both should not confess. Is this not a method of transferring themselves from the top left-hand box where they do not want to be to the bottom right-hand box where they would rather find themselves?

Sadly, however, the advantages of consultation are illusory if both parties are primarily concerned with personal interest. For suppose that they have entered into an undertaking that both will keep quiet. Each prisoner, when his interrogator appears, must make a decision whether or not to keep to the agreement which he has made. But that decision is itself a move in a game, and the matrix for the game is the same as before, except that 'breaking agreement' must be substituted for 'confession' and 'not breaking agreement' for 'not confessing'. So each prisoner will break the agreement he has made in order to minimize the disadvantage if the other breaks the agreement.

What the prisoners need is a method of making their agreement irrevocably binding. It would, for example, be in their interests to find a third party who could police the treaty and wreak some terrible penalty on either of them if he broke his word. The threat of such punishment would be beneficial to each of them, since it would deter him from straying from the 0, 0 box in the misconceived hope of finding +15 in the Caribbean.

The possible relevance of the Prisoners' Dilemma to the arms race is clear. Simply replace confession with nuclear armanent and non-confession with disarmament. As a result you will have something which looks remarkably familiar, namely two contestants who feel forced to arm themselves even though they admit that they would both be better off if bilateral disarmament could be arranged (Figure 3).

		B (USSR)	
		Arm	Disarm
A (US)	Arm	−2, −2	+15, −15
	Disarm	−15, +15	0, 0

Figure 3

How are the figures in the arms race matrix calculated? In particular, since the arms race might lead to mutual extermination, why is the disutility associated with joining in the race (upper left box) a modest −2, whereas the disutility associated with being disarmed in the face of an armed foe is −15? Does this valuation imply that it is better to be dead than red?

In fact the difference in the figures relates as much to the probability of various outcomes as to their intrinsic nastiness. The large negative score of −15 for being disarmed in the top right-hand box is based on the thought that in such a situation there is a *high* probability of major political disadvantage ('becoming red'). If the Western Alliance laid down its arms it is *possible* (as idealists point out) that the Soviet Union would do likewise, but I am cynical enough to think that this would be a very unlikely eventuality. It would be much more probable that the party which had kept its nuclear armaments would take advantage of the opportunity to use nuclear blackmail. On the other hand, I am assuming in this paper that the party which had given up its arms would be prudent enough to give way if the other side resorted to nuclear blackmail, and thus (contrary to some opinions) that if one side unilaterally disarmed a nuclear holocaust would be unlikely. Such, at any rate, is the basis of the +15, −15 figures.

What of the −2, −2 score in the top left compartment? If nuclear holocaust followed B's strategy in the top left box with the same probability as that with which political conquest follows his strategy in the top right, then the negative scores in the top left would be far higher than −15, provided that one makes the (presumably widespread) assumption that being red is in itself preferable to being dead.

The claim, however, that the arms race instantiates the Prisoners' Dilemma matrix relies on the theory of nuclear deterrence, the theory that the possession by both sides of nuclear armaments makes a nuclear exchange highly unlikely, since each side is frightened off the use of his weapons by the near-certainty of retaliation.

The question of whether nuclear deterrence works will be my major concern in the second half of the chapter. But at this juncture I want to make the point that if the theory of nuclear deterrence does work then it will justify assigning small negative scores to the top left even though nuclear extermination is so much worse than political conquest. For the figures are arrived at by means of a function which takes as its arguments both the objectionability rating of the various possible outcomes and their probabilities. In other words, better a very low probability of being dead than a very high probability of being red.

Why is the figure for disarmament in the face of an armed foe −15? There are those who maintain that unilateral disarmament makes a nuclear attack more, rather than less, likely, or at any rate that it does little to increase one's security. If this were true, -15 would be optimistic, perhaps disastrously so. But note that by disarmament I mean laying down one's arms and then adopting an extremely co-operative and ingratiating stance towards one's enemy. It is surely clear that such a 'hearthrug' policy would remove many of the dangers associated with jettisoning nuclear arms but retaining substantial conventional weaponry and the belligerence that goes with it.

The thrust of the argument is that if nuclear deterrence works then we are in a Prisoners' Dilemma matrix. But if we are in a Prisoners' Dilemma matrix than unilateral disarmament makes very little sense at all. What possible reason could there be for abandoning -2 in favour of -15? (I shall be examining one reason—altruism—which might be suggested presently.)

Provided that the scores in the other boxes remain as shown, then the efficacy of deterrence will be a sufficient condition for the matrix to be Prisoners' Dilemma. It might seem natural to take it to be a necessary condition as well. Unilateralists in practice often try to discredit the deterrence theory, and, given this natural assumption, they would in so doing be by implication attacking the Prisoners' Dilemma argument against disarmament.

What of multilateral disarmament? Even if we are in the Prisoners' Dilemma matrix, no one could deny that we would be better off all round if we could get ourselves into the 0,0 box. The practical difficulty is to find a way into it. We saw in the case of the Prisoners' Dilemma itself that a formal agreement between the prisoners not to confess was useless if not backed up by any sanction. A policeman to enforce the agreement might be effective in their case.

It has often been argued that a justification of the state and its judicial apparatus is that it enforces a mutually beneficial agreement between persons who would otherwise be engaged in a costly struggle between one another ('the state of nature'). This Prisoners' Dilemma foundation for political philosophy is particularly associated with Hobbes. But notoriously there is a difficulty in fully applying to international relations the so-called 'domestic analogy' with the internal affairs of the state. In the case of the prisoners a third party might enforce the agreement and make it binding. In the state we have the police and the law-courts. But what can fill their place to enforce a binding agreement between nations? Who can be so starry-eyed as to believe that the United Nations could perform this function?

On the other hand, the fact that no obvious solution is available to the problem of multilateral disarmament, to the problem of forming an effective agreement in an atmosphere of mutual distrust, is not a reason for abandoning a search for a solution. If we are in a Prisoners' Dilemma matrix then the importance of multilateral disarmament is emphasized by the fact that unilateral disarmament is no way out of the problem. This is a point to which the leaders of nations would do well to pay heed, since their protestations of adherence to the multilateral ideal are sometimes belied by their actions.

The last topic which I want to examine in this section is the question of altruism. One common reaction to the Prisoners' Dilemma is to assert that the difficulty is caused by the fact that both prisoners (or superpowers) base their reasoning on self-interest. If one party, far from objecting to the other scoring at his expense, actually regarded it as a desirable object to secure a high rather than a low score for his 'opponent', then he would be prepared to refrain from confessing (or prepared to disarm). And if both participants saw things in this way then they might finish up in the bottom right-hand box after all.

To some extent the argument which I shall offer in Section II makes this response redundant. For my suggestion there will be that *even if* one bases one's reasoning entirely upon self-interest it can *still* be shown that disarmament is preferable to armament.

At this point, however, I have two negative comments to make on the suggestion that altruism as a policy might extricate us from the impasse. The first is that if one is to argue for a policy of disarmament (whether multilateral or unilateral) one would be well advised to devise something which has a chance of convincing one's fellow citizens. Perhaps sufficiently large numbers of Britons (not to mention Americans and other allied races) are motivated by burning altruistic ideals, or could have those ideals inculcated into them, sufficient numbers, that is, to give the altruistic argument for disarmament a decent chance of success. But I fear that this is not so, and some support for this pessimistic thought is provided by the results of public opinion polls on the subject of unilateralism.

A complication here is that the argument for the possession of nuclear arms is not presented in a way that appeals purely to self-interest either. On the contrary elements will creep into the argument which appear to be (and perhaps are) altruistic: references are made to the welfare of presently subjugated Poles and of future generations of all nationalities who need to have Western democracy preserved for their benefit. Such ingredients cloud the issue. Possibly they show that there are aspects of the debate which transcend the Prisoners' Dilemma framework. Certainly they mean that appeals to altruism by the disarmer are liable to be trumped by further appeals to altruism by his opponent.

The second point which I wish to make about altruism is simply that altruism as a general policy is no more attractive or effective than self-interest. Here we come to a point which philosophically is of really first-rate interest, and owing to shortage of space I shall simply utter some dogma with perfunctory support in argument.

The problem is this: if altruism is adopted as the basis of strategic decisions then other matrices can be devised which present exactly the same kind of problems for the altruist as those which the Prisoners' Dilemma posed for the self-interested.

Figure 4 is an example of an Altruists' Dilemma. If two altruists are playing this game, then each will adopt choice 2 to avoid the risk of the 'opponent' finishing up with -15, and thus they will finish up in the bottom right box. But each would rather be in the top left box, where the other party is better off than in the bottom right.

		B	
		1	2
A	1	+2, +2	+15, −15
	2	−15, +15	0, 0

Figure 4

So the altruist, although he may arrive at a more satisfactory rapprochement in the Prisoners' Dilemma, is liable in the long run to find life no more rewarding an affair than the self-interested does. It might be suggested that the answer lies in some sort of compromise: be an altruist when it leads to the most satisfactory results and self-interested when that pays off better. But the merits of this proposal are chimerical. For the upshot of a strategy adopted in a particular situation can only be judged satisfactory or otherwise against the fixed background of some consistent view about one's goals in life. A policy of oscillating between altruism and self-interest does not constitute such a background but is instead a form of philosophical schizophrenia. Indeed, many of the decisions taken during one's altruistic phases will come to be a source of bitter regret during one's periods of self-interest.

II

In the previous section I argued that if deterrence theory were correct we would be caught in the trap of the Prisoners' Dilemma. Multilateral disarmament would be difficult and unilateral disarmament would be irrational. In what follows I shall try to work out matrices describing rather more complicated sets of choices which are arguably closer to those which we shall soon find ourselves facing. First I am going to consider whether deterrence is likely to work in current conditions and those likely to obtain in the near future. The question to be tackled is not whether to disarm but whether firing our missiles would ever be preferable to not firing them.

In its classic form the theory of nuclear deterrence is based on the concept of mutually assured destruction ('MAD'), the notion, that is, that if either side launches a nuclear attack on the other the party which had been attacked would be able to reciprocate with a devastating onslaught on the cities of the aggressor. This requires the possession by each side of a more or less invulnerable second-strike capability, an ability to respond from 'invulnerable' submarines, aircraft in flight, or hardened missile silos.

In my view if MAD exists its presence will serve as an extremely effective nuclear deterrent. To see why this is so, consider a somewhat degenerate matrix where the choices of the two players are between firing their rockets with nuclear warheads or not doing so (Figure 5).

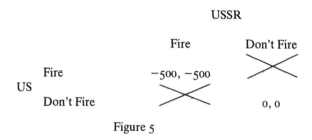

Figure 5

The mammoth negative figures in the top left box reflect the fact that if either party fires, a nuclear exchange ensues resulting in catastrophic losses to both sides. Why are two of the boxes scored out? Nominally, I suppose, if one side fired and the other did not then the firer might hope to gain some advantage (although quite what, if his opponent were a victim of nuclear devastation, is less than clear). But since the whole point of this game is that if one side fires the other side will always retaliate, the only rational course for a participant is to discount the top right and bottom left boxes altogether, and assume that firing will always move him into the top left box.

The game is easy to play, since the choice is between firing and earning −500 or not doing so and earning 0. So if MAD, and therefore nuclear deterrence, obtains, the modest negative figures in the top left box of the Prisoners' Dilemma matrix, which obtain when neither side disarms, are perfectly appropriate to the arms race. They should, however, be less advantageous than 0 (say, −2 as above), since the chance of a nuclear exchange starting by accident is never to be discounted, nor should we forget the potentially ruinous cost of the weaponry.

So much for MAD. Let us now consider what matrix is appropriate for a very different kind of strategic situation, namely one where both contestants have what I shall call first-strike capacity (possibly diverging from the standard use of this term by strategists). In my usage of the term a contestant has first-strike capacity when he has the ability of destroy *all* his opponent's weapon delivery systems in a single attack in such a way as to prevent his opponent retaliating with nuclear arms (note that to possess a first-strike capacity in this sense requires one to be able to evade or disable the enemy's early warning system).

Figure 6 is not too far off the mark for the appropriate matrix.

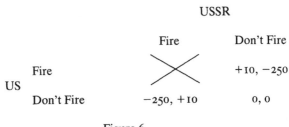

Figure 6

Here the figures for disutility associated with being fired on may be somewhat arbitrary. I am taking it that having all your rocket silos destroyed by nuclear attack is definitely bad news, since there is radioactive fall-out to contend with on top of massive immediate loss of life from other causes, but that it is not as bad as having your cities wiped out as in the MAD scenario. The firer in the top right and bottom left boxes earns +10 because he does not himself become the victim of nuclear attack, having knocked out the enemy's weapons. He does indeed obtain political advantage, but I have reduced this from 15 (as in the Prisoners' Dilemma matrix) to 10 since the conquest of an opponent who has suffered extensive nuclear attack must be less advantageous than the gains to be reaped from defeating him by nuclear blackmail.

Obviously as the matrix stands the rational course (in that situation) is to fire, since if I do not fire I will achieve either 0 or −250, whereas firing will bring in +10.

The top left box is crossed out since the nature of the game is that he who has been fired upon cannot himself fire. This is not strictly speaking correct since both parties might fire simultaneously, with a resulting score of −250, −250. This is perhaps a relatively unlikely event, although it should not be discounted completely if both contestants are following the same course of reasoning at the same time.

These notional figures for the top left box do not, however, provide any further reason for hesitation. Suppose that I am deliberating about whether to fire at a time t. The enemy may or may not fire at t. If he does fire at t my position if I do fire simultaneously is no worse than if I do not fire (−250 in each case). But if he does not fire at t I am much better off if I do fire then. So I should fire—and as soon as possible, since the probability of his firing during the next ten minutes is greater than the probability of his firing during the next five.

Another possible 'game' is one in which, say, the US does have first-strike capacity but the USSR does not. The matrix looks like Figure 7.

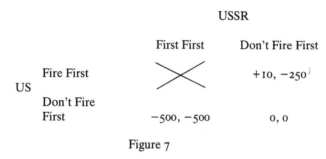

Figure 7

The figures in the bottom left box have changed. If the USSR attacks first, the US can retaliate in the usual way familiar from MAD, since the USSR, unlike the US, does not have first-strike capacity. I am assuming that a Soviet attack would be on American cities (hence an American figure of −500 rather than −250 in the bottom left box). The available strategies have been changed from firing to firing first and from not firing to not firing first: in the case of the US, firing does not imply firing first. Not firing first *includes* both firing second and not firing at all (although in the case of the Russians, firing second is not a possibility; note also that I have assumed that the Americans, if attacked, would retaliate, so that in the bottom left-hand box the US not firing first is taken to be the US firing second).

By reasoning which we have already examined the rational course for the US must be to fire as soon as possible in the hope that she will be firing first. The USSR, on the other hand, is faced with a very different problem. If she stays in the game her best hope (and it is a slim one) is that if she does not fire then the Americans may fall victim to some mental aberration and fail to fire either, in which case she will escape with a near-miraculous 0. But in any case she should operate on the policy of maximizing her minimum pay-off, which dictates that she should not fire, thus making her minimum pay-off (or worst possible loss) −250 rather than −500.

The Soviet Union would, however, be much better advised to withdraw from the game represented by this matrix altogether by finding some method of unilateral disarmament and/or surrender. For her minimum pay-off will then be the −15 of the Prisoners' Dilemma (equals political conquest), and this is a great deal better than the virtual certainty of −250.

The moral of the matrices involving first-strike capacity on the part of one or both of the contestants is that such a capability constitutes a nuclear incentive rather than a nuclear deterrent to its possessor, whereas to the player unfortunate enough not to possess it when his opponent does it serves not only as a deterrent but also as a powerful reason for pulling out of the arms race altogether.

If one or both sides has a first-strike capability where does this leave the matrix for armament/disarmament?

Consider first the case where both sides have first-strike capacity. If we assume that both sides are aware of their first-strike capacity, then we can take it for the purposes of the calculation that the chance of the US firing first (and therefore last) is exactly the same as the probability of the USSR doing so. One might be tempted at first, therefore, to construct a matrix like Figure 8.

The figures of −120 are reached by the following reasoning. Where both sides are armed and possess a first-strike capability, I have taken it that the chances of either side firing first are equal to each other (I ignore, for this calculation, the possibility of neither firing or both firing simultaneously). Now if the chances of either of two things happening are equal, one says in probability theory about each of the outcomes that the probability of it happening is 1/2 or 0.5 (in more popular parlance this is often referred to as a

'50 per cent chance'). I calculate, therefore, that the utility to a side
of being armed is the pay-off for making a first-strike multiplied by
0.5, plus the pay-off for being the victim of a strike multiplied by
0.5. But the pay-offs in question are +10 and −250 respectively (see
Figure 5, top right-hand box). So the 'utility' of being armed is
$(10 \times 0.5) + (−250 \times 0.5) = (10 \times 0.5) − (250 \times 0.5) = 5 − 125 = −120$.

USSR

		Arm	Disarm
US	Arm	−120, −120	+15, −15
	Disarm	−15, +15	0, 0

Figure 8

But there is something seriously misleading about the matrix. It
suggests that the rational thing to do in these circumstances (on a
policy of maximizing one's minimum pay-off) would be to disarm,
and in a sense this is true, but the seemingly pacific nature of this
conclusion masks the fact that undertakings to disarm may be either
sincere or insincere, and it is yet to be determined whether a sincere
undertaking is more or less advantageous than an insincere one.

To convey to one's opponent an intention to disarm and to
persuade him of one's sincerity takes a certain period of time.
During the period when one was setting one's unilateral disarmament in motion (I'll call this the 'disarmament period') one could
instead fire one's weapons—for obvious reasons this can be called a
policy of 'insincere disarmament'. Provided that the opponent did
not fire during the disarmament period (an important proviso) the
resulting pay-off will be +10 instead of the −15 of unilateral
disarmament.

At first sight this suggests a straightforward advantage in making
an *insincere* promise to disarm. But there are further complications
which I have not yet mentioned. For one thing if I sincerely promise
to disarm there is a greater than zero probability that the other side
will fire on me during the disarmament period (this is so whether or

not *he* has undertaken to disarm, since any such undertaking to disarm may be insincere). This shows, incidentally, that my original Figure 8 will not do as it stands, since the disutility of disarming when the other side does not must be worse than -15. Furthermore, the advantages of making an insincere promise to disarm are complicated by the fact that there is a greater than zero probability of the other side firing on me during the disarmament period, in which case I will not collect my $+10$.

To construct a suitable matrix for the decision between sincerely disarming and insincerely disarming is, therefore, not without its complications. More detailed discussion of how the various utilities are arrived at has been relegated to an Appendix. But the conclusion can be summarized in a few words: the matrix for the sincere/insincere disarm game will be Prisoners' Dilemma, provided that (a) the chance of the US firing upon the USSR during the disarmament period is not lower than $1/25$ (i.e. a 4 per cent chance), and that (b) the corresponding chance of the USSR firing during that period is not lower than $1/25$. But it would be realistic to assume that the probabilities in question would be higher than this—probably much higher.

What this would mean in practice is singularly depressing. When I say that the sincere/insincere matrix would be Prisoners' Dilemma I mean that both sides would be driven by the logic of the game into making an insincere promise and firing within the disarmament period, even though both would be better off making a sincere promise. If both sides had a first-strike capacity, therefore, the chances of nuclear conflict would be high indeed. For either both sides retain their first-strike capacity or at least one of the sides enters into a process of 'disarmament' (whether sincere or insincere). In the first case, as Figure 6 shows us, each side has an incentive to fire. If both sides 'disarm' then, as I have just argued, each side will be driven by Prisoners' Dilemma reasoning into firing within the disarmament period. I have not considered in detail the case where just one side 'disarms', but it should be clear that, by the same reasoning as in the case where both 'disarm', the 'disarmer' will see it to be to his advantage to be insincere.

The same kind of reasoning does not, however, apply in the case where one side has first-strike capacity and the other does not, and the matrix for the arm/disarm game is in that case nothing like the Prisoners' Dilemma. Firing first is not a serious option for the side which does not have first-strike capacity but is threatened by a foe who does (as we've seen—Figure 7, bottom left)—the pay-off is −500. So his only realistic choice is between disarming sincerely and keeping his arms but doing nothing with them. To present the matrix for such a game requires the same kind of probabilistic complication as in the case where both sides have first-strike capability, so this exercise too has been consigned to the Appendix. But it will not come as a great surprise to learn that in the long term it will be more to the advantage of the party who lacks first-strike capacity to disarm than to retain his arms.

I remarked in the first section that if the success of the deterrence theory were a *necessary* condition for the arms race matrix to be Prisoners' Dilemma then the unilateralist who attacked the deterrence theory would be by implication attacking the use of Prisoners' Dilemma reasoning in this context. The recent course of the argument shows that it is not strictly true that the deterrence theory is a necessary condition for the matrix to be Prisoners' Dilemma. It is a necessary condition for the matrix to be Prisoners' Dilemma that the pay-off for (sincerely) disarming should be worse than that for keeping one's arms. *One* situation which can produce such a relative arrangement of pay-offs is where deterrence obtains, but it is not the only such situation, since we also have a worse pay-off for disarmament if the risks of disarmament equal or exceed those associated with keeping one's weapons *and using them*.

The following does seem, however, to be true. The success of the deterrence theory is a condition which must obtain if *both* of the following are to be true: (a) the matrix is Prisoners' Dilemma, (b) the Prisoners' Dilemma reasoning leads one to keep one's arms but *not* use them. So the unilateralist is right to see if he can overturn the deterrence theory, since his main target is the person who maintains that Prisoners' Dilemma reasoning should lead us to keep our arms in order to minimize the danger of them being used.

There are two points remaining which I propose to examine. The first is the question whether either or both sides are at all likely to obtain first-strike capacity, and the second the practical implications of that likelihood.

The first of these issues has been extensively discussed, and there appear to be two main schools of thought. Both agree that the accuracy with which nuclear warheads can be delivered to their targets has increased, and will continue to increase, to a remarkable degree, and both agree that there has been a change in policy from targeting the warheads on cities to aiming them at enemy missile systems (the so-called 'counter-force strategy'). But the two parties disagree on the question of whether the implications of these developments is a move towards first-strike capacity.

The opinion that the increase in accuracy portends the coming of first-strike capacity is eloquently stated in Professor Michael Pentz's booklet 'Towards the Final Abyss?'.[2] To have first-strike capacity is to have a very high probability of knocking out *all* the enemy's missile firing sites in one strike. Pentz points out that quite a small increase in accuracy can make an enormous qualitative difference in this respect. For example, if there are 1,000 Soviet launching sites (not so far from the truth in fact) then a 0.99 probability for each American missile of destroying the Russian silo it is aimed at will give a very low probability (0.99^{1000}, which is scarcely greater than 0) of knocking out *all* the Soviet sites in one attack. But an increase in accuracy of American missiles such as to give each a 0.99998 probability of knocking out its target will tip the scales dramatically, since the chance of disabling *all* the Russian launching sites will now have increased to something which is scarcely smaller than 1. But the US is striving to produce just such an increase in accuracy in its weapons, and Pentz therefore concludes that it is aiming to have first-strike capability by the end of the decade.

Let us note two points which are produced in response to this.

The first is simply the assertion that the counter-force strategy, and the increase in accuracy which goes with it, is not intended to produce a first-strike capability but is instead designed as part of the deterrent strategy called 'flexible response'. But, whatever the current intentions of, say, the controllers of the Pentagon, once the increased accuracy exists the possibility of using it for first-strike purposes will exist. There is no guarantee at all that future leaders of nations will not come to relish and use it. The technological

[2] J. D. Bernal Peace Library Pamphlet, 1980.

developments imply progress towards a first-strike policy by implication even if the intentions which accompany them are innocent.

The second response to Pentz's type of argument is to point out that not all Soviet warheads are launched from rocket silos. There can also be movable delivery systems in aircraft and, most significantly, submarines. The US could not realistically suppose itself to be capable of a first strike until it had licked the problem of how to target weapons on these comparatively elusive missile launchers.

Now it is true as far as I know that the US is not currently able to identify the positions of Soviet submarines once they have left port, and it is true that until they are able to do so there will still be a deterrent against an American first strike. But how much comfort should the Soviet Union derive from that fact? It appears to me that Soviet euphoria on this score would be sadly out of place. Even if the US is not currently trying to develop an effective submarine tracking system (which seems unlikely), and even if the US has not yet realized the possible significance of its counter-force strategy, it is surely only a matter of time before it *does* realize the significance and pull out all the stops in the attempt to remove the remaining obstacles to a first-strike capacity.[3]

It is perfectly reasonable, therefore, to see the arms race as now being a race to achieve first-strike capacity.

Let us suppose, then, that it is highly probable that at least one side will eventually achieve first-strike capability. How should we take this into account in planning our (i.e. NATO's) present strategy in the arm-disarm game?

I take the strategy of arming here to consist not just in possessing arms but in striving to develop them as well. Strictly speaking there are at least three options open, namely (1) keeping one's weapons and not developing them, (2) developing them, and (3) disarming. In practice, however, we can safely ignore the first of these strategies, since not to develop is to invite the other side to acquire first-strike capacity when one does not have it oneself, and if that occurs one will be worse off than if one disarmed now (basically because

---

[3] On this, see F. Barnaby, *The Nuclear Arms Race—Control or Castastrophe?*, Proceedings of the British Association for the Advancement of Science 1981 (London, 1982), pp. 33–4.

one then has the risk that the enemy may make a first strike before one has managed to disarm—Figure A3 in the Appendix is the relevant matrix).

Effectively, therefore, the choice is between technological development and disarmament. Now it only makes sense to persist with development of weapons if the worst pay-off, the one which should be avoided by the rational principle that one should maximize one's minimum pay-off, comes from disarming (when the other side is still armed) rather than from meeting armament with armament. If both sides continue to develop their weapons there are three possibilities open: we get first-strike capacity and they do not, we do not and they do, or both do (*ex hypothesi* we are ignoring the possibility that neither will).

In the first eventuality we get a positive pay-off of less than 15 (+15, representing bloodless conquest, is the *best* we can hope for, and this will not be achieved if the other side fails to resign when he observes our superiority). In the second eventuality we get a negative pay-off worse than the present disarmament pay-off (see the last paragraph but one and the part of the Appendix referred to there). In the third case we get a pay-off determined by the probabilistic calculations consigned to the Appendix (Figure A1 is the relevant matrix); it will almost certainly be worse than the present armament pay-off of −2 (Figure 3)—indeed if the probability of the other side attacking us during the disarmament period is around 0.1 or higher then the figure is worse than the present disarmament pay-off of −15.

How, then, is one to construct a matrix for develop/disarm on the basis of these three possible outcomes of development? I am afraid that I do not know. I do not see how one is to compute the probabilities of the various relevant outcomes in even the roughest way. To illustrate this point, let us consider two possible ways of calculating the score for armament (when the other side arms), one of which makes it sensible to arm and the other sensible to disarm.

Suppose first that the probability of my side obtaining first-strike capacity before the other is 0.45 (= 9/20), that the probability of the reverse happening is also 0.45, and that the chance of both obtaining it at once is 0.1.

To all intents and purposes the third eventuality can be ignored, since its contribution to the final figure will be so small. The utility of developing one's weapons, therefore, I shall compute as the score for winning the first-strike race times the probability of this happening, *plus* the score for losing the race times the probability of *that* happening (this sum will in practice, of course, turn into a subtraction since the second figure will be negative).

I remarked before that the *best* which can be hoped for from obtaining first-strike capacity before the opponent is +15 (if he resigns). There is also a chance that he will not resign and that my score will therefore be reduced by such factors as the devastation of parts of the enemy's territory and nuclear fall-out. Let us therefore reduce the score for winning the first-strike race to 13. The chance of me winning this race we have supposed to be 0.45, and 0.45 times 13 is approximately 6.

Let us also assume that if the opponent wins the first-strike race then my side will be sufficiently prudent to surrender and disarm (clearly the pay-off will come out worse if we do not make this assumption). The second component in our calculation is, therefore, the pay-off for disarming when the other side has obtained first-strike capacity multiplied by the probability of him winning the first-strike race. Now I have already explained that to calculate the pay-off for disarmament when the other side can make a first-strike, one must know the probability of him attacking during the disarmament period. Let us suppose it to be relatively small, say 0.1. If we feed this probability into the relevant formula (which is in fact $-[(250 \times p2) + 15(1 - p2)]$, where $p2$ is the probability of attack— see the Appendix) the pay-off for disarmament when the other side has first-strike capacity comes out as -38.5. So the second component in the calculation comes out as -38.5×0.45, which is approximately -17.5. So on these assumptions the utility of developing one's arms is the sum of 6 and $-17.5 = -11.5$. But the score for disarming now is -15, so on these assumptions one would be better advised to develop one's weaponry.

Compare this, however, with the result one obtains if one keeps everything as before except that one allows a probability of attack during the disarmament period of 0.2 instead of 0.1. The positive component in the pay-off remains 6 as before. But the pay-off for disarmament when the other side has first-strike capacity becomes

−62, so the negative component in the calculation becomes −62 times 0.45, which is approximately −28. On these new figures, therefore, the score for developing one's weapons becomes 6 − 28, which is substantially less appealing than the disarmament pay-off of −15.

Reflection on the dramatic difference between these two ways of doing the calculation suggests an important moral. If one is to decide the merits of a policy of armament on the basis of a game-theoretic matrix in an age when the advent of first-strike capability is very probably imminent, some way must be found of assigning values to a number of crucial variables. The contrast I drew highlighted the importance of just one of these, the probability of attack during the disarmament period. I would not care to lay a bet on whether the higher or the lower probability of the two mentioned in this context is the more plausible. Do not dismiss the higher figure of 0.2 out of hand, however, for you should remember that it is by no means clear that a future government would in a precipitate manner disarm once it suspected that the other side had first-strike capacity. If it did not then the effective disarmament period might be quite prolonged, and the probability of being attacked consequently higher. Nor is it certain that a government would have speedy intelligence that the enemy had acquired such a capability.

There are, moreover, a number of assumptions relied upon in both the sample calculations which I supplied which might be changed quite radically with a consequent change in the armament pay-off. For example the figure of +13 for the result of achieving first-strike capacity before the other side may be much too high (since a drift of devastating fall-out from enemy territory might be a highly likely result of the use of such capacity) or, alternatively, too low (since perhaps the surrender of the enemy would be almost inevitable under such circumstances). Again, how is one to calculate the chances of either or both the sides obtaining first-strike capacity? If my side could be seen to be a strong favourite to obtain that capacity first then this would certainly increase the advantages for me (and decrease those for the enemy) of continuing with technological development.

Some of these uncertainties may be simply a product of my ignorance. Perhaps there is somewhere in the Pentagon a Dr

Strangelove seated in front of a computer terminal who can supply you on demand with accurate calculations of the probability of the United States obtaining first-strike capacity before the Soviet Union, who can make a truly reliable estimate of the amount of fall-out which would follow on a United States first strike and calculate the probability of that fall-out blowing across the Bering Straits and down the West American seaboard. But this is improbable. There are so many shortcomings in our ability to foretell the future course of events, so many deficiencies in such matters as intelligence gathering and weather forecasting, that to put a confident figure on the relevant probabilities on the basis of the available information is only marginally more sensible than consulting the entrails of goats.

Where, then, does this uncertainty leave us? Some might be tempted to reply that it leaves us with no certain conclusion at all, but they would be wrong. It is true that I cannot say whether we are still in a Prisoners' Dilemma matrix, since I am quite unable to tell what figures should be inserted in the top left box. But it does not follow that there is no rational procedure for making a decision between armament and disarmament. For the choice is between a strategy with a (more or less) known disutility and a strategy whose pay-off *may* be worse than the known disutility or *may* be better. The rational course for an agent faced with such a choice will normally be to choose the known evil rather than embark upon uncharted waters, and it is only when unusual special features obtain that this may cease to be the preferred option.

Consider a little fantasy which by analogy may throw some light on the correct reasoning to adopt. I am forced by a dictator with a warped sense of humour to undergo a curious ordeal. I am faced with two boxes, one of which I must open. If I open the first box a hand, clad in a boxing glove, will emerge on the end of an arm and hit me forcefully in a painful spot (this is a definite consequence of opening the first box). If I open the second box one of two things will happen: either a whirling blade will emerge and cut off both my legs, or I will be presented with a new set of hi-fi equipment. I have absolutely no way of calculating the relative probabilities of these two results of opening the second box. For all I know dismemberment may be far the more, or far the less, probable.

If I found myself in the situation described in this version of the story I should certainly be inclined to open the first rather than the second box, even though the painful consequence is not one that I should relish. The conclusion which I am urging about the arms race is that if you would act like me in the imaginary situation then you should also regard disarmament as a more attractive prospect than joining in the race to first-strike capability. It may help, however, to quell any remaining doubts if I mention two sorts of special circumstances which would be relevant, circumstances which I suggest are not present in the arms race.

There is some resemblance between my fantasy and the puzzle known as 'Newcomb's Problem'.[4] In Newcomb's Problem, however, there is additional evidence which may give support to opening the second box. A near parallel to this in our story would be a regular correlation in the past between opening the second box and doing well. I did admit earlier that if we had good evidence of some kind that we were going to obtain first-strike capability before the other side this might make it relatively sensible to press on. But no evidence of *this* kind exists in the real life situation, no observed correlation between entering the first-strike race and winning it.

Another kind of feature which might be present relates to the preference scale of the dictator's victim. He *might* regard a blow in, say, the groin as worse than the loss of both legs. If so, he would be well advised to open the second box. There is a rough parallel to this in the arms race if a participant regards political conquest as so awful that he thinks that nuclear devastation is no worse. But for those of us who do not share this 'better dead than red' sentiment such considerations should not affect our reasoning.

My concluding claim, therefore, is that in joining in the first-strike race one is buying a pig in a poke, a pig which has an unknown probability of possessing a savage bite. If a method of disarming unilaterally can be discovered this is the more rational option even if it leads to political subjugation.

---

[4] A description and comprehensive bibliography of this puzzle may be found in Ellery Eels, *Rational Decision and Causality* (Cambridge, 1982).

APPENDIX

Our first task is to construct a matrix for the strategic decision between sincerely disarming and insincerely disarming (i.e. firing one's weapons during the disarmament period). The left-hand box pay-offs for the US in such a matrix might come out like Figure A1.

USSR

	Insincere	Sincere
US Insincere	$10(1 - p1) + (-250 \times p1)\ldots$	
US Sincere	$-[(250 \times p2) + 15(1 - p2)]\ldots$	

Figure A1

Here p1 and p2 are probability variables—their values are fractions between 0 and 1. p2, for example, is the probability of the USSR attacking the US during the disarmament period, $1 - p2$ is the probability of this not happening (since the only possibilities are for such an attack to happen and for it not to happen, and the probabilities must add up to 1). Let t be the time at which the US will fire (if not previously fired upon) in pursuance of a policy of insincere disarmament. Then p1 is the probability of the USSR attacking the US before t, and $1 - p1$ is the probability of this not happening. Thus the top left figure for the US, for instance, represents the pay-off for the US if she makes a surprise strike during the disarmament period times the probability of that happening *plus* the (negative) pay-off for the US for being attacked before she can attack times the probability of that happening.

Some features of the matrix are worth pointing out. The US figure in the bottom left box is negative whatever value is assigned to p2. Furthermore, although the US figure in the top left box may be either positive or negative (depending on what value is assigned to p1), the US pay-off in the bottom left is always worse than her pay-off in the top left since p2 is bound to be larger than p1 (the strategy of insincere disarmament, remember, is a strategy of firing before the end of the disarmament period, preferably as soon as possible).

Although the top left pay-off *can* be positive, the probability of attack during the disarmament period must be very low for this to be the case. The watershed is a value of p_1 between 0.03 and 0.04: if p_1 is 0.03 then the pay-off is $10(1 - 0.03) + (-250 \times 0.03) = 9.7 - 7.5$, while if p_1 is 0.04 then the pay-off is $10(1 - 0.04) + (-250 \times 0.04) = 9.6 - 10$.

Two further points: the figures in the bottom right box where both sides disarm are (as usual), 0, 0. And the pay-off for a policy of insincere disarmament when the other side is sincerely disarming (e.g. the US top right pay-off) is positive—given that the sincere disarmer is not going to attack, the pay-off to the insincere party is, if Figure 6 is to be believed, $+10$.

Provided that the value of p_1 is 0.04 or greater and the corresponding probability for the USSR top left figure is at least 0.04, then the matrix will have the shape shown in Figure A2, where $A < E$ and $B < D$ (i.e. $-E$, for instance, is a worse pay-off than $-A$). If the value of p_1 is the same as the corresponding probability for the USSR, and likewise for p_2, then $A = B$ and $D = E$, with the result that the matrix will be straightforward Prisoners' Dilemma. But even if we do not make this assumption, the reasoning appropriate to the matrix will still be like the Prisoners' Dilemma in that each side will be insincere in order to maximize its minimum pay-off, even though each would have been better off if both had been sincere.

		USSR Insincere	Sincere
	Insincere	$-A, -B$	$+C, -D$
US	Sincere	$-E, +C$	0, 0

Figure A2

The same reasoning does not, however, apply in the case where one side has first-strike capacity and the other does not, and the matrix for the arm/disarm game is in that case nothing like the Prisoners' Dilemma. For the side which does not have first-strike capacity but is threatened by a foe who does, firing first is (as we've seen) not a serious option, the pay-off being -500. So his strategy alternative to sincerely disarming is keeping his arms but doing nothing with them. Let us assume that it is the USSR which has the first-strike capacity and the US which does not.

Let us say that the disarmament period lasts from now to t, and let us consider the pay-offs over a period from now to t+, where t+ is later than t. Let p3 be the probability of the USSR attacking the US between now and t+, and let p2 be the probability of the USSR attacking the US during the disarmament period. The matrix for the relevant decision will now look like Figure A3.

USSR

		Keep arms	Disarm
US	Keep arms	$-250 \times p3 \ldots$	
	Disarm	$-[(250 \times p2) + 15(1 - p2)] \ldots$	

Figure A3

The figure of $-250 \times p3$ stands unadorned in the top left box because in the event of the USSR not attacking the US (probability $1 - p3$) the pay-off to the US will be o. The bottom left figure is the same as in Figure A1.

The important point about this matrix is that the later we take t+ to be the higher the value of p3, whereas the bottom left figure remains the same whatever t+ may be. There is a t+ in the future, therefore, such that over the period till that t+ disarmament is the best bet, so in the long run the matrix is not Prisoners' Dilemma.

NOTES ON CONTRIBUTORS

THOMAS NAGEL is Professor of Philosophy at New York University. He is the author of *The Possibility of Altruism* (1970), *Mortal Questions* (1979), and *The View From Nowhere* (1986).

DAVID HUME (1711–76) ranks among the greatest of British philosophers. He was also celebrated for his historical works and his essays on political and economic topics. His chief philosophical works are *A Treatise of Human Nature* and *An Enquiry Concerning the Principles of Human Morals*.

JAMES RACHELS is Professor of Philosophy at the University of Alabama at Birmingham. He is the author of *The End of Life: Euthanasia and Morality* (1986) and *The Elements of Moral Philosophy* (1986).

JUDITH JARVIS THOMSON is Professor of Philosophy at the Massachusetts Institute of Technology. She is the author of *Acts and Other Events* (1977), and *Rights, Restitution, and Risk* (1986).

MICHAEL TOOLEY is Professor of Philosophy at the University of Western Australia. He is the author of *Abortion and Infanticide* (1983).

JOHN HARRIS is Senior Lecturer in Philosophy in the Department of Education, University of Manchester. He is the author of *Violence & Responsibility* (1980) and *The Value of Life: An Introduction to Medical Ethics* (1985).

JOHN STUART MILL (1806–73) was a leader of the British utilitarian school. He is best known for his essay *On Liberty*, but wrote widely on utilitarianism, logic, the position of women, and economics. He was Member of Parliament for Westminster from 1865 to 1868.

LOUIS PASCAL is an independent researcher in the field of overpopulation. His philosophical interests include especially issues in ethics arising from the population explosion; human nature; and the nature of consciousness. He has published two papers in *Inquiry*.

JONATHAN GLOVER is Fellow of New College, Oxford. He is the author of several books on ethics and editor of *The Philosophy of Mind* (1976), which is also published in this series.

DEREK PARFIT is a Senior Research Fellow at All Souls College, Oxford, and also teaches as a Visitor at New York University. He is the author of *Reasons and Persons* (1984).

R. M. HARE is Graduate Research Professor at the University of Florida, Gainesville. He was White's Professor of Moral Philosophy at Corpus Christi College, Oxford, until 1983. His books include *The Language of Morals* (1952), *Freedom and Reason* (1963), and *Moral Thinking* (1981).

JANET RADCLIFFE RICHARDS is Lecturer in Philosophy at the Open University, and author of *The Sceptical Feminist: A Philosophical Enquiry* (1980).

PETER SINGER is Professor of Philosophy and Director of the Centre for Human Bioethics at Monash University, Melbourne, Australia. His publications include *Animal Liberation*, *Practical Ethics*, *The Expanding Circle*, *The Reproduction Revolution* (with Deane Wells), and *Should the Baby Live?* (with Helga Kuhse).

NICHOLAS MEASOR is Lecturer in Philosophy at the University of Leicester. He has published articles on a wide range of philosophical topics, in particular space, time, and personal identity.

BIBLIOGRAPHY

GENERAL

Many of the best examples of applied ethics are to be found in journal articles, particularly in *Philosophy and Public Affairs*, which began publication in 1971, and more recently in the *Journal of Applied Philosophy*, which published its first issue in 1984. *Ethics* also publishes some applied articles. More specialized journals include *Environmental Ethics*, the *Journal of Medical Ethics* and *Bioethics*. Because of the large number of articles on each of the topics listed below, I have restricted the suggestions for further reading to books. Many of these are anthologies, containing some of the more important articles. Most books contain bibliographies which will guide the reader to other books and articles in the specific field.

Readers not familiar with ethical theory may wish to begin with an introduction to this area. J. Rachels's *The Elements of Moral Philosophy* (1986) is brief, clear, and alert to the applications of ethical theory. More advanced works include R. Hare, *Freedom and Reason* (1963) and *Moral Thinking* (1981); J. Rawls, *A Theory of Justice* (1971) and R. B. Brandt, *A Theory of the Good and the Right* (1979).

Moving on to applied ethics itself, useful general anthologies include:

RACHELS, J., *Moral Problems* (3rd edn., 1979).
WASSERSTROM, R., *Today's Moral Problems* (2nd edn., 1979).
NARVESON, J., *Moral Issues* (1983).
VELASQUEZ, M., and ROSTANKOWSKI, C., *Ethics: Theory and Practice* (1985).

Death, Suicide, and Euthanasia

Lucretius, *On The Nature of Things* (various editions) Bk. 3, 830–1094.
  M. Pabst Battin and D. Mayo (eds.), *Suicide: The Philosophical Issues* (1980).
GLOVER, J., *Causing Death and Saving Lives* (1977) chs. 1–8, 13–15.
WILLIAMS, G., *The Sanctity of Life and the Criminal Law* (1958) ch. 8.
KUHSE H. and SINGER, P., *Should the Baby Live?* (1985).
SINGER, P., *Practical Ethics* (1979), ch. 7.
STEINBOCK, B., (ed.), *Killing and Letting Die* (1980).

COHEN, M., NAGEL, T. and SCANLON, T. (eds.), *Medicine and Moral Philosophy* (1981) Pt. IV.
RACHELS, J., *The End of Life* (1986).
HARRIS, J., *The Value of Life* (1985), chs. 1–4.
REGAN, T., (ed.), *Matters of Life and Death*, 2nd edn., 1986.
DOWNING, A. B. and SMOKER, B. (ed.), *Voluntary Euthanasia: Experts Debate the Right to Die* (1986).

Abortion

TOOLEY, M., *Abortion and Infanticide* (1984).
GRISEZ, G., *Abortion: The Myths, the Realities and the Arguments* (1969).
BRODY, B., *Abortion and the Sanctity of Human Life: a Philosophical View* (1975).
SUMNER, L. W., *Abortion and Moral Theory* (1981).
FEINBERG, J. (ed.), *The Problem of Abortion* (1973).
GLOVER, J., *Causing Death and Saving Lives* (1977), chs. 9–11.
SINGER, P., *Practical Ethics* (1979), ch. 6.
HARRIS, J., *The Value of Life* (1985), chs. 6–8.
REGAN, T. (ed.), *Matters of Life and Death,* 2nd edn., 1986.

Capital Punishment

EZORSKY, G. (ed.), *Philosophical Perspectives on Punishment* (1972).
GLOVER, J., *Causing Death and Saving Lives* (1977), ch. 18.
HART, H. L. A., *Punishment and Responsibility* (1968).
REGAN, T. (ed.), *Matters of Life and Death,* 2nd edn., 1986.

World Poverty

AIKEN, W. and LA FOLLETTE, H. (eds.), *World Hunger and Moral Obligation* (1977).
BROWN, P. and SHUE, H. (eds.), *Food Policy* (1977).
SHUE, H., *Basic Rights* (1980).
SINGER, P., *Practical Ethics* (1979), ch. 8.
FISHKIN, J., *The Limits of Obligation* (1982).
HARRIS, J., *Violence and Responsibility* (1980).
DOWER, N., *World Poverty: Challenge and Response* (1983).
BEITZ, C., COHEN, M., SCANLON, T. and SIMMONS, A. (eds.), *International Ethics* (1985), Pt. V.
REGAN, T. (ed.), *Matters of Life and Death,* 2nd edn., 1986.

Ethics and Optimum Population

BARRY, B. and SIKORA, R. (eds.), *Obligations to Future Generations* (1978).
BAYLES, M. (ed.), *Ethics and Population* (1976).

BAYLES, M., *Morality and Population Policy* (1980).
PARFIT, D., *Reasons and Persons* (1984), Pt. IV.

Feminism, Equality, and Reverse Discrimination

RADCLIFFE RICHARDS, J., *The Sceptical Feminist* (1981).
MIDGLEY, M. and HUGHES, J., *Women's Choices: Philosophical Problems Facing Feminism* (1983).
JAGGAR, A., *Feminist Politics and Human Nature* (1983).
COHEN, M., NAGEL, T. and SCANLON, T. (eds.), *Equality and Preferential Treatment* (1976).
GOLDMAN, A., *Justice and Reverse Discrimination* (1979).
SINGER, P., *Practical Ethics* (1979), ch. 2.

Animals and the Environment

GODLOVITCH, R., GODLOVITCH, S. and HARRIS, J. (eds.), *Animals, Men and Morals* (1972).
SINGER, P., *Animal Liberation* (1975).
SINGER, P., *Practical Ethics* (1979), chs. 3, 5.
CLARK, S., *The Moral Status of Animals* (1977).
REGAN, T., *The Case for Animal Rights* (1984).
REGAN, T. (ed.), *Matters of Life and Death*, 2nd edn., 1986.
REGAN, T. and SINGER, P. (eds.), *Animal Rights and Human Obligations* (1976).
FREY, R., *Interests and Rights: The Case Against Animals* (1980).
FREY, R., *Rights, Killing and Suffering* (1983).
MIDGLEY, M., *Animals and Why They Matter* (1983).
ELLIOT, R. and GARE, A., *Environmental Philosophy* (1983).
SHRADER-FRECHETTE, K., *Environmental Ethics* (1981).
PASSMORE, J., *Man's Responsibility for Nature* (1974).
McCLOSKEY, H. J., *Ecological Ethics and Politics* (1983).

War and Nuclear Deterrence

WALZER, M., *Just and Unjust War* (1977).
WASSERSTROM, R. (ed.), *War and Morality* (1970).
SCHELL, J., *The Fate of the Earth* (1982).
BLAKE, N. and POLE, K. (eds.), *Objections to Nuclear Defence* (1984).
BLAKE, N. and POLE, K. (eds.), *Dangers of Deterrence* (1984).
MacLEAN, D. (ed.), *The Security Gamble: Deterrence Dilemmas in the Nuclear Age* (1984).
BEITZ, C., COHEN, M., SCANLON, T. and SIMMONS, A. (eds.), *International Ethics* (1985), Pt. III.

INDEX OF NAMES